Democratization in Africa

A *Journal of Democracy* Book

•

BOOKS IN THE SERIES

Edited by Larry Diamond and Marc F. Plattner

Capitalism, Socialism, and Democracy Revisited (1993)

Nationalism, Ethnic Conflict, and Democracy (1994)

Economic Reform and Democracy (1995)

The Global Resurgence of Democracy, 2nd ed. *(1996)*

Civil-Military Relations and Democracy (1996)

Consolidating the Third Wave Democracies (1997)
(with Yun-han Chu and Hung-mao Tien)

Democracy in East Asia (1998)

Published under the auspices of

the International Forum for Democratic Studies

Democratization in Africa

*Edited by Larry Diamond
and Marc F. Plattner*

The Johns Hopkins University Press

Baltimore and London

Chapter 16 originally appeared in the *Journal of Democracy*, January 1999; chapter 10 appeared in the October 1998 issue; chapter 2 appeared in the July 1998 issue; chapters 1, 3, 13, 14, and 15 in the April 1998 issue; chapter 9 in the January 1998 issue; chapter 4 in the July 1997 issue; chapters 11 and 12 in the April 1997 issue; chapter 5 in the July 1996 issue; and chapters 6, 7, and 8 in the January 1996 issue.

The Johns Hopkins University Press
2715 North Charles Street
Baltimore, Maryland 21218-4363
http://www.press.jhu.edu

Library of Congress Cataloging-in-Publication Data

Democratization in Africa / edited by Larry Diamond and Marc F. Plattner.
    p.   cm. — (A Journal of democracy book)
    Originally published in Journal of democracy.
    Includes bibliographical references and index.
    ISBN 0-8018-6272-8 (alk. paper). — ISBN 0-8018-6273-6 (pbk. : alk. paper)
    1. Democracy—Africa.   2. Africa—Politics and government—1960–
I. Diamond, Larry Jay.   II. Plattner, Marc F., 1945–
III. Series.
JQ1879.A15D4639   1999
320.96'09'045—dc21   99–20503
                                           CIP

A catalog record for this book is available from the British Library.

CONTENTS

III. African Ambiguities

ACKNOWLEDGMENTS

This volume brings together 16 essays, dealing with various aspects of democratization in Africa, that were originally published in the *Journal of Democracy* between 1996 and 1999. The idea of compiling such a collection was first proposed to us by Joel D. Barkan, coauthor of the chapter on Kenya and also a valued member of the Research Council of the International Forum for Democratic Studies, the mini-think tank that has grown up around the *Journal*. A professor of political science at the University of Iowa who teaches courses on African politics, Joel felt that such a volume would be valuable not only for general readers but for use in college classrooms. We thank him for his suggestion, and hope that the final product meets his expectations.

The *Journal* has published extensively on Africa, but space constraints made it impossible for us to include in the current volume all the relevant articles that appeared in the *Journal*'s pages during the past few years. We are conscious of the fact that we were compelled to omit not only some fine articles but also treatments of some very important countries. We regret these omissions, but we believe that the collection presented here nevertheless offers a broad, diverse, and insightful set of reflections on the dilemmas of democratization in Africa in the 1990s.

There are many institutions and individuals whom we would like to thank for their contributions to this volume and to our work more generally. First among these is the Lynde and Harry Bradley Foundation, which has provided the *Journal* with generous financial assistance since its launching. For the past two years the Donner Canadian Foundation has supported a full-time internship at the *Journal* that has been indispensable to its smooth functioning. The Smith Richardson Foundation and the Carnegie Corporation of New York have each provided financial support for other aspects of the International Forum's work that has redounded to the benefit of the *Journal*. And our parent organization, the National Endowment for Democracy, has enthusiastically supported our efforts in every possible way.

Many present and former members of the *Journal* staff have contributed to the editing and production of the essays that appear in the pages that follow: Phil Costopolous, Mark Eckert, Zerxes Spencer, Annette Theuring, Miriam Kramer, and Stephanie Lewis. The production of this volume was superbly handled by Stephanie Lewis, who has also skillfully guided the *Journal* into the use of PageMaker desktop publishing software. The index reflects not only the diligence and perspicacity but also the experience (this is his second index for us) that Mahindan Kanakaratnam brought to the task of compiling it.

Finally we wish to thank our editor Henry Tom and his colleagues at the Johns Hopkins University Press for their customary efficiency in bringing out this volume, our eighth *Journal of Democracy* book.

INTRODUCTION

Larry Diamond

During the 1990s, the third wave of global democratization finally
reached the African continent. This African wave was widely dubbed
"the second liberation" (underscoring the betrayed hopes surrounding
the liberation from colonial rule in the 1960s), but as Crawford Young
notes, it was actually the third wave of efforts to inaugurate democracy
in Africa. It began in February 1990 with two events that would prove
to be momentous. In Benin, popular protests against the corrupt, bankrupt 17-year rule of Mathieu Kérékou led to a "National Conference of
Active Forces of the Nation" that effectively seized power from the
dictator and launched a transition to democracy. The model of the
Conférence Nationale would subsequently be borrowed, with mixed
success, by a number of other Francophone African countries seeking a
path out of autocracy.[1] In South Africa, the apartheid regime, realizing
that it was running out of time to negotiate a peaceful transition to a
more viable, open, and nonracial political order, released Nelson
Mandela from nearly three decades in prison and lifted its ban on the
African National Congress, the principal political organization
representing the hopes for liberation of the country's vast black
majority. This was the beginning of a turn away from repression toward
negotiation and a transition to democracy in South Africa. Coinciden-
tally, in that same month, the Constituent Assembly of Namibia, which
(as South West Africa) had been ruled for seven decades by South
Africa, approved a liberal, democratic constitution under which the
country gained independence the following month.

When these events occurred in early 1990, in the aftermath of the
sudden implosion of communism in Eastern Europe, there were only
three democracies in Africa: Botswana, the Gambia, and Mauritius.
Each had been continuously democratic since independence, but only
Mauritius had seen an alternation of the party in power. Many other
African countries had attempted democracy, some of them (like
Nigeria, Ghana, and Sudan) repeatedly, but all had failed. What had
prospered instead were a variety of military and one-party regimes,

TABLE—AFRICAN REGIMES IN 1998, BY REGIME TYPE
AND AVERAGE FREEDOM HOUSE SCORE*

LIBERAL DEMOCRACIES	ELECTORAL DEMOCRACIES	PSEUDO-DEMOCRACIES	AUTHORITARIAN REGIMES
1.5	**3.0**	**4.0**	**5.0**
Cape Verde	Ghana	Ethiopia	Eritrea
Mauritius	Madagascar	Senegal	Nigeria
São Tomé &	Seychelles	Sierra Leone	Swaziland
Príncipe		Uganda	
South Africa	**3.5**		**5.5**
	Central African	**4.5**	Djibouti
2.0	Republic	Burkina-Faso	Mauritania
Benin	Mozambique	Comoros	
Botswana		Gabon	**6.0**
	4.0	Tanzania	Congo-Brazzaville
2.5	Guinea-Bissau	Zambia	
Malawi	Lesotho	Zimbabwe	**6.5**
Namibia			Burundi
	4.5	**5.0**	Congo-Kinshasa
3.0	Liberia	Chad	Rwanda
Mali		Côte d'Ivoire	
			7.0
		5.5	Equatorial
		Guinea	Guinea
		Kenya	Somalia
		Togo	Sudan
		6.0	
		Angola	
		Cameroon	
		The Gambia	
		Niger	

*Liberal democracies are those countries rated "free" by Freedom House. Electoral democracies are also listed as democracies but not rated as "free." Pseudodemocracies have multiparty competitive elections that fall short of international standards of free and fair competition. All other regimes are classified simply as "authoritarian."
Sources: Adrian Karatnycky, "The Freedom House Survey: The Decline of Illiberal Democracy," *Journal of Democracy* 10 (January 1999): 112–25; and Freedom House, *Freedom in the World: The Annual Survey of Political Rights and Civil Liberties, 1997–1998* (New York: Freedom House, 1998).

many of them characterized as "neopatrimonial" because of the degree to which a single domineering leader personified and, in effect, owned the political system. So thin was the democratic terrain in Africa in the 1970s and 1980s that many academic and political observers accepted as democracies several regimes (most notably Senegal, but also Zimbabwe) that were at best semidemocracies, permitting multiparty elections but controlling the electoral process and repressing or coopting opposition so that defeat of the ruling party was impossible. The democratic label was also sometimes extended to one-party rule in Kenya and Tanzania, where intraparty elections for parliament were sufficiently contested so that as many as half of the incumbents lost their seats.

The democratic wave of the 1990s left few African states

untouched.[2] Michael Bratton reports in chapter 2 that of the 48 states in sub-Saharan Africa, only four had not held a competitive, multiparty election at the national level by the end of 1997. And one of those four, Nigeria, held a national election that was annulled by the military in 1993 and finally looked set to complete a democratic transition in the first half of 1999. As Bratton's essay and others in this volume make abundantly clear, many of Africa's new, competitive elections were deeply flawed and even blatantly rigged. But the mere fact that dictators felt compelled to legalize opposition parties and submit at least to the appearance of democratic competition represents a sea change in the postindependence politics of Africa. And many transitions signified real political openings.

The current state of democracy in Africa is open to differing assessments, as readers of this volume will discover. But no one can dispute that there has been a retreat "from *abertura* [the term for political opening in Brazil] to closure," as Richard Joseph terms it in the title of his essay opening this book. For Joseph, the "virtual miracle" of a new wave of democratic transitions in Africa rather quickly gave way to a state of "virtual democracy," or what is often termed "pseudodemocracy." A growing number of African regimes, Joseph argues, contrive the illusion that they are governed by democratic institutions and practices in order "to satisfy prevailing international norms of 'presentability.'" Where competitive multiparty elections did give birth to democracy, many newly elected leaders, like Frederick Chiluba in Zambia and Charles Taylor in Liberia, degraded fundamental features of the democratic process. So have the new generation of African leaders who promised a new liberation after seizing power by force of arms, such as Meles Zenawi in Ethiopia and Yoweri Museveni in Uganda. Elsewhere, authentic democracy (even of the limited electoral type) was preempted by wily, long-serving dictators who repressed, coopted, or outmaneuvered their newly legalized opponents, or by military officers who traded their uniforms for business suits (or flowing traditional robes) and then manipulated the electoral process to put an appearance of civilian constitutionalism on their dictatorial rule. Archetypes of the former type of virtuality were Daniel arap Moi in Kenya, Paul Biya in Cameroon, Omar Bongo in Gabon, Gnassingbé Eyadéma in Togo, and Henri Konan-Bédié in the Côte d'Ivoire. The archetype of the latter charade was Jerry Rawlings in Ghana, but even as Ghana gradually grew into a genuine democracy, other West African soldiers followed the path of legitimation through pseudodemocracy in 1996. They were Ibrahim Mainassara in Niger and Yahya Jammeh in the Gambia. As Joseph notes, the Nigerian military dictator Sani Abacha was preparing to follow suit, staging a phony transition amidst a reign of political terror. Indeed, Abacha had arranged for himself to receive the presidential nomination of all five recognized political parties. However, in a stroke of deliverance for the country, he suddenly died in mid-1998 (some months after the publication of Joseph's essay), reportedly after being poisoned by some of his fellow officers.

The retreat away from democracy in Africa is documented by Michael Bratton's analysis of founding and second elections in Africa during the 1990s. Even the early wave of founding elections (1989–94) in 29 countries was far from flawless; only a little more than half of these 54 contests (which included separate parliamentary and presidential elections in some countries) were internationally recognized as "free and fair" (and then often not without qualifications). In the subsequent three years, however, founding elections (15 in 11 countries) were manifestly less democratic. None was generally recognized by international observers and domestic monitors as "free and fair;" none was accepted by the losers (in contrast to 60 percent of the earlier founding elections); and most of them were boycotted. "As the 1990s progressed," Bratton observes, "leaders became adept at accommodating the international norm for competitive elections, while at the same time learning to manipulate them to their own ends." Thus, during the 1995–97 period, the second elections that were held in 16 countries were more often boycotted by the opposition and much less often (30 percent) recognized as free and fair. Overall, Bratton judges, the quality of the electoral process worsened in nine countries and improved in only two, Ghana and São Tomé. And in roughly half of Africa's new democracies, promised local-government elections were held late or not at all. For Bratton, as for Joseph and many other observers of Africa, Zambia stands as one of the starkest and most unfortunate examples of the retreat from democratic progress. "The Zambian case encapsulates many of the trends evidenced in other new African multiparty regimes, including the disqualification of leading candidates, the spotty coverage of voter registration, the lack of internal democracy in ruling parties, the abuse of government resources during the campaign, and the growing hostility of governments toward watchdog groups."

The trend toward declining political competitiveness and entrenchment of ruling parties and presidents is recognized as well in the other contributions to Section I of this volume. With the states of Francophone Africa particularly in mind, Célestin Monga, a native of Cameroon, captures in chapter 4 the frustration that so many African democrats have felt at the ability of longtime authoritarian rulers "to retain power by circumventing the new rules of the game and keeping a grip on military power and the public fisc." He notes the pervasive narrowness of the political arena, the suppression of civil society, the new and more subtle means by which the press has been intimidated and subdued, and the variety of tactics incumbent rulers have used to manipulate the electoral process and delegitimize opposition (sometimes to the point of challenging the very nationality of their principal presidential challengers).

These harsh realities are acknowledged both by E. Gyimah-Boadi and Crawford Young, but they arrive at more hopeful overall assessments. Despite the many renewed authoritarian practices, Gyimah-Boadi (in chapter 3) sees important trends toward liberalization in Africa. Progress is perhaps most pronounced in his own country, Ghana—one of the two that Bratton identifies as recording clear institutional progress in its second elections. But elsewhere on the continent as well, there is a new concern for constitutionalism, and some constitutions have introduced important liberal innovations to limit the discretion of state officials, protect private property, decentralize power, and provide for judicial review. Parliaments are constrained by extremely poor physical and financial resources and an autocratic culture of executive domination, but in some countries they are making a comeback as representative institutions with greater legal authority and popular prestige. Civil societies, too, suffer "severe material and organizational deficiencies" and frequent intimidation and repression even in formally democratic states, but they have not lost their energy and zeal for democratic reform. Africa's nongovernmental organizations (NGOs), frequently with small-scale assistance from international donors, are working to guard civil liberties, advocate economic and political reforms, monitor elections, strengthen democratic institutions, and educate citizens for democracy. Certainly the tradition of independent association in Africa is a long one. But what is new, in Gyimah-Boadi's view, is the vibrancy and focus of a whole new generation of NGOs that are "dedicated to the promotion of democratic governance and human rights."

The guarded optimism of Crawford Young's "balance sheet" in chapter 5 derives in part from his more historical perspective. Against the backdrop of Africa's repeated democratic failures and variety of authoritarian doctrines, the current decidedly mixed picture does represent progress. Only a few transitional regimes (Rwanda, Burundi, Algeria, Congo-Brazzaville) have descended into the escalating communal violence that authoritarian rulers have frequently cited as a reason for their indispensability. Elsewhere, more constitutional and participatory processes have shown promise of a greater ability to manage ethnic conflict, while showing "the need for thoughtful statecraft to devise constitutional formulas that can accommodate ethnic, religious, or racial differences." Democracy has worked to bring extraordinary developmental progress in Botswana and Mauritius, and may now be beginning to do so in Ghana, which with Uganda has been a leader in implementing economic reform. Not all of Africa's democratic experiments will survive, Young concludes, "yet many countries have experienced important changes beyond the most visible one of multiparty elections: a freer and more vocal press, better respect for human rights, some headway toward achieving the rule of law."

This progress is evident when one examines the annual Freedom House ratings for Africa. In 1989, just before the third wave washed over Africa, only three African countries were rated as "Free," a standard that might be taken as loosely equivalent to "liberal democracy."[3] Moreover, these three states (Botswana, Mauritius, and the Gambia) were the only electoral democracies in Africa. Eleven African states were rated as "Partly Free" (but mostly with scores near the bottom of that category), and 33 of the then 47 states in sub-Saharan Africa were rated "Not Free." By the end of 1998, the number of electoral democracies in Africa had mushroomed to 17 and the number of "Free" states had increased to nine, while the number of "Not Free" states had shrunk from 33 to 19.[4] (For a classification of all African regimes at the end of 1998, see the Table at the beginning of this article). These trends were reflected as well in the improvement in overall levels of freedom in Africa. If we take the average of the two Freedom House scores for political rights and civil liberties (each varying from 1, most free, to 7, least free), the overall average score for Africa in 1989 was 5.61.[5] By the end of 1998, this average score had improved markedly, to 4.42.[6] This improvement of more than a point on the seven-point scale well exceeds the global improvement in freedom scores since the start of the third wave.[7] Yet, indicative of Richard Joseph's assessment about the increasingly "virtual" state of democracy in Africa, there are now 19 pseudodemocracies in the region, two more than the number of electoral democracies. In sum, the glass may be only "one-third full," and then only murkily, but it contains considerably more than it did a decade ago.

South Africa: An African Success?

Perhaps the greatest hope for democracy in Africa, and the most vivid demonstration of the march of democracy on the continent, lies in South Africa. Certainly, South Africa is today the most powerful and influential liberal democracy on the continent, and its constitution is in some respects one of the most liberal in the world. Despite serious outbreaks of political violence, postponed elections in some local areas, and a frightening wave of violent crime, South Africa has managed to construct and maintain the political institutions of democracy. It is easy to forget that just a decade ago many observers, both South African and foreign, believed the country was on the edge of a full-scale racial civil war. The peaceful negotiation of a new, democratic, nonracial political order was widely viewed as a political miracle, and owed much to the exceptional vision and courage of political leaders on all sides, particularly Nelson Mandela. As the report of a 1998 International

Forum for Democratic Studies conference on South African democracy concluded, "those inclined to optimism can find much evidence of democratic progress: Civil liberties are intact more than three years into the new order; democracy remains the preference of more than two-thirds of citizens; and government actions and policies are subject to vigorous and vocal public debate."[8] However, as the essays in Section II demonstrate, the apartheid system—with its grotesque, racially based inequalities and its incessant manipulations of racial and ethnic animosity—has left behind formidable challenges for the new democracy, including acute economic distress and a wave of violent crime.

The contradictory nature of South Africa's situation is conveyed in all five of the chapters in Section II. The first three of these essays were published in January 1996, less than two years after the country's historic April 1994 founding elections and a few months before the adoption in May 1996 of the country's permanent constitution. While they have been overtaken by events in some of their details, their analysis continues to capture the painful dilemmas and immense possibilities of South Africa's democracy.

In chapter 6, Wilmot James and Daria Caliguire depict the problems confronting one of South Africa's most democratically dynamic sectors, civil society. The peaceful nature of South Africa's transition owes much to the long tradition of mobilization by thousands of NGOs and social-movement groups that resisted racial domination, defended human rights, promoted community development, and, in the words of James and Caliguire, provided "humane anchors and safe havens to a people victimized by apartheid." They estimate that at the time of the April 1994 elections, there were some 54,000 such organizations in the country. This represents an extraordinary source of democratic energy, independent of the state. However, as they demonstrate, the first years of democracy have ironically been a time of recession for civil society. With many of their leaders drafted into politics and government (or business), and with foreign donors shifting their funding to the state and larger-scale, more bureaucratic NGOs, many organizations have gone out of business. The dangers to civil society have been compounded by the corporatist mentality of many officials in the new ANC government, who would prefer to see civil-society organizations licensed by the state and responsive to its direction.[9] Yet the failure of an early effort to impose such constraints legislatively suggests the resilience of South Africa's democratic culture. And as some NGOs have moved to a larger, more bureaucratic scale, with extensive international grant funding, they have made impressive contributions to the spread of democratic values and ideas, the education of voters, the strengthening of parliamentary and local government institutions, the measurement of public opinion, and the preservation of a pluralistic social order. In fact, it would be difficult to find an NGO that has done more for democratic development on the African continent than the one which James himself has led for several years as executive director, the Institute for Democracy in South Africa (Idasa).

No problem is more vexing for South Africa than how to manage its deep racial and ethnic divisions. This challenge has attracted the creative attention of some of the world's leading theorists of ethnic conflict and democratic institutional designs.[10] Debates over institutional design have centered in particular on the virtues of power-sharing or "consociational" models, in which the power of an electoral majority is constrained constitutionally by requirements for proportional representation, special majorities, and broadly inclusive coalition cabinets. In chapter 7, Vincent T. Maphai takes a more nuanced approach. He argues that power-sharing along the lines of Arend Lijphart's consociational model can overcome the perils of a transition by giving each key actor a stake in the new system and giving minorities a brake on the power of a natural majority. To some extent, this is what the transitional South African constitution did, guaranteeing cabinet representation to any party winning more than five percent of the national vote, and thus producing a fairly inclusive "government of national unity." For South Africa, this and related provisions were "an essential precondition of democratization," the minimum that the ruling (predominantly white) National Party (NP) would accept. However, as Maphai notes, "government by grand coalition has its costs," and these were underscored when the NP finally withdrew from the coalition government in 1996. Like other critics of the model, Maphai argues that consociational bargains are "not the cause of tolerance, but the result." This compels a rethinking of the entire concept of a "deeply [and by implication, enduringly] divided" society. Like a growing number of scholars of ethnicity, Maphai sees ethnic divisions as much more fluid, and he notes the surprisingly low level of overt racial and ethnic campaigning (or militant racial voting) in the 1994 founding elections. Whatever the constitutional provisions, Maphai believes that pragmatic power-sharing is effectively mandated by South Africa's complex structure of power—which finds blacks dominant in the political arena but whites in the economic one, and different balances of strength in other sectors, such as the media, the military, and the police. He notes as well the potential problems for democratic competition and accountability of indefinite power-sharing. For these reasons, Maphai does not reject the model but believes that constitutional mandates for power-sharing are best employed as a purely transitional mechanism (which is what they were rendered when the permanent constitution dispensed with them).

South Africa's other most important cleavage is socioeconomic. Comparative data show South Africa to have one of the most unequal distributions of income in the world, with the richest 10 percent of the population earning 47 percent of annual income.[11] As Charles Simkins notes in chapter 8, an added problem with this inequality is its extraordinary correlation with race, more so than in any other country in the world. "The average per-capita income of blacks is about one-eighth that of whites," and the gaps in public services for the two communities are at least as large. Three-quarters of rural blacks live in poverty. This, even more than the past political repression, is the bitter legacy of apartheid. And it has placed enormous pressure on the new ANC government to try to meet a staggering backlog of needs for schools, potable water, jobs, and all the other elements of economic development. The government's chosen instrument for meeting this challenge was the Reconstruction and Development Program (RDP). However, as Simkins notes, it was constrained from the start by tepid economic growth, high budget deficits, and the need to restrain spending in order to maintain macroeconomic stability. The government has had more success at the latter goal than many of its critics would have expected. But as Simkins shows, the RDP was slow to get off the ground and was hampered by massive infrastructural and bureaucratic deficits as well. (By 1997, the RDP was abandoned altogether in favor of a more liberal, less redistributionist program known as Growth, Employment, and Redistribution, or GEAR.) Simkins concludes that "it will take a generation to reduce poverty from a mass condition to a state experienced by a small group of unfortunates," and like most economists, he argues that the real engine of poverty alleviation will have to be investment in the formal sector to create jobs.

The overriding political challenge for South Africa is whether it can consolidate democracy, and if so what type of democracy it will consolidate. These are the principal questions addressed in chapters 9 and 10. To examine progress toward consolidation, Robert Mattes and Hermann Thiel review in chapter 9 the growing body of evidence from public opinion surveys (which are now regularly conducted by Idasa). This evidence presents a mixed picture of public support for and commitment to democracy. In the abstract, most South Africans (three-quarters in 1995) believe democracy is a good form of government. But many of them comprehend democracy more in terms of material progress than of procedural guarantees like multiparty elections and minority rights. When asked to make a more demanding judgment— whether "democracy is always best," even if it does not work—56 percent of South Africans still endorsed democracy in 1997 (up from 47 percent in 1995). The clear majority preference for democracy, the growth in this preference over the preceding two years, and the dramatic drop in the proportion of the public who opt instead for "a strong leader who does not have to bother with elections," are all signs of apparent growth in the legitimacy of democracy, which may represent a somewhat more positive picture than Mattes and Thiel perceive. At the same time, the authors note a growing racial gap in public opinion about politics and democracy. In 1997, 61 percent of blacks said "democracy is always best," but only 39 percent of whites. Yet whites are much more likely than blacks to identify regular elections, party competition, and free speech as essential to democracy. They are also less likely to be satisfied with national conditions, to approve of government performance, and to be optimistic about the future. These racial differences in values and perceptions are another element of apartheid's legacy, and a prominent challenge on the path to consolidation.

For Hermann Giliomee in chapter 10, the primary challenge ahead is the quality and competitiveness of South Africa's new democracy. In contrast to Maphai, Giliomee believes the model of a "deeply divided" society is both theoretically valid and applicable to South Africa. He argues that, with the ANC's firm hold on the majority black electorate offering little prospect of electoral alternation in the foreseeable future, power-sharing constitutional provisions would be much more suitable than the largely majoritarian provisions that South Africa has settled on in its permanent constitution. Beyond the termination of power-sharing in the cabinet, he points with concern to that constitution's weak form of federalism and thin provisions for minority or cultural rights, as well as the absence of constitutional court judges "whose known views . . . on issues like federalism and cultural rights accord with those of minority parties." The new framework, he predicts, will give rise to a dominant-party system, in which the ANC will use its sweeping control over state power and patronage to cement the support of key constituencies and to rule unchallenged for some time to come. Given the illiberal record of dominant parties in semideveloped countries and especially in Africa, Giliomee worries that South Africa's emerging system could come to resemble its counterparts in semidemocratic Mexico and Malaysia more than the period of Congress party dominance in India. The danger is exacerbated, he feels (as do Mattes and Thiel), by the highly centralized character of most South African political parties, which are able to maintain tight party discipline through the closed-list system of proportional representation and the constitutional provision enabling "party leaders to expel from Parliament any member who defies party discipline or crosses the floor" to join another party.

Like Simkins and others, Giliomee also worries about the political implications of South Africa's economic distortions. These include not only the huge income and wealth disparities between the races, but widening class differences among blacks (who make up three-quarters of the population). Annual surveys cited by Mattes and Thiel show that the income gap between the poorest and richest fifths of black households is even greater than that between whites and blacks as a whole. This gap is heavily driven, Giliomee suggests, by the power of South African organized labor, which has used strikes and demonstrations to press for higher wages and more rigid labor markets at a time of high unemployment (24 percent) and anemic economic growth (barely 2 percent). What South Africa needs instead, Giliomee, Simkins, and other economic liberals argue, is greater labor market flexibility and other economic reforms to generate a policy climate conducive to investment. But this would require the ANC to confront one of its core constituencies. Following the 1999 national elections, it will fall to Nelson Mandela's almost-certain successor, Deputy President Thabo Mbeki, to tackle the formidable task of generating balanced and sustainable economic growth. Even if one takes a less skeptical view than Giliomee of the scope for political pluralism and the security of minority rights under the new constitutional regime, real progress on this economic front is essential if South Africa's democracy is to thrive in the twenty-first century.

African Ambiguities

Since its December 1996 national elections moved it past the threshold of electoral democracy, Ghana has also attracted much attention among observers looking for, and optimistic about, democratic progress in Africa. Since the mid-1980s, Ghana has complied with World Bank-style structural adjustment and economic reform measures more vigorously than almost any other African country. However, its politics and state have been dominated for almost two decades ago by a single, charismatic, and overpowering leader, former Flight Lieutenant Jerry Rawlings. Rawlings set up an authoritarian mobilizational regime upon seizing power for the second time at the end of 1981, and he has controlled Ghana's government ever since. As we see in chapters 11 and 12, by Terrence Lyons and E. Gyimah-Boadi respectively, Rawlings continues even to this day to manifest the neopatrimonial style and intolerance of opposition characteristic of most African leaders. But under pressure from below, in civil society, and from outside, among various donor organizations and states, Rawlings has liberalized the political system as well as the economy. The first step came in 1992, when voters approved a new constitution, the ban on political parties was lifted, and Rawlings resigned from the air force to contest the presidency at the helm of his own new party (which succeeded his mass movement). The November 1992 elections were so flawed, however, that the opposition parties boycotted the subsequent parliamentary elections, leaving Rawlings' National Democratic Congress (NDC) with virtually all the seats. The December 1996 elections were a dramatically different story. Rawlings was reelected, but only after being compelled to campaign seriously in a strongly contested race. The opposition parties won a third of the parliamentary seats. Most importantly, in contrast to 1992, the election was widely judged by both domestic and international actors to be free and fair.

In the difference between Ghana's 1992 and 1996 elections lie some important lessons for democratic development in Africa. As both Lyons and Gyimah-Boadi show, there were important institutional innovations, induced in part by the deliberations of a broad Inter-Party Advisory Committee. The electoral commission was made much more independent of government and partisan influence. The voters' register was completely revised. Extensive voter education efforts were undertaken, and Ghanaian NGOs fielded over 4,000 independent poll-watchers to supplement the 60,000 candidate agents present at nearly every polling station. This systematic domestic vote-monitoring enabled Ghana to use for the first time in its history one of the most important tools for preventing electoral fraud, a "parallel vote tabulation." By this technique, competing parties and nonpartisan actors are able to watch the votes as they are counted at the polls, receive copies of the officially reported count, and tabulate for themselves the vote totals at the constituency and national levels. These efforts were made possible by extensive financial and technical support from international democracy donors, international pressure on Rawlings to permit a more transparent process, and an enormous organizational effort by a broad range of Ghana's civil society organizations. Growing pluralism in the mass media also made a more competitive election possible.

Although the 1996 elections were (to quote Lyons) "an encouraging step forward in the democratization process," many obstacles remain. As Gyimah-Boadi shows, Ghana continues to be plagued by many of the problems that bedevil democratic politics generally in Africa: government and ruling party intolerance; weak and ineffectual opposition parties; entrenched ethnic political cleavages and resentments; a notable lack of intraparty democracy; central state dominance of district government; scant democratic accountability of military and security forces; and widespread misuse of state resources to support the ruling party. The 1996 elections were fought on a more level playing field, but it was one still heavily tilted in favor of the ruling party. That party is so intertwined with state institutions and resources that, in Gyimah-Boadi's view, "the NDC could become a frozen-in-place majority party, driving the opposition to despair of the ballot box as a route to power." For Ghanaian democrats, the challenge ahead is to strengthen opposition parties, civil-society organizations, the independent press, and the official agencies of horizontal accountability so that they "can restrain undemocratic governmental impulses" and build the foundations of a more liberal and sustainable democracy.

For all its flaws, Ghana's progress stands out in comparison with the democratic detours and dashed hopes suffered by many other African countries. The final four chapters look at four of these cases. In chapter 13, Joel D. Barkan and Njuguna Ng'ethe assess Kenya's democratic prospects following a December 1997 election in which, for the second time since Daniel arap Moi legalized opposition parties in 1991, hopes for a democratic alternation in power were frustrated by ruling party machinations and fractious ethnic divisions among the opposition. As in 1992, the electoral process in 1997 got off to a pseudodemocratic start when Moi—who has emerged as one of Africa's most corrupt and cynical rulers since succeeding to the presidency on Jomo Kenyatta's death in 1978—rejected domestic and international appeals for an independent electoral commission. The commission then grossly malapportioned electoral constituencies to favor the ruling party, while state security forces harassed and physically abused opposition politicians, their supporters, and civil society organizations. Worse still, as in 1992, the regime fomented deadly ethnic violence to terrorize and disorganize opposition strongholds. However, with his legitimacy in shreds, "Moi beat a tactical retreat" and opted for limited negotiations with the opposition. This produced some important institutional reforms to make the electoral commission more independent and the process more inclusive and fair. As in Ghana, the combination of institutional reforms, massive civil society mobilization (with the churches in each case playing a major role), and extensive international assistance produced an impressively comprehensive election monitoring effort. This in turn stimulated voter turnout and enabled significant opposition gains in parliament. In these developments, Barkan and Ng'ethe perceive democratic progress that can be built upon to negotiate a genuine regime transition, if soft-liners in the ruling party and pragmatists in the opposition can find a way to continue their dialogue and prevail against hard-liners.

Perhaps no case of political change in Africa is more ambiguous than that of Uganda, which Nelson Kasfir analyzes in chapter 14. Since his National Resistance Movement (NRM) took control in 1986 after a long military struggle, Yoweri Museveni has provided more decent and stable government than Uganda has known in decades. This has brought recurrent elections at both the national and village levels, middling levels of freedom, and (with aggressive economic reforms) the most rapid economic growth in Africa in recent years. All of this, however, has come in the strange form of what the NRM labels "no-party democracy." Uganda is the only African country to liberalize its politics while clinging to the African refrain of the 1960s and 1970s that competing political parties only foster ethnic divisions. Yet its political and economic success has won it acceptance from Western governments that have heavily pressured authoritarian regimes like Moi's. For Kasfir, the Ugandan case is puzzling because "Uganda has never been as democratic, either at the village or the national level, as it is today," but it is not the system of "no-party democracy" that has made it so. While parties are barred from political activity, the principles behind this hybrid system are otherwise poorly articulated. "Popular democracy" has worked at the village level to stimulate democratic participation, both in electing village councils and in making community decisions. Above the village level, the regime's institutional architecture of "resistance councils" involves several tiers of indirect representation, and the regime's commitment to "parliamentary democracy" remains vague and ill-defined. Indeed, as Kasfir notes, these forms of participatory and representative democracy are an odd, if not illogical, fit, and the regime has done little to square them other than to tacitly allow parties to compete beneath the veneer of a formal ban. As for the NRM itself, without internal democracy, "without institutions, without ideology, and finally, without a rationale that can justify its no-party democracy, it no longer has any existence apart from its leader."

Chapter 15, by John A. Wiseman, analyzes a country that has gone from one of Africa's few true democracies in the 1970s and 80s to one of its many pseudodemocracies today. In fact, until President Dawda Jawara was toppled from power in a July 1994 coup, the Gambia had the longest-standing democracy in Africa. The cabal of young officers who seized control, led by the new head of state Colonel Yahya Jammeh, trotted out all the usual excuses for their takeover. But whatever their frustrations with 29 years of rule by a single man and party, Gambian parties and civil society organizations strongly condemned the overthrow of constitutional rule. There followed the familiar African cycle of repression and resistance. For 30 months the military regime abused the press, arrested dissidents, pressured and stacked the judiciary, and brutally assaulted the rule of law. Then, in classic pseudodemocratic fashion, Jammeh and his regime created a party-movement that monopolized the political field until shortly before elections were called. With firm control of an electoral process so flawed that Western organizations abandoned monitoring efforts, and with a sweeping ban on all the former parties and politicians, Jammeh won the presidency and then a huge parliamentary majority in elections riddled with violence, partiality, and intimidation. In Wiseman's view, the "transition" was an improvement over "undiluted military rule." But in leaving this former bastion of liberal pluralism in the grip of a harshly repressive regime, the Gambia's pseudotransition has underscored the vulnerability of African democracy—and the courage of countless activists and journalists who are struggling to restore it.

As Wiseman notes, many observers saw Jammeh's maneuvers as a test run for the plans of Nigerian military dictator Sani Abacha to legitimize his own dictatorship through a pseudoelection. Those plans were derailed by Abacha's sudden death in June 1998. His military successor expedited a more authentic transition, with fresh political parties and elections at all levels. The schedule was to culminate in a presidential election on 27 February 1999, shortly after this book went to press. However, as Peter M. Lewis demonstrates in chapter 16, Nigeria is a country devastated by 15 continuous years of plundering, lawless military rule. The oil-based economy has been decimated by gross mismanagement and "new extremes of predation." Addicted to the huge financial rewards of power, the "armed forces have become habituated to ruling," and will look for the thinnest pretext to overthrow the politicians once more. Party politicians have themselves rarely risen above their own instinct for corruption, fraud, and opportunism, which brought down the Second Republic (1979–83). Moreover, they remain divided along ethnic and regional lines that were dangerously inflamed during the last decade and a half of rule by northern, Muslim military presidents. Indeed, northerners have led Nigeria's governments for all but four of its nearly 40 years of independence, and the 1993 annulment of the first election of a southerner (Chief Moshood Abiola) to the presidency profoundly wounded the body politic.

As in so many other African countries, the brightest aspect of a grim picture in Nigeria has been the tenacity and imagination with which many elements of civil society—including human rights and prodemocracy groups, academics, journalists, trade unions, and the bar association—have fought unprecedented repression, terror, and abuse of power by the militarized state. Even civil society, however, has been "subdued by repression and economic malaise," as well as by the ethnic and regional divisions that plague politics. A new civilian republic will be an enormous relief to a country exhausted by military dictation and larceny. But that republic will have to move quickly to craft a new, fairer, and more inclusive federal bargain, with meaningful devolution of economic and political power. It will also face daunting challenges of constraining military prerogatives, controlling corruption, and reviving a moribund economy. As Lewis concludes, "In view of its wealth and its regional importance, the ramifications of success or failure will extend well beyond Nigeria's borders."

Prospects for African Democracy

It did not take long for the promise of Africa's second liberation to evaporate in many countries. Transitions to electoral democracy were aborted, repressed, or outmaneuvered by wily dictators in roughly a dozen countries. Democracy has already broken down in Zambia, Niger, and the Gambia, replaced with its pale imitation of pseudo-democracy. In several other countries, such as Angola, Sierra Leone, Congo-Kinshasa, and Somalia, civil war and state collapse have pushed the question of democracy to the background as societies struggle for political order of any kind.

In the language of the social sciences, Africa's past democratic failures and current democratic recession are "overdetermined." The multiple obstacles identified in this volume include pervasive poverty, economic ruin, and the near-absence of a true middle class; the depth and tenacity of ethnic and regional divisions; the weakness of political parties, legislatures, courts, bureaucracies—political institutions of all kinds; the tradition of deference to "big men" and the larger culture of corruption and neopatrimonialism; state decay and its attendant rampant "crime, gangsterism, and warfare" (to quote Richard Joseph); and the divisions among powerful forces in the international community, which have led to the acceptance of pseudodemocracies that fail to meet supposed standards of good governance.

All of this is true, but it is only half true. Poverty did not prevent several other countries in Africa and Asia from developing and maintaining democracy. As Crawford Young and Vincent Maphai (as well as others) show in this volume, identity politics in Africa are more fluid and amenable to institutional incentives than pessimists allow. State decay can be arrested if political institutions begin to win legitimacy, respond to citizens, control corruption, and develop a rule of law. In large measure, that is what the struggle for genuine democracy is all about.

For the past three decades, there has been no lack of reasons to be pessimistic about Africa's future. But a more balanced reading is called for. As noted above, there is significantly greater political freedom and more space for civil society in Africa today than a decade ago. Even as some states have disintegrated, others are moving forward to reconstruction. There is also a new ideological and intellectual climate. Unlike during the false start of the first liberation that came with decolonization, Africa today evinces a new political sobriety that is hardened (and even jaundiced) by experience, but not without hope. Political ideologies, illusions, and excuses have fallen into disrepute: African socialism, Afro-Marxism, the integral state, the vanguard single-party state, the patrimonial keeper of ethnic peace, the military as modernizer, the military as social reformer—all of these excuses for authoritarian rule and "developmental dictatorship" have been roundly, and probably enduringly, discredited. Within sub-Saharan Africa, only in Uganda does a political ruler still mobilize majority support for a no-party state, and even there President Yoweri Museveni has used intimidation and state power to inflate his support at the polls. Moreover, political pluralism is growing in Uganda, and the issue of returning to a multiparty system will be revisited in a 1999 referendum.

As I have argued elsewhere (building on the work of Richard L. Sklar),[12] if we view democracy in developmental terms, as emerging in

fragments or parts by no fixed timetable or sequence, then the presence
of one fragment of democracy can provide space or inspiration for the
emergence of others. From this perspective, every increment of
democratic progress is significant and should be encouraged. Thus the
presence in pseudodemocracies of legal opposition parties that may
compete for power and win some seats in parliament, along with the
greater scope for civil society groups to organize and educate the
people, can provide foundations for eroding the hegemony of the ruling
party and pressing democratization further at some point to achieve a
(more or less) "free and fair" election.[13] This process is occurring now
in Mexico as civil society and opposition parties become stronger and
more resourceful. Even as Jerry Rawlings was reelected in 1996, Ghana
crossed the threshold to electoral democracy. As Crawford Young
observes, "Chicanery by incumbents can backfire, for denatured
elections lose much of their legitimating value." By the same token,
although electoral democracy may coexist with very significant levels
of hidden military power, judicial inefficacy, political and police
corruption, and human rights violations, the ability to turn the ruling
party out of power (at the center as well as in various state and local
governments) is a crucial threshold for democratization, especially
given Africa's harshly authoritarian experience. Most liberal democracies that do emerge in Africa will probably do so after passing
through, or even slipping back to, some period of "merely" electoral
democracy. The key is to keep the system moving forward, to
institutionalize whatever fragments or "parts" of democracy may have
emerged, and to avoid their displacement or perversion by yet another
in a long succession of military or executive coups.

As much as anything, Africa needs time to work with and become
habituated to democratic institutions, to shape them to fit its particular
cultural and political circumstances, and to allow them to sink deep
roots of commitment among all major political players and the public
at large. Time in itself is an important determinant of institutionalization.
Political parties, legislatures, judicial systems, civic organizations,
and other key structures of democracy cannot develop institutional
capacity, coherence, complexity, adaptability, autonomy, and broad
support unless they are permitted to operate continuously without
interruption.[14]

Is the glass two-thirds empty or one-third full? The truth is that the
situation of democracy in Africa is very fluid. Many of the remaining
African authoritarian regimes, especially the pseudodemocracies, have
weaker domestic support bases and face more vigorous and organized
opposition, especially in civil society, than in the past.[15] Some of the
pseudodemocracies, such as Kenya and Tanzania, at least have more
political pluralism and freedom than in the recent past. At the same
time, most of the new democracies are also fragile, and increasingly

Africa is haunted by the specter not just of authoritarianism but of the breakdown or disintegration of the state altogether. Because of the low legitimacy and pervasive weakness of state structures of all kinds, Africa would seem to be the region of the world where the future of democracy in the coming decade or two is most open-ended. That should be not a counsel for despair, but rather an invitation to democratic forces—in politics and civil society, in Africa and the international community—to learn from the mistakes of the past and deepen their commitment.

Africa's new democracies are still young and unconsolidated, but they are not doomed to failure by poverty and backwardness. Their peoples clearly want them to succeed. If they can find the resources and the strategies to develop their institutions and generate even modest economic growth, they can survive against the odds. And if, a decade from now, one can point to even a few more African democracies— particularly ones so large and powerful as South Africa and Nigeria— with some of the economic dynamism and political stability of Botswana and Mauritius, they will become important models for their neighbors. At that point, Africa will truly enter a new era.

NOTES

1. As Crawford Young notes in chapter 5, "National conferences drove incumbents from power in Mali, Niger, Congo-Brazzaville, and Madagascar; they failed to do so in Gabon, Zaire, and Togo, but still changed the 'rules of the game.'"

2. Our focus here is on the (currently) 48 states of sub-Saharan Africa, although Crawford Young expands his survey in chapter 5 to examine the five Arab states of North Africa as well.

3. Liberal democracy goes beyond the provision for regular, free, and fair electoral competition to provide for extensive individual and associational freedoms, secured through a rule of law that is enforced by an independent judiciary; it also requires the absence of "reserved domains" of power for the military or other forces not either directly or indirectly accountable to the electorate, and the presence of various means of "horizontal accountability" beyond an independent judiciary to constrain executive power. For a fuller discussion of the distinction, see Larry Diamond, *Developing Democracy: Toward Consolidation* (Baltimore: Johns Hopkins University Press, 1999), ch. 1.

4. This improvement is despite the fact that the "Not Free" category now takes in a wider range of countries (including those with an average score of 5.5) than the classification did in 1989.

5. Freedom House, *Freedom in the World, The Annual Survey of Political Rights and Civil Liberties, 1989–1990* (New York: Freedom House, 1990), 312–13.

6. In recent years, the criteria for evaluation applied by Freedom House have become somewhat more rigorous, complicating efforts to compare scores in countries (or average scores for regions) across long spans of time. However, this would tend to bias the more recent scores in a more authoritarian direction. The fact that Africa's 1998 freedom scores are considerably more liberal than those for 1989, despite the

more exacting standards, underscores how real the progress of freedom has been in Africa.

7. Globally, the average freedom score improved from 4.47 in 1974 to 3.58 in 1997, less than one point on the scale. See Larry Diamond, *Developing Democracy*, 27, Table 2.3.

8. Louise Stack, "Democratic Consolidation in South Africa: Progress and Pitfalls," Report at a conference by the same title, sponsored by the Centre for Policy Studies (Johannesburg) and the International Forum for Democratic Studies (Washington, D.C.), in Johannesburg, 16–17 February 1998. The report is available online at: www.ned.org/page_6/safrica/intro.html#intro.

9. These problems of civil society are hardly unique to South Africa, E. Gyimah-Boadi's essay makes clear. For a more extensive treatment, see his article, "Civil Society in Africa," *Journal of Democracy* 7 (April 1996): 118–32.

10. In addition to the works by Arend Lijphart cited in chapter 7, see Donald L. Horowitz, *A Democratic South Africa? Constitutional Engineering in a Divided Society* (Berkeley: University of California Press, 1991).

11. Of more than 90 countries for which recent data is reported, only Kenya and Brazil exceed this measure of South Africa's income inequality, and they do so by less than one percentage point. World Bank, *World Development Report 1998/99* (New York: Oxford University Press, 1999), Table 5, 198–99.

12. Richard L. Sklar, "Developmental Democracy," *Comparative Studies in Society and History* 29 (October 1987): 686–714, and "Towards a Theory of Developmental Democracy," in Adrian Leftwich, ed., *Democracy and Development: Theory and Practice* (Cambridge, England: Polity Press, 1996): 25–44. My perspective is articulated more extensively in *Developing Democracy*.

13. This is one important implication of the empirical finding of Michael Bratton and Nicolas van de Walle that the frequency of elections (even if opposition parties were forbidden to compete in them) and the percentage of opposition seats in the legislature prior to 1989 both had significant positive correlations with the level of democracy (as measured by the absolute level of political rights) in 1994. See their *Democratic Experiments in Africa: Regime Transitions in Comparative Perspective* (Cambridge: Cambridge University Press, 1997).

14. For a seminal theoretical perspective on institutionalization, see Samuel P. Huntington, *Political Order in Changing Societies* (New Haven: Yale University Press, 1968): 12–24. One reason why India, Sri Lanka, Jamaica, and other British Caribbean states had more postindependence success with democracy than most African states is that the former countries had much longer periods of practice with electoral competition and participation and partial self-rule before independence. By contrast, democratization occurred much more rapidly under British rule in Africa, and more rapidly still (if at all) under French and other colonial rule in Africa. Africa's second liberation has also experienced very rapid transitions from authoritarian rule. Bratton and van de Walle calculate a median interval of less than three years between the onset of the transition and the accession to office of a new government. They note that this has left "precious little time" for democratic procedures to take root, and is bound to make the challenge of consolidating these new democracies "problematic in years to come." Bratton and van de Walle, *Democratic Experiments in Africa,* 1997.

15. See, for example, Masipula Sithole's trenchant account of "Zimbabwe's Eroding Authoritarianism," *Journal of Democracy* 8 (January 1997): 127–41. We regret that space constraints did not enable us to include this fine essay in our book.

I

Assessing Africa's Third Wave

1

AFRICA, 1990–1997: FROM *ABERTURA* TO CLOSURE

Richard Joseph

Richard Joseph is Asa G. Candler Professor of Political Science and former fellow at the Carter Center of Emory University in Atlanta. His essay "Africa: The Rebirth of Political Freedom" appeared in the Fall 1991 issue of the Journal of Democracy. *He is the author of* Democracy and Prebendal Politics in Nigeria: The Rise and Fall of the Second Republic *(1987), and he edited the Carter Center bulletin,* Africa Dēmos, *from 1989 to 1994. He is the editor of* State, Conflict, and Democracy in Africa *(1999).*

Writing in these pages in 1991, I noted that a "virtual miracle" seemed to be leading Africa away from authoritarianism and toward democratic governance.[1] So rapid and extensive were the democratic developments at the time that I urged caution in assessing their consequences. What few analysts anticipated, however, was that the democratic wave in Africa would crest so quickly or that the countercurrents would surface so swiftly.

Africa's political opening or *abertura* (a Portuguese term that entered comparative political discourse as a description of Brazil's gradual transition from military to elected government) had similar characteristics to those experienced elsewhere in the years before and after the end of the Cold War: the termination of single-party dominance; relegalization of opposition parties; restored freedoms of association, assembly, and expression; and constitutional reforms leading to competitive elections. In my 1991 essay, I discussed the salient features of seven African models of transition. These included: 1) the national conference; 2) government change via democratic elections; 3) coopted transitions; 4) guided democratization; 5) recalcitrance and piecemeal reforms; 6) armed insurrections culminating in elections; and 7) conditional transitions. Given the rapid, unpredictable pace of change, these categories were admittedly preliminary. With few exceptions, they have since culminated in variants of what I have termed "virtual democracy."[2] What distinguishes this type of regime is the illusory nature of its democratic institutions and practices, and the fact that they are deliberately contrived to satisfy prevailing international norms of "presentability."

The following is a brief review of these seven provisional models and their generally disappointing results. During ten momentous days in early 1990, the first national conference in the small West African country of Benin stripped President Mathieu Kérékou, an autocratic ruler for 17 years, of all his executive powers. Over the next few years, however, other African leaders became so skillful in denying, pro-longing, and neutralizing national conferences that the latter were gradually transformed into instruments for regime consolidation.[3] Free elections, which had seemed to signal Africa's coming of age and its capacity to oversee the peaceful, democratic replacement of one government by another, followed national conferences in becoming exercises that mainly legitimized, rather than undermined, incumbent regimes. The next three models—coopted transitions, guided democratization, and recalcitrance and piecemeal reforms—are best seen today as having produced exemplars of virtual democracy. The sixth model, armed insurrections culminating in elections, was pri-marily a mechanism for transferring or legitimizing power after years of armed conflict.[4] Finally, conditional transitions, in which threats to regime dominance by militant groups also jeopardized prospects for democracy, have evolved into unconditional denials of any transition, as exemplified by the brutal conflict in Algeria.

Political Renewal and Political Violence

Of the many factors impeding constitutional democracy in Africa, none appears more significant than the upsurge of political violence. Reflecting his skepticism about the recomposition of power in Africa behind the facade of democratization, Achille Mbembe proposed closer scrutiny of "regimes which long relied on modes of authoritar-ian governance [and] are making an about-turn and verbally espousing democratic ideals."[5] More attention, in his view, should be directed to the crime, gangsterism, and warfare prevalent in both functioning and collapsed states in Africa. Instead of political transitions, Mbembe speaks of revising formulas and structures of domination, which rely upon the coexistence of warfare and civil politics.

Following Mbembe, we can distinguish cases in which warfare leads to the collapse of civil politics from those in which warfare and civil politics coexist. Often there is no clear demarcation between organized groups that pursue political objectives and those responsible for the criminalization of state and society through drug trafficking, mineral smuggling, embezzlement of public funds, money laundering, and other fraudulent practices.[6] In rethinking the course of political renewal in Africa, analysts should pay more attention to the role of political violence.

Since Sani Abacha seized power in Nigeria in November 1993, state-sponsored violence there has steadily intensified. Numerous security agencies track, harass, and often eliminate individuals considered a threat to the regime. Opponents of the Abacha government, among them such prominent figures as Alfred Rewane, Kudirat Abiola, Ken Saro-Wiwa, and Shehu Yar'Adua, have been systematically brutalized and killed, both within and outside prison. Yet the use of political assassination as an instrument of rule can be traced to the very start of the military government's "democratic transition" program, when the dynamic journalist Dele Giwa was blown up by a parcel bomb in October 1986.[7]

In 1995, former British foreign secretary Douglas Hurd described Nigeria as a country of "growing cruelty." Today, brute force has become the main currency of political control, whether in the form of mass executions of alleged coup-plotters; prolonged detentions under inhumane conditions without trial; targeted assassinations; or physical harassment of journalists, human rights monitors, and political opponents. Nevertheless, a veneer of civility shrouds the political arena, with the regime sanctioning political parties, conducting elections for various assemblies, and allowing independent groups to function under the constant threat of arrest or physical attack. Regime spokesmen continue to insist that the transition program is on course, and portray its critics as misguided persons seeking to tarnish the country's image. Bolstered by oil income, the Abacha regime has perpetrated a reign of terror. As its opponents are driven to contemplate armed struggle or palace coups, the regime preempts these threats with greater violence, the use of *agents provocateurs,* and further expansion of the security forces. In Nigeria, political renewal and political violence have become tightly interwoven: Today, there is little hope for the former without an effective response to the latter.[8]

In Kenya, President Daniel arap Moi's resort to political violence as a means of retaining power while making piecemeal concessions to the opposition is well known. Therefore, I shall discuss the lesser known but highly similar cases of Cameroon and Togo. Both countries are ruled by regimes that have remained in power for over three decades. In Cameroon, Paul Biya replaced Ahmadu Ahidjo as president in 1982, having served as his vice-president for several years. Togo's Gnassingbé Eyadéma masterminded a military coup in 1967, and has ruled his country ever since. In the early 1990s, the governments of both these countries came under significant challenge. In Cameroon, Biya restored political liberties but refused to convene a national conference, while in Togo, a national conference forced Eyadéma to share power with a transitional government in 1991–92.[9] Despite the *abertura* that saw the reemergence of full political contestation in both countries, pervasive state violence coupled with bogus elections gradually succeeded in dividing, coopting, and subduing the opposition. Today, Cameroon and Togo are archetypical virtual democracies, possessing many of the institutional features of liberal democracy (such as regularly scheduled elections) while their governments systematically stifle opposition behind a mask of legitimacy.

Another country that often eludes criticism and even enjoys a certain international cachet because of its positive economic growth is Burkina Faso. In October 1987, Blaise Compaoré, a prominent member of the military government, plotted the assassination of its radical leader, Thomas Sankara. Shortly thereafter, the other key members of the junta were also eliminated. In order to consolidate and legitimize his seizure of power, Compaoré had to overcome two important obstacles: Burkina Faso's tradition of genuine transitions to elected governments, and the existence of numerous political associations and militant trade unions. In a grim prelude to competitive party politics, Compaoré's government subjected moderate and radical forces alike to harsh repression. Although opposition parties boycotted the 1992 elections in protest, the government went ahead with them. Duly elected, the Compaoré regime has since succeeded in establishing complete dominance over Burkinabe society, in attracting substantial foreign private and public capital, and in conducting plebiscitary elections against token opposition.

In English-speaking Africa, the archetypical example of both *abertura* and subsequent political closure has been Zambia. In 1991, President Kenneth Kaunda, head of the government for 27 years, ceded to opposition and international demands for a return to multiparty elections, and was defeated at the polls. Although the government of the victorious Movement for Multiparty Democracy (MMD), led by President Frederick Chiluba, could have proceeded to construct a constitutional democracy in compliance with its promises, it opted instead for a virtual democracy. Chiluba's elected government arrested outspoken journalists and civil society activists; detained political opponents; used mysterious bombings as a pretext for imposing states of emergency; and amended the Constitution to bar Kaunda from competing in the 1996 elections. In six years, Chiluba has taken Zambia back to the worst period of what had been, by prevailing African standards, relatively mild authoritarian governance under Kaunda. What is more alarming is the ease with which Chiluba has manipulated voter support and development aid to withstand demands to follow a more democratic course.

Bullets, Ballots, and Regime Change

In explaining political trends in African countries that attained independence in the 1960s, analysts have noted that these new states had emerged from colonial rule only to be caught up in the bipolar rivalry of the Cold War. East-West geopolitics facilitated their movement toward authoritarianism. The end of the Cold War both helped and hindered Africa's *abertura* of the early 1990s, spurring democratic transitions as well as armed struggles. At first, these seemed to be different kinds of phenomena. What is now evident, however, is the convergence and interpenetration of the two sets of dynamics.

In December 1989, a small band of armed men headed by Charles Taylor entered northeastern Liberia in an attempt to overthrow the repressive regime of Samuel Doe. After a few months of fighting, during which both sides terrorized the civilian population, Taylor and his men managed to encircle the capital city of Monrovia. Doe, however, could not be dislodged. After diplomatic efforts to end the impasse failed, a Nigerian-led regional peacekeeping force entered the country in August 1990. During the next seven years, warlord factionalism in Liberia and military domination in Nigeria became symbiotically linked. The Liberian factional leaders engaged in predatory activities to support their irregular forces, and many officers of the peacekeeping force followed suit. Eventually, Taylor made a pact with Abacha: The Nigerians would guarantee the former's physical security as his troops were disarmed and he prepared for national elections. In return, the Abacha regime could proclaim the peacekeeping mission—to which Nigeria had contributed considerable resources—a success. Moreover, both Abacha and Taylor could take credit as "democratizers." By conceding to this scenario in giving Taylor and his National Patriotic Party an overwhelming victory in the July 1997 elections, the war-weary Liberian electorate seized the opportunity to vote for the person most likely to end the war—the one who had started it and had kept it going in his quest for power.[10]

In East Africa, Ethiopia and Somalia were once heavily armed by Cold War adversaries. When Siad Barre was driven from power in January 1991, the Somali state dissolved into Somali clan society. Unless a warlord or some coalition of factions acquires the military capacity to reunite the country through force, the Somali state may never reemerge. In neighboring Ethiopia, a bloody civil war resulted in the May 1991 overthrow of the Marxist-Leninist regime of Mengistu Haile Mariam by two disciplined and politicized armed forces, the Eritrean People's Liberation Front (EPLF) and the Tigre People's Liberation Front (the latter constituting the core of the Ethiopian People's Revolutionary Democratic Front, or EPRDF). After Mengistu's defeat, the EPLF had the easier path to political hegemony in newly independent Eritrea, as it had trounced both its Eritrean and Ethiopian opponents during the war.

In Ethiopia, the U.S. government had given the EPRDF the go-ahead to take control of Addis Ababa in order to avoid the chaos and anarchy that had gripped Monrovia in 1990. Such an external blessing, however, was conditioned on the movement's promise to establish a democratic government. Ethiopia's new government, led by Meles Zenawi, was left with the task of satisfying a number of competing imperatives—conducting democratic elections from a minority ethnic base while retaining power as the fruit of its armed victory; reassuring international donors of his regime's commitment to democratic pluralism while maintaining its Leninist core; and respecting freedoms of assembly, organization, and expression in a country that had never previously enjoyed them (and in which many political groups preferred to settle disagreements by resort to arms). Since 1991, the new regime has achieved a high degree of presentability and has overcome or defused many of these challenges. Yet the democratic system, established to satisfy external patrons, is wholly virtual in nature. Today, the Ethiopian government systematically detains journalists and opponents, brushes off a catalogue of human rights condemnations, manipulates elections, and writes constitutions to produce predetermined results, all the while attracting lavish international development aid and enjoying the privilege of being treated as a close U.S. ally in the region.[11]

> *In much of Africa, armed force still confers the basic right to rule, which is then ratified by elections.*

A fundamental premise of a successful *abertura* is that state power must eventually be legitimized by a democratic vote. Since the 1970s and 1980s, this principle has been upheld by political systems in many once-authoritarian countries throughout Southern Europe and South America. In much of Africa, however, armed force still confers the basic right to rule, which is then ratified by elections. In the Gambia, Niger, Burundi, and Sierra Leone, army coups dislodged representative governments in the mid-1990s. In the first two countries, controlled elections were held to legitimize this seizure of power. In Burundi, Pierre Buyoya, a military officer who had been praised for ceding power after his electoral defeat in 1993, was restored to power in July 1996 when the Tutsi-dominated army overthrew a civilian coalition government. Only in Sierra Leone was the ruling junta not permitted to obtain legitimacy via controlled elections, thanks to Nigerian intervention. The Nigerian government led the call for international sanctions, then launched a military assault to force the junta to restore Sierra Leone's elected president, Ahmad Tejan Kabbah, who was overthrown in May 1997. Meanwhile, Nigeria's own elected president, Moshood Abiola, remains imprisoned without trial for a fourth year.

What has further signaled the emergence of a new paradigm in late twentieth-century African politics is a sequence of events that can be traced back to Uganda's fraudulent elections of 1980 and that culminated in 1997 in the forcible overthrow of dictator Mobutu Sese Seko in the former Zaire. After the defeat of his minor political party in Uganda's 1980 elections, Yoweri Museveni organized a National Resistance Army (NRA) that eventually swept to power. In January 1986, his forces decided to seize all power rather than share it with other opponents of the former regime of Milton Obote. Having started out as a minor political player in a brutalized nation, Museveni succeeded through force of arms and skillful political management in generating a profound geostrategic shift in east and central Africa. The political arm of the NRA, the National Resistance Movement (NRM), has garnered extensive support and tacit acceptance of its hybrid political system from Western powers and international donors.

Beginning with a crossborder incursion from Uganda into Rwanda in 1990, high-ranking Tutsi members of the NRM sought to replicate the Ugandan experience. After seizing power in Rwanda in the wake of that country's April–May 1994 genocide, the Rwandan Patriotic Front (RPF) later sought to extend the NRM's model of regime change to Zaire. When the Alliance des Forces Démocratiques pour la Libération du Congo (AFDL) launched its military campaign against the Mobutu regime, it did so with considerable RPF assistance and even guidance. Today, the regimes in all three countries rely on their armed might, refuse to share power with other opponents of the former governments, and have won grudging international acceptance of their right to "democratize" in their own way and at their own pace.

A dramatic demonstration that might is still the basis of right in Africa, rather than the reverse, occurred in Congo-Brazzaville. Since 1993, this central African nation had been the site of intermittent warfare among militias organized by leading politicians. Hostilities resumed in June 1997, and four months later the militia of head-of-state-turned-warlord Denis Sassou-Nguesso defeated the elected government of Pascal Lissouba with the strategic help of the Angolan government and the tacit compliance of France. A numbed international community barely issued a murmur of protest about this return by force of arms of a dictator who had been made to confess his failings by the national conference in 1991, and who had been eliminated in the first round of presidential elections in 1992. New elections had been scheduled for July 1997, but were postponed because of the armed conflict. Shortly after seizing power in October 1997, Sassou-Nguesso announced that his regime would conduct proper elections in due course. Angola, which had sent troops and planes to help Sassou-Nguesso's final onslaught, was simply asked to withdraw them.

These events have greatly reduced hopes for a deepening and broadening of the *abertura* in many countries. Africa is once again regarded internationally as a continent of mixed governance—of a few states with genuine democratic features and many others in which democracy is valued only as camouflage. Despite the significant increase in the number of elected governments since the 1980s, the virtual nature of most of the democracies established and the recognition accorded regimes imposed by armed force suggest that democratization in the new global era should be examined within a broader framework of the reconfiguration of state power.

The International Dimension

I have suggested above that Africa's stalled *abertura* cannot be understood without considering the simultaneous upsurge in armed conflicts. Equally important in explaining both the *abertura* and subsequent closure in African politics is the extensive influence of international actors. My perspective differs in this regard from that of Michael Bratton and Nicolas van de Walle, who argue that "although international factors played an important part in explaining democratization, they remained secondary." These authors also contend that analysis of democratization "is likely to be more fruitful if focused on political rather than economic factors," and anchor their study to the premise that "African regime transitions are primarily explicable in terms of domestic political struggles . . . in a context of inherited institutions."[12]

Based on close monitoring of and personal involvement in several African transitions since 1990, I have advanced a different interpretation that does not privilege political factors over economic ones or domestic struggles over international action. Crucial to my analysis is the interplay among these intersecting factors and forces. Elsewhere, I have argued that democratic outcomes in Africa are the consequence of a dynamic interplay among three forces—regimes, domestic opponents, and external agencies—and that the international drive to impose market-based solutions in the form of structural adjustment programs was intrinsic to the *abertura*.[13]

Following independence from colonial rule, as African regimes grew increasingly monopolistic and their economies atrophied, the gap between claims to "juridical statehood" and the reality of domestic failure to achieve "empirical statehood" widened.[14] The ability of African states to procure resources from the international system proved critical to their survival. The relentless search for financial and other resources came to characterize African politics in the postcolonial era. As the Cold War drew to an end, external leverage that the West had used to promote economic liberalization during the 1980s was initially applied to promote political liberalization. By the mid-1990s, however, external concerns for order, regional security, and market-based reforms encouraged political closure and the return to largely rhetorical endorsements of democratization. Moreover, as presentability became the effective criterion for obtaining the stamp of international approval, both African regimes and their foreign sponsors engaged in democracy as illusion.[15]

As long as African countries fail to negotiate the passage from "quasi-statehood" to "empirical statehood," licit and illicit transfers of resources across their boundaries will be vital to the sustenance of their governments. Christopher Clapham emphasizes the "extroverted" character of African politics, by which he means that developments on the continent are heavily influenced, and often determined, by external forces. His perspective contributes to our understanding of the tenuous nature of Africa's *abertura*. The fiscal crisis that gripped most African states in the 1980s forced them to accept increased dictation by international agencies and bilateral donors. As domestic revenues dried up, regimes reluctantly agreed to remove constraints on private market development in order to ensure continued access to international aid. Many analysts felt that private markets would undermine the political monopolies of regimes and provide resources to sustain a competitive party system.

After initially viewing structural adjustment reforms as threats to state-dominated economies and their patronage networks, African rulers have slowly adapted to the demands of the international community. However, this "political adjustment," to use Jeffrey Herbst's formulation, only partially promotes the liberalization that outsiders anticipated.[16] Generous aid packages accompany structural adjustment programs, and are replenished regularly so long as recipients promise to implement acceptable economic reforms. Gradually, African leaders evolved from being adversaries to becoming allies of external agencies. In the long term, increased economic development may well provide the basis for viable competitive politics. In the short term, however, increases in Africa's economic growth have strengthened the commitment of external donors to work with existing regimes, whatever their provenance and internal character, and have led them to ease demands for political pluralism, except in egregious cases such as Kenya and Nigeria.

As Clapham observes, external resources have always been vital to regime survival in Africa and have become particularly critical since the end of the Cold War. Western powers achieved some initial success in using this leverage to compel recalcitrant rulers to open up their political systems. Just as in the economic realm these rulers had mastered the art of promising external agencies what they demanded while doing only what was unavoidable, so too did they learn to cede ground to demands for democratization while using its very instruments to effect closure of the transition.[17] Robert Bates has perceptively argued that only when African rulers have to negotiate with their own citizens for the resources to govern will a genuine transition away from authoritarianism become possible.[18] From Clapham's perspective, the African experience since 1990 suggests the inverse of the Bratton and van de Walle hypothesis. Domestic tensions in political and civil society in Africa can be neutralized as long as regimes procure sufficient external resources to keep their opponents at bay.[19] Thus by a curious paradox, "extroversion" renders African states vulnerable to international pressure for political and economic change, but this same phenomenon has made it possible for both incumbent and new regimes to adjust to external demands, secure enhanced resources, and use this support to tighten their grip on power. External actors consequently find themselves as deeply enmeshed today in the political dynamics of closure as they were in those of *abertura*.

The international environment, of course, is not a cohesive but a competitive one, and this factor has also facilitated political closure in Africa. To take one example, France's fear of U.S. incursions into its postcolonial empire has enabled autocratic rulers in several African countries to overcome strong domestic and external challenges since 1990. France has provided financial resources to its former colonies whenever a serious threat has arisen. The persistence of armed conflict and genocidal wars in Africa has prompted foreign leaders to push for greater political order on the continent. Diplomatic efforts to strengthen African states therefore converged with international attempts to promote economic liberalization, providing African rulers enhanced leverage against their domestic opponents. Many of the latter are giving up the struggle and settling for a share of power in reconstituted national governments, a model that has been fine-tuned in Senegal since 1991, and is now being advanced in Cameroon, Côte d'Ivoire, and even Kenya.

The message being sent by these developments is that Africa is not ready for competitive democracy but only for a lesser system that French-speaking scholars derisively call "démocratie tropicalisée." Nevertheless, as the cases of Botswana, Mauritius, Benin, Ghana, and South Africa demonstrate, political contestation can help transform African countries into constitutional democracies. Where such progress has not occurred, ruling groups have often deliberately acted to impede it, as the cases of Nigeria, Zambia, and Rwanda exemplify.[20] The role of international actors in facilitating Africa's *abertura* must not be underestimated, but neither should their capacity to hasten or slow down the closure presently under way.

African Closure in Comparative Perspective

A number of scholars are now examining the decline in the pace and depth of democratization worldwide. In an insightful essay entitled "Is the

Third Wave Over?" Larry Diamond advances a three-fold typology of democracies—liberal democracy, electoral democracy, and pseudo-democracy.[21] Liberal democracy is a robust version of Robert Dahl's polyarchy. While falling short of liberal democracy, electoral democracy at least provides "a sufficiently fair arena of contestation to allow the ruling party to be turned out of office."[22] Countries that hold multiparty elections without fair contestation are considered pseudodemocracies. Diamond devotes most of his attention to the "hollowness" of the electoral democracies that have emerged since the late 1970s, and to the growing gap between them and genuine liberal democracies. He points out that the former, many of which are to be found in Latin America, stop at the electoral stage of democracy, which is enough to achieve "international legitimacy and economic rewards."[23]

African countries, Diamond observes, are held to an even lower threshold: "All that is required is the presence of opposition parties that can contest for office, even if they are manipulated, hounded, and robbed of victory at election time."[24] There are many points of overlap between Diamond's analysis and that presented here. Diamond recognizes, for example, the positive and negative consequences of the international dimension of contemporary transitions and the importance of what I refer to as presentability. Despite the dismissive connotation of the designation "pseudodemocracies," Diamond believes, following Richard Sklar, that such systems include democratic features that may be developed over time. I have adopted and adapted the term "virtual democracy" to emphasize the significance of "virtuality"—of ritual and symbol, of appearance and presentability—in these regimes. The image of men and women in poor countries queuing up *en masse* to vote is a powerful one. When opposition parties boycott such balloting on the grounds that existing conditions preclude a fair election, they often become targets of criticism for refusing to perform their appropriate roles.

While Diamond frequently refers to constitutionalism and the rule of law as intrinsic elements of the armature of liberal democracy, my studies suggest the need to give them even greater consideration. Whether or not countries make a successful transition to democracy depends in large part on their respect for constitutionalism, the rule of law, and judicial independence. In Zambia, it was the survival of these very institutions throughout the single-party period that facilitated the transfer of power in 1991. Their deliberate weakening today under Chiluba foreshadows the restoration of authoritarianism. A reverse process is occurring in both Benin and Ghana. Mathieu Kérékou and Jerry Rawlings undermined these institutions when they ruled as autocrats, but have shown respect for their operations since they were elected as presidents of democratic polities.

While Diamond and other analysts of contemporary democratic

transitions wrestle with the limitations of electoralism, they anchor their framework to its attributes.[25] Greater attention must be devoted to the possibilities for democratic development outside the electoral arena and to assessments of their broader impact. As Sklar observes, all that is good in political life may not be definable as democratic, and most political systems are mixed in nature.[26] Sklar's argument alerts us not just to the importance of oligarchical features in Western political systems—such as upper legislative chambers and supreme courts—but also to the rich array of traditional institutions in Africa that often provide some accountable, if not strictly "democratic," governance within myriad local communities.

> **The rebirth of political freedom and the resurgence of political violence took place simultaneously as consequences of the end of the Cold War.**

In an exercise similar to Diamond's, Thomas Carothers explores the reasons why the global democratic revolution "has cooled considerably," and why, in the case of Africa, it has not fulfilled hopes for a "continent-wide shift to democracy."[27] Part of the problem, he contends, is that the drive toward democratization in the early 1990s seemed to override concern for the assumed prerequisites of liberal democracy—including economic wealth, political history, culture, and class development. The result, Carothers argues, has been the emergence of "semi-authoritarian" regimes, fashioned in direct response to external incentives. His description of what I have called virtual democracies is on target. To obtain international attention, approval, and aid, rulers conduct "a balancing act in which they impose enough repression to keep their opponents weak and maintain their own power while adhering to enough democratic formalities that they might just pass themselves off as democrats."[28]

Carothers' essay could just as well have been entitled "Democracy as Illusion," for he demonstrates how, after the introduction of such key elements of pluralist democracy as independent media, opposition parties, legislatures, and periodic elections, these elements are drained of their vitality in ways that do not trigger adverse responses from Western powers and international donors. He concludes that the enlargement of democracy should be abandoned as an overriding goal of U.S. foreign policy. My own conclusion, based on a similar assessment of post-1990 developments, is that scholars should actively analyze and criticize configurations of power that involve the adoption and distortion of democratic institutions, rather than simply recommend policy adjustments based on their acceptance.

In a provocative essay, Fareed Zakaria examines the upsurge of what he calls "democratic illiberalism."[29] Elected governments in emergent democracies "are routinely ignoring constitutional limits on their power and depriving their citizens of basic rights and freedom,"[30] signaling the absence from their systems of "constitutional liberalism." Zakaria's essay should spur more attention to the difficult task of developing constitutionalism as a means of preventing monopolies of power and abuses of office in countries that lack a liberal tradition. Avoiding the teleology implicit in many studies of emergent democracies, Zakaria argues that contemporary combinations of democracy and illiberalism may be neither temporary nor transitional, and that Western liberal democracy may just be one of many possible outcomes. He recognizes the "electoralist trap" that has ensnared advocates of democracy and is also aware of the peculiarities of contemporary democracy-as-presentability: "In an age of images and symbols, elections are easy to capture on film," thereby making democracy "part of the fashionable attire of modernity."[31]

Contemporary democratization, I would conclude, must be studied as part of a complex set of national and global dynamics including: 1) the insistence on the sovereign rights of states over those of peoples; 2) the reinforcement of personalist rule by external actors; 3) the freer flow of financial resources, which reduces the leverage of any particular major power, such as the United States; 4) the overlapping of global crime syndicates with transnational political networks (enabling rulers to draw resources from both the official and the "shadow" state); 5) the upsurge in ethnic and religious movements; 6) and the pressures to restore political order after the turmoil and upheavals of the *abertura*. The rebirth of political freedom and the resurgence of political violence took place simultaneously as consequences of the end of the Cold War. The convergence and interpenetration of these dynamics have yielded a complex pattern of regime change. Far from generating a mood of "democratic pessimism," these circumstances should invite a renewed commitment to investigate their essential features as a prelude to devising more appropriate theories of democratic development. Political closure in Africa and elsewhere, which followed the global *abertura,* should therefore encourage the opening of new lines of inquiry and analysis.

NOTES

1. Richard Joseph, "Africa: The Rebirth of Political Freedom," *Journal of Democracy* 2 (Fall 1991): 11–24.

2. See Richard Joseph, "Democratization in Africa After 1989: Comparative and Theoretical Perspectives," *Comparative Politics* 29 (April 1997): 363–82.

3. Such an assessment applies most clearly to Gabon, Togo, and Zaire. In Congo, Niger, and Madagascar, national conferences contributed, in a more disorderly fashion than in Benin, to regime change. Everywhere else—in Cameroon, Côte d'Ivoire, and Nigeria, for instance—the government crushed or outmaneuvered conference advocates.

4. This formulation can be applied to all post-1989 examples in Africa: Ethiopia, Liberia, Mozambique, Namibia, and South Africa. With the exception of Angola, where insurgents led by Jonas Savimbi refused to accept their electoral defeat in 1992, elections in general have proven an effective exit from the stalemate of warfare.

5. Achille Mbembe, "Democratization and Social Movements in Africa," *Africa Dēmos* 1 (November 1990): 4.

6. See Jean-François Bayart, Stephen Ellis, and Béatrice Hibou, *La criminalisation de l'état en Afrique* (Brussels: Editions Complexe, 1997).

7. See Ray Ekpu, "Nigeria's Embattled Fourth Estate," *Journal of Democracy* 1 (Spring 1990): 106–16.

8. For a fuller discussion, see Richard Joseph, "Autocracy, Violence, and Ethno-Military Rule in Nigeria," in Richard Joseph, ed., *State, Conflict, and Democracy in Africa* (Boulder, Colo.: Lynne Rienner, 1999).

9. See Jean-Germain Gros, "The Hard Lessons of Cameroon," *Journal of Democracy* 6 (July 1995): 112–27.

10. This summary is based on several visits by the author to Liberia and neighboring countries from 1991 to 1994 in connection with peace initiatives. I conducted two subsequent research visits in 1995 and 1997 financed by a grant from the United States Institute of Peace.

11. These observations are drawn from the available scholarly literature and other reports as well my personal engagement (1989–94) in conflict-resolution efforts, first between the Mengistu regime and its adversaries, and then between the EPRDF and its opponents.

12. Michael Bratton and Nicolas van de Walle, *Democratic Experiments in Africa: Regime Transitions in Comparative Perspective* (Cambridge: Cambridge University Press, 1997), 221. I concur, however, with their emphasis on institutionalization in this important study.

13. See my "Democratization in Africa After 1989," and "Reconfiguration of Power in Late Twentieth-Century Africa," in Richard Joseph, ed., *State, Conflict, and Democracy in Africa.*

14. Christopher Clapham, *Africa and the International System: The Politics of State Survival* (Cambridge: Cambridge University Press, 1996); and Robert H. Jackson and Carl G. Rosberg, "Why Africa's Weak States Persist: The Empirical and the Juridical in Statehood," *World Politics* 35 (October 1982):1–24.

15. Several media reports on the visit of U.S. secretary of state Madeleine Albright to seven African nations in December 1997—only one of which (South Africa) had a democratically elected government—emphasized this point. See Hugh Dellios, "Faking It in Africa," *Chicago Tribune,* 4 January 1998; and Howard W. French, "Albright in Africa: The Embraceable Regimes," *The New York Times,* 16 December 1997.

16. Jeffrey Herbst, "The Structural Adjustment of Politics in Africa," *World Development* 18 (July 1990): 949–58.

17. I first heard Marina Ottaway advance this notion of "closure" during a workshop in April 1996, although I use it here more narrowly than she does. See Marina Ottaway, ed., *Democracy in Africa: The Hard Road Ahead* (Boulder, Colo.: Lynne Rienner, 1997), 3.

18. See Robert Bates, "The Economic Bases of Democratization," in Richard Joseph, ed., *State, Conflict, and Democracy in Africa.*

19. This is what happened for several years in the former Zaire, which experienced an expansive *abertura* in 1990–92. A supreme master at using the extroversion of his vast country to political advantage, President Mobutu overcame all challenges and was only dislodged by armed force after he became fatally ill.

20. On Rwanda, see the insightful analyses by Timothy Longman of the defeat of the *abertura* (1990–94) in "Rwanda: Chaos from Above," in L.A. Villalón and P.A. Huxtable, eds., *The African State at a Critical Juncture* (Boulder, Colo.: Lynne Rienner, 1997), 75–91; and "State, Civil Society, and Genocide in Rwanda," in Richard Joseph, ed., *State, Conflict, and Democracy in Africa.*

21. Larry Diamond, "Is The Third Wave Over?" *Journal of Democracy* 7 (July 1996): 20–37.

22. Ibid., 25.

23. Ibid., 32.

24. Ibid., 30.

25. In fact, the very hollowness of the electoral democracies that Diamond discusses suggests the need for a broader approach to democratization than the dominant Schumpeter-Huntington framework. See my own formulation in "Democratization in Africa After 1989."

26. See *African Renewal,* Conference on African Renewal, Massachusetts Institute of Technology, 6–9 March 1997; and Richard Sklar, "African Polities: The Next Generation," in Richard Joseph, ed., *State, Conflict, and Democracy in Africa.*

27. Thomas Carothers, "Democracy Without Illusions," *Foreign Affairs* 76 (January–February 1997): 85–99.

28. Ibid., 91.

29. Fareed Zakaria, "The Rise of Illiberal Democracy," *Foreign Affairs* 76 (November–December 1997): 22–43.

30. Ibid., 22.

31. Ibid., 40 and 42.

2

SECOND ELECTIONS IN AFRICA

Michael Bratton

Michael Bratton, professor of political science at Michigan State University, spent 1998 in South Africa. He is the coauthor, with Nicolas van de Walle, of Democratic Experiments in Africa: Regime Transitions in Comparative Perspective *(1997). An early version of this article appeared in a chapter, coauthored with Daniel Posner, in* State, Conflict, and Democracy in Africa, *edited by Richard Joseph, copyright ©1998 by Lynne Rienner Publishers, Inc. Parts of the original chapter are used with permission of the publisher.*

The early 1990s saw a wave of competitive multiparty elections in Africa. These contests can be described as "founding" elections in the sense that they marked for various countries a transition from an extended period of authoritarian rule to fledgling democratic government. By the middle of the 1990s, this wave had crested. Although founding elections continued to be conducted in African countries that were latecomers to the political-reform bandwagon, they took place less frequently than earlier in the decade. Meanwhile, in countries that had experienced early regime change, expiring electoral cycles gave rise to a groundswell of "second" elections. Less glamorous than the landmark contests that gave birth to democracy, these events nevertheless held out the possibility that democratic routines might be deepened.

The consolidation of democracy involves the widespread acceptance of rules to guarantee political participation and political competition. Elections—which empower ordinary citizens to choose among contestants for top political office—clearly promote both sorts of rules. But analysts do not agree on the role that elections play in the consolidation of democracy. Some, like Samuel P. Huntington, use electoral criteria for measuring consolidation: the so-called two-turnover test.[1] Against such an approach, Terry Karl has raised the specter of a "fallacy of electoralism."[2] As experience with "illiberal" democracies shows, elections can coexist with systematic abuses of political rights and the disenfranchisement of much of the population.[3]

I hold a middle view in this debate: While seeking to avoid the electoral fallacy, I try not to commit its antithesis—what Seligson and Booth call the "anti-electoralist fallacy"[4]—by assuming that elections *never* matter for democratization. I recognize that elections do not, in and of themselves, constitute a consolidated democracy. This end-state also requires civil rights and due process of law; checks on arbitrary executive power; civilian control of the military; and an independent press and civil society. In a consolidated democracy, citizens and politicians alike accept that this array of institutions is the only legitimate arrangement for governing public life.

But while elections and democracy are not synonymous, elections remain fundamental, not only for installing democratic governments, but as a necessary requisite for broader democratic consolidation. The regularity, openness, and acceptability of elections signal whether basic constitutional, behavioral, and attitudinal foundations are being laid for sustainable democratic rule. It is meaningful to study elections for the simple reason that, while you can have elections without democracy, you cannot have democracy without elections. If nothing else, the convening of scheduled multiparty elections serves the minimal function of marking democracy's survival. The most immediate concern for many of Africa's fragile new democracies is whether they will endure at all. By recording the occurrence of a second competitive election, we can at least confirm that democratic gains have not been completely reversed by executive fiat or military coup.

In assessing second elections, the empirical tasks are straightforward. The first concerns electoral *quantity*. Are second elections held? And if so, do they take place on time? The answers here help ascertain how strictly officeholders subject themselves to the rule of law. Incumbents who respect electoral schedules (rather than illegally altering election timing to increase their chances of holding on to power) acknowledge that good governance requires observance of at least some constitutional constraints.

Next come questions of electoral *quality*. Exactly how free and fair are second elections? Definitive judgments are difficult whenever the quality of elections varies across different stages of the process. For example, flawed voter-registration exercises or highly unfair campaigns may be followed by relatively open and free balloting. But to the extent that observers report gross deficiencies at any stage of an election, its integrity can be called into dispute. In addition, one must consider whether an election is boycotted by opposition parties. Whereas widespread involvement by various political parties probably indicates the absence of major electoral deficiencies, a boycott seems to signal a lack of agreement on the rules of the democratic game. Yet the

TABLE 1—TRENDS IN FOUNDING ELECTIONS IN SUB-SAHARAN AFRICA, 1989–1997

Chronology of Election	No. of Countries	No. of Elections (Pres. & Leg.)	Opposition Boycott[1]	Free and Fair[2]	Leadership Alternation[3]	Losers Accept[4]	Voter Turnout[5] (% Reg. Voters) (mean)	Winner's Vote Share (Pres. Elecs.) (mean)	Winner's Seat Share[6] (Leg. Elecs.) (mean)
Early (1989–94)[7]	29	54	6 (11.1%)	30 (55.5%)	11 (37.9%)*	32 (59.2%)	63.3%	61.4%	62.7%
Late (1995–97)[8]	11	15	11 (73.3%)	0 (0.0%)	1 (6.6%)*	0 (0.0%)	66.8%	69.1%	72.0%
All	40	69	17	30	12	32			
All (Percent)			(24.6%)	(43.5%)	(30.0%)*	(46.3%)	64.1%	63.4%	65.3%

Notes:

1. An opposition boycott occurs if any party withdraws in protest from the election. In most cases, boycotts are partial with some parties participating and others standing back.

2. The "free and fair" determination is based on the preponderance of judgments reported by international election observers and domestic election monitors.

3. Leadership alternation refers to electoral turnover of chief political executives.

4. Loser acceptance is established when minority parties do not mount a legal challenge to the election of a president, or when they accept parliamentary seats following a legislative election.

5. Wherever possible, turnout is measured as total valid votes as a percentage of registered voters.

6. Winner's seat share refers to the proportion of seats won by the largest party in the legislature, which, for bicameral systems, is regarded as the lower house. Data on founding legislative elections are taken from the variable LEGSEATS in Michael Bratton and Nicolas van de Walle et al., *Political Regimes and Regime Transitions in Africa: A Comparative Handbook* (East Lansing: Michigan State University Press, 1996).

7. All other data on early founding elections are taken from Michael Bratton and Nicolas van de Walle, *Democratic Experiments in Africa: Regime Transitions in Comparative Perspective* (New York: Cambridge University Press, 1997), Tables 7 and 8.

8. Data on late founding elections were collected for this article from *Africa Research Bulletin, Election Notes, Parliamentary and Presidential Elections Around the World, Elections Today, NDI Reports, Journal of Democracy,* and *Marches tropicaux.*

* Numbers refer to countries rather than elections. Percentages are calculated using the number of countries as a denominator. All other figures and percentages refer to elections.

quality of boycotted elections can be ambiguous; we should remain alert to the possibility that a boycott, rather than reflecting a flawed electoral process, can be a ruse by opposition parties that have concluded that they stand no chance of winning.

This brings us to a third set of questions concerning electoral *meaning*. Because political power involves intangible elements like the legitimacy of government, elections are contested in symbolic as well as empirical terms. In new democracies, where elections are not yet fully institutionalized, contenders vie to win votes and seats but they also struggle to control the interpretation of outcomes. Elections that result in regime transition or leadership alternation are usually un-equivocal, signifying a break with the past. Those in which incumbents retain power are harder to interpret because they involve judgments about whether the vote enhances or reduces a sitting government's mandate. In part, an election's legitimacy can be gauged by objective indicators such as the winner's shares of votes or seats. But even these are subject to interpretation, for example in the light of turnout rates or considerations of campaign context and conduct.

In Africa, disputes about the meaning of multiparty elections tend to be directed externally at foreign aid donors, especially when funding decisions hinge on a verdict of "free and fair." Because the stakes are high—the continuation of balance-of-payments support or project aid—disputes over interpretation come to the fore after the election. Winners deploy the informational and coercive instruments of the state to reinforce their claim to have received a mandate, while losers try to undermine this assertion by arguing that the process was rigged. The competition to assign meaning takes place before various audiences— elite and mass, domestic and international—that may apply different standards of judgment. Thus analysts are forced to interpret diverse claims of electoral quality, understanding all along that the contending parties seek to interpret the meaning of elections in order to promote their own interests.

Founding Elections, 1989 to 1997

In *Democratic Experiments in Africa,* Nicolas van de Walle and I documented the nature of "early" founding elections in Africa.[5] These events were widespread, with 54 elections occurring in 29 countries during a brief five-year period of transition from 1990 to 1994 (see Table 1). More than half of these early founding elections—30 out of 54—reflected the will of the electorate, inasmuch as reputable election observers ruled them free and fair. They were marked by relatively high turnout (averaging 64.1 percent of registered voters) and convincing victories (with winners averaging 63.4 percent of valid votes in presidential elections). Most importantly, in a momentous break with past patterns of leadership succession in Africa, these contests resulted in the peaceful ejection of sitting presidents in 11 countries (plus three more turnovers where incumbents declined to run). In sum, the postcolonial generation of African political leaders proved unable to survive truly democratic elections.

Since that time, multiparty elections have become commonplace in sub-Saharan Africa. By the end of 1997, only four countries in the region had failed to complete a competitive contest during the 1990s: Nigeria, Somalia, Swaziland, and Zaire. All others had held either first founding elections (40 cases) or regular competitive polls (5 cases). "Late" founding elections (i.e., those held *after* 1994) did not usually result in leadership alternation, however; more often than not, sitting presidents found ways to survive. As the 1990s progressed, leaders became adept at accommodating the international norm for competitive elections, while at the same time learning to manipulate them to their own ends. In general, the later founding elections were held in Africa, the poorer the quality of their conduct and the lower the likelihood that incumbents would lose.

Table 1 summarizes the features of the 15 late founding elections held in 11 African countries between January 1995 and December 1997. In some respects, these contests resembled the early founding round, for instance in terms of relatively high turnout (averaging 66.8 percent). In other respects, late founding elections revealed novel trends. There were opposition boycotts, for example, in 11 out of the 15 cases. Concomitantly, election observers were unable to endorse *any* of these elections as fully meeting international standards, calling into question the integrity of the polling, the campaign, or the electoral rules. This undistinguished record stands in marked contrast to the more than half of African elections that observers ruled free and fair during 1990–94.

Strikingly, leadership turnover occurred in only one case after 1994. In Sierra Leone in February 1996, civilian leader Ahmad Tejan Kabbah displaced coup-maker Brigadier Julius Maada Bio (who did not run) in an election in which "a military connection was the kiss of death for vote-seekers."[6] In all other cases of late founding elections, the incumbent was returned and election winners commonly increased their margins of victory (with vote and seat shares averaging 69.1 and 72 percent in presidential and legislative elections, respectively). Almost invariably, losers refused to accept the results.

How can this trend of declining quality of founding elections be explained? With the exception of Tanzania, late founding elections were all held in countries whose leaders had come to power by military coup or, in the cases of Ethiopia, Liberia, and Uganda, by dint of a guerrilla military victory. The person presiding over (and competing in) the election was a soldier who had doffed his uniform to run as a civilian. His commitment was usually less to democracy than to shoring up his international and domestic standing by catering to the new expectation that African political leaders ascend to office via elections. Not surprisingly, the imperfect elections sponsored by such calculating leaders did little to advance the cause of democratization on the African continent. The lower quality of late founding elections was perhaps predictable: Because the most reluctant political reformers were the last to concede elections, they departed furthest from the democratic ideal.

Second Elections, 1995 to 1997

During the same period, 1995 to 1997, African countries that had embarked early on political reforms entered a second round of elections. Having completed early founding polls (with various degrees of success), these countries came due again for regularly scheduled polls. A list of 16 such countries and 23 second elections is presented in Table 2.

This list excludes countries whose democratic transitions were reversed by military coup before second elections could take place. Melchior Ndadaye's elected government in Burundi survived all of four months before being overthrown by the Tutsi-led military in 1994. In Sierra Leone, the elected government lasted little more than a year before falling in 1997 to adventurer Johnny Paul Koroma. In Congo-Brazzaville, deposed dictator Denis Sassou-Nguesso fought his way back to power with the help of the Cobra militia; second elections were canceled amid the fighting between rival ethnic factions. By the end of 1997, four of Africa's 17 new democracies (Burundi, Congo-Brazzaville, Niger, and Sierra Leone) and one longstanding multiparty regime (the Gambia) had succumbed to military takeovers. And the long-awaited ouster of Mobutu Sese Seko in Congo-Kinshasa (formerly Zaire) came not after founding elections, but after the military victory of a leader who modeled his transitional regime on no-party principles. Thus any doubt that a backwash of democratic reversals had begun in Africa was surely dispelled by late 1997.

Yet soldier-politicians have not had everything their own way in the current era of global democratization. Military coups failed as often as they succeeded, in part due to a changing international environment in which both donor countries and neighboring African governments withheld recognition and support from unelected regimes. Attempted coups have been blocked by international interventions, for example, by the French in Comoros and the South Africans in Lesotho. Successful coups have been followed by political isolation. And since the ouster of coup-maker Koroma by Nigerian-led forces in Sierra Leone in February 1998, soldiers even run the risk of facing the forced restoration of elected leaders. Reflecting the widespread influence of

TABLE 2—SECOND ELECTIONS IN SUB-SAHARAN AFRICA, 1995–1997*

Country	Date[1] (Type)[2] of Election	Held on Time[3]	Opposition Boycott	Free and Fair[4]	Quality Trend[5]	Leadership Alternation[6]	Losers Accept	Voter Turnout (% Reg. Voters)	Winner's Vote Share (Pres. Elec.)	Winner's Seat Share (Leg. Elec.)
Namibia	12/7/94 (G)	Yes?	No	Yes	unchanged	No	Yes	76.1	74.5	73.6
Niger	1/12/95 (L)	Yes	No	Yes	unchanged	Yes?	Yes	35.0	—	34.9
Benin	3/28/95 (L)	Yes	No	Yes	unchanged	Yes?	Yes	75.9	—	24.1
	3/3/96 (P)	Yes	No	Yes?	worsened	Yes	Yes	86.8	52.5	—
Côte d'Ivoire	10/22/95 (P)	Yes	Yes	No	worsened	No	No	56.2	95.2	84.0
	11/26/95 (L)	Yes	No	No	worsened	No	Yes?	48.9	—	69.4
Cape Verde	12/17/95 (L)	Yes	No	Yes	unchanged	No	Yes	76.5	—	—
	2/18/96 (P)	Yes	No	Yes	unchanged	No	Yes	43.4	80.0 (est.)	—
Comoros	3/6/96 (P)	Yes	No	Yes?	unchanged	Yes?	Yes	62.0	61.2	85.7
	12/1/96 (L)	Yes?	Yes	No	worsened	No	No	low	—	—
São Tomé	6/30/96 (P)	Yes	No	Yes	improved	No	Yes?	67.5	52.2	—
Mauritania	10/11/96 (L)	Yes	No	Yes?	unchanged	No	Yes?	30.0 (est.)	—	88.6
	12/12/97 (P)	Yes	Yes	No	worsened	No	No	74.0?	90.2	—
Madagascar	11/3/96 (P)	Yes	No	Yes?	worsened	Yes	Yes?	49.7	50.7	—
Zambia	11/18/96 (G)	Yes?	Yes	No	worsened	No	No	58.7	72.6	87.3
Ghana	12/7/96 (G)	Yes?	No	Yes	improved	No	Yes	77.9	57.4	66.0
Gabon	12/15/96 (L)	No	Yes	No	unchanged	No	No	not available	—	76.6
Mali	4/30 & 7/20/97(L)	Yes	Yes	No	worsened	No	No	21.0	—	88.4
	5/11/97 (P)	Yes	Yes	No	worsened	No	No	28.4	95.9	—
Burkina Faso	5/11/97 (L)	Yes?	No	No	worsened	No	No	44.0	—	90.9
Cameroon	5/18/97 (L)	Yes	No	No	unchanged	No	No	not available	—	60.6
	10/12/97 (P)	Yes	Yes	No	worsened	No	No	81.0?	92.6	—
Kenya	12/29/97 (G)	Yes	No	No	unchanged	No	No	67.0	40.4	51.4
All (n=16)	23	22	8	7		2	8			
All (Percent)		(95.6%)	(34.8%)	(30.4%)		(8.7%)	(34.8%)	55.8%[7]	70.4%	70.1%

*For Notes to Table 2, see bottom of facing page.

the democratic idea, soldiers who seize power now find it essential to promise citizens and the international community that they will convene competitive elections as soon as possible.

Indeed, military rule is now exceptional in Africa. Thirteen of Africa's 17 new democracies have retained civilian rule, and most have held second elections on time (see Table 2, column 3). Just one multiparty regime has so far failed to adhere to its electoral cycle, and then only temporarily. President Omar Bongo breached Gabon's 1990 Constitution, abandoned a written accord between the ruling and opposition parties, and ignored a Constitutional Court ruling calling for National Assembly elections before 8 June 1996. Instead, he re-appointed the prime minister whose term had expired and hinted that he would bring family members back into government. Commentators speculated that Bongo was worried that his party would lose the impending legislative elections, forcing him to appoint an opposition premier and relinquish control over the crucial ministries of finance, oil, and internal security.[7] In the end, however, Bongo allowed disputed elections to go forward six months late on 15 December 1996, and his party was returned with an increased majority.

The other 22 second elections in Africa's civilian regimes have all been convened in timely fashion. In a few cases the elections were held several weeks after a due date (see "Yes?" in Table 2, column 3). In Zambia, the government and opposition could not agree on the starting date used to calculate the expiration of the electoral cycle; in Ghana, the delay was incurred against the wishes of the government so that presidential and parliamentary elections could be held on the same day. Yet even where incumbents exploited their discretion over scheduling to the utmost, elections were held with sufficient timeliness to satisfy at least the spirit of the law. In other cases, elections were actually called

---

* *Notes to Table 2:*

1. For two-round elections and for elections that last more than one day, the date of the election refers to the first day of polling. Dates are given as month/day/year.

2. G stands for general election, P for presidential, and L for legislative. Elections are dubbed "general" if a presidential and legislative poll are held concurrently on the same day or days; otherwise, elections are listed separately.

3. Elections that are called early or held on time according to the electoral timetable are scored as "Yes." If elections are only slightly delayed, i.e., held within three months of the scheduled date, the score is "Yes?" This category is included in the calculation of the total number and percentage of elections that were timely.

4. "Yes?" refers to qualified "free and fair" judgments by observers or cases where observers did not agree on the quality of the election. This category is not included in totals.

5. Quality trend is measured by change, if any, between founding and second contests in reported judgments by observers on whether the elections were free and fair.

6. Leadership alternation refers only to presidential elections. "Yes?" indicates instances in which a new party (or party coalition) took over control of the national legislature as the result of a second election. This category is not included in totals.

7. Excludes questionable official turnout figures for presidential elections in Mauritania and Cameroon.

ahead of time. For example, parliamentary elections were held prematurely in Niger in January 1995 when the ruling coalition broke up and the National Assembly was dissolved. In Madagascar, the impeachment of President Albert Zafy, a legislative decision that was later upheld by the High Constitutional Court, led to early presidential elections in November 1996. In all other eligible countries, second presidential and legislative elections were held precisely on schedule.

Unfortunately, the same cannot be said for local-government elections. In perhaps half of Africa's new democracies, these were held either late or not at all. Again, Gabon was a main offender: Bongo postponed municipal polls on five separate occasions, saying each time that more time was needed for preparations. While incumbents had self-serving reasons for avoiding exposure at the polls, there was some truth to the claim that logistically demanding local elections were beyond the financial and administrative capacity of poorer African countries (though not of Gabon, which runs budget surpluses). In Malawi, local polling had to be put off because of a government fiscal crisis and international donors' unwillingness to pay. Obviously, until elected local governments are established or restored, the task of building democracy in Africa will remain seriously incomplete.

The Quality of Second Elections

Did the quality of second elections, like that of the late founding contests with which they overlapped, also decline? The best standard for comparison is a country's own recent history. Here the findings are less encouraging, with performance worsening in 11 out of 23 cases (see Table 2, column 6). Indeed, as a group, Africa's liberalized regimes experienced fewer acceptable elections during 1995–97 (30.4 percent) than in their own founding round in 1990–94 (55.5 percent).

Take some examples. In Côte d'Ivoire, President Henri Konan-Bédié introduced a new electoral code stipulating that a presidential candidate had to be both born of Ivorien parents and resident in the country for at least five years, thereby effectively sidelining Alassane Ouattara, his only serious rival. Bédié marshaled his main assets—the ruling party's patronage machine, the paramilitary *gendarmerie,* and backing from France—to engineer landslide victories in both the presidential and legislative polls. As in Zambia, where similar doctoring of the rules took place, the incumbent appeared determined to "rig an election he would probably have won anyway."[8] In Comoros, where the presidential election of March 1996 went relatively smoothly, the legislative election of December 1996 was a disaster. Voter turnout was reportedly low following the arrest of two former prime ministers and a series of arson attacks in the run-up to the election.[9] In a searing symbol of electoral decline, the central administrative building in Moroni was burned to the ground, destroying ballot boxes and other electoral materials.

Although incumbent parties were returned to power in these cases, the poor quality of the elections cast doubt upon the legitimacy of the resulting governments. In Côte d'Ivoire and Comoros, these outcomes represented a measure of institutional continuity, since neither of these countries had strong democratic records. Zambia, on the other hand, had held a model founding election in 1991 and therefore enjoyed a much more promising start. It stands as perhaps the clearest example of the trend of declining quality of second elections in the sub-Sahara region. The Zambian case encapsulates many of the trends evidenced in other new African multiparty regimes, including the disqualification of leading candidates, the spotty coverage of voter registration, the lack of internal democracy in ruling parties, the abuse of government resources during the campaign, and the growing hostility of governments toward watchdog groups.[10]

In another unfortunate precedent from one of Africa's most promising new democracies, the second legislative elections in Mali in April 1997 were badly bungled. Polling stations failed to open, voting materials were in short supply, and inaccurate voter lists prevented voters from casting their ballots. The organization of the elections was so poor that the courts ultimately annulled the results, and the election had to be rerun four months later. Suspicions that these obstacles were not entirely accidental led the two main opposition alliances to announce boycotts; incumbent Alpha Oumar Konaré therefore won the second presidential election of May 1997. Although he got 96 percent, the 28 percent turnout made it a less-than-ringing endorsement.

Africa-wide trends, however, obscure a couple of exceptions. In Ghana and also in the island republic of São Tomé and Príncipe, the quality of elections improved as dubious earlier proceedings were succeeded by more open and transparent contests. In São Tomé, the second presidential election of July 1996 was the first to feature more than one candidate. In Ghana, observers uniformly praised the conduct of the December 1996 second elections, singling out the independence and professionalism of the national Electoral Commission and the determination of voters peacefully to exercise their political rights as "positive step[s] forward in the strengthening of Ghana's democracy and its electoral process."[11] Interestingly, although incumbents were returned to office in these improved second elections, the losers accepted the results. While hardly conclusive, this suggests that Africans are beginning to focus less on the removal of individual strongmen and more on the creation of lasting electoral institutions.

Generally, second elections were not marked by leadership alternation; clear presidential turnover occurred in only two cases (see Table 2, column 7).[12] In Benin in March 1996, Nicéphore Soglo was

ejected by the same voters who had swept him to power in one of
Africa's landmark democratic transitions just five years earlier. Soglo
(though reportedly privately bitter at the result) honorably hailed the
principle of multiparty elections: "My greatest consolation comes from
the conduct of my fellow countrymen . . . all the people of Benin were
the winners."[13] In an equally close but more sharply disputed contest,
leaders alternated in Madagascar in a drawn-out electoral process.
Having tried to delay the second round of voting and charging malfeasance in vote counting, former president Zafy eventually conceded
defeat in early 1997. In both these cases, second elections restored
former strongmen who had been ousted in founding elections. Yet
while Kérékou of Benin proclaimed that he had been "born again," not
only as a Christian but also as a democrat, Ratsiraka of Madagascar
showed less indication of having changed his autocratic spots.

Everywhere else in sub-Saharan Africa, sitting leaders weathered
second elections. Most often, voters reaffirmed their support for political reform by reelecting leaders who had first obtained office during
the regime transitions of the early 1990s. Providing that voters had not
been entirely disillusioned by an incumbent's economic management,
they generally sought continuity in political leadership in the aftermath
of turbulent interludes of regime transition. Additionally, voters probably chose to give incumbents another term in office before passing
judgment on whether the government had delivered on its promises.

The Meaning of Second Elections

What, then, was the meaning of second elections? To be sure, sitting
governments and their opponents differed in their views of these
events, as indicated by the increased frequency of opposition boycotts,
usually to protest an incumbent's efforts to bend electoral rules or
monopolize electoral resources. As Table 2 (column 4) shows, protesting parties stayed away from nearly a third of second elections, a
higher rate than in founding elections (24.6 percent), especially early
ones (11.1 percent). Opposition boycotts were a surefire way to call the
integrity of an election into question. Table 2 confirms that every
boycott of a second election was accompanied by unfavorable reports
on that election from observers and monitors. Not unexpectedly, there
was also a strong correlation between boycotts and the refusal of losers
to accept the results of elections.

Especially where boycotts occurred, the announcement of results
was immediately followed by a new competition to assign meaning to
elections. The default position for election losers—sometimes supported by watchdog nongovernmental organizations (NGOs)—was to
level allegations that the elections had been rigged, whether or not
electoral fraud could be definitively proven. Reelected governments

responded to these allegations by pointing to peaceful polls and to participation by multiple candidates and parties as evidence that democratization remained fundamentally on course. Both sides directed their appeals to the international community, which is the principal source of funds for both government and NGO development budgets.

For example, an intense struggle over the meaning of second elections consumed Zambia's political discourse during the weeks following the November 1996 vote. Both President Chiluba's victorious Movement for Multiparty Democracy (MMD) and the opposition parties had much at stake in the verdict. The MMD stood to lose the balance-of-payments support that it needed to prevent the economy from slipping back into the stagnation of the Kaunda era. The opposition parties, trounced at the polls, stood to lose the leverage over the government that they derived from the sympathy of the donor community. In press conferences and newspaper editorials, each side aggressively presented its own version of how the elections should be read.

Other participants expressed their own interpretations. International donors chose to make Kaunda's exclusion the centerpiece of their objections, correctly asserting that no election could be fair when a major opposition candidate was barred from competing. Somewhat overlooked in the discourse, however, were the views of those who voted. By largely ignoring the opposition boycott and granting the MMD a second term, most Zambians indicated that they hoped that the "old man" (Kaunda) would quietly step aside from politics. Many also supported the idea that candidates whose ancestries were not "authentically Zambian" should be barred from running for president and saw nothing wrong with altering the Constitution to uphold this principle.[14] Thus different audiences judged the election differently. What was undoubtedly a flawed election from the standpoint of most outside critics was far more acceptable to most Zambians.

At a minimum, opposition boycotts signaled a lack of full agreement on the rules of the political game. Flawed second elections thus had contradictory implications for democracy: While stimulating civil society and mobilizing it against manipulation by incumbents, they undercut consensus on procedures for constituting governments. In most African countries, opposition boycotts of flawed elections raised the alarm that even elected leaders would stoop to political abuse in order to remain in power. In the final analysis, however, an opposition's rejection of a flawed election did not deny the legitimacy of elections per se. If anything, the boycotters' emphasis on electoral violations (rather than on the fact that elections were being held in the first place) served to underscore the basic agreement emerging among all participants that elections are the only acceptable institutional device for choosing top leaders.

Participation and Competition

For the most part, leaders have not chosen to meddle with rules of political participation as a means of maintaining power. Civilian leaders reluctantly accept that citizens have political rights to be enfranchised, to vote, and to be consulted about policy in some fashion. Cases may be found—in Kenya and Cameroon, for example—of deliberate tampering with voter rolls in order to exclude voters from known opposition strongholds. More widespread are tardy election planning, inadequate systems of voter identification, and outdated voter registers. Yet despite opposition claims, these problems are just as likely to be attributable to the state's fiscal and administrative weakness—and to growing voter indifference—as to premeditated interference on the part of politicians.

Instead of trying to control participation, incumbents have doctored the rules of political competition by restricting entry to candidacy for office. In Africa's personalistic political regimes, such rule changes usually involve disqualifying principal rivals for the presidency, though dissident ruling-party candidates for parliamentary seats may also be sidelined. This finding confirms that the biggest challenge in getting to democracy, especially from the mass-mobilizing one-party systems that were so common in Africa, is not so much the expansion of political participation as the introduction of genuine political competition. It also suggests that, although a normative consensus may be emerging in Africa around the principle of broad popular participation, there is still fundamental disagreement on the rules for open political contests.

With few exceptions, second elections also confirm that polling procedures and vote counting are not principal sources of electoral malfeasance in Africa. If rigging occurs, it does so long before polling day in the form of vote-buying and political intimidation. Indeed, (notwithstanding election-day debacles in Mali and Tanzania,) observers increasingly distinguish between the growing efficiency and effectiveness of polling administration on the one hand and persistent problems with election rules or campaign conduct on the other. Incumbents who are intent on retaining office have found "wholesale" rule changes (concerning who competes) to be a far more effective means of controlling outcomes than seeking to influence votes individually at the "retail" level (i.e., who participates).

Comparisons between Table 1 and Table 2 show clear trends in political participation and political competition. Voter turnout fell between founding and second elections (from an average of 64.1 to a mean of 55.8 percent). To some extent, this is to be expected as elections become routine and as their stakes get smaller. Yet in some countries (like Niger and Mali) turnout rates were low enough to indicate an electorate seriously disengaged from the political process. And, in other countries (like Mauritania and Cameroon), incumbent strongmen revived the discredited expedient of inflating turnout figures, a practice that only added fuel to their opponents' rejection of election results. Yet in most places, election observers and monitors commented that voters displayed great seriousness of purpose; at least a core of African citizens seemed to have become attached to political rights and wished to keep exercising them regularly.

Political competition also declined as winners increased their margins of victory from first to second elections. Whereas the winning candidates or parties averaged 63.4 percent of the presidential votes and 65.3 percent of the legislative seats the first time around (see Table 1), these figures increased to 70.4 and 70.1 percent respectively in the second elections (see Table 2). To be sure, leadership alternation was associated with close races, suggesting that vigorous contestation was becoming routine in places such as Benin and Madagascar. But where incumbents were returned, it was usually with increased majorities, and often thanks to opposition boycotts (as in Côte d'Ivoire and Mali).

Indeed, the trend is toward entrenchment of incumbent presidents and domination by ruling political parties. In the 13 countries that have held second presidential elections, the winners beat their rivals by a margin of two to one in no less than seven cases (see Table 2, column 10). In the 14 countries that have held second parliamentary elections, ruling parties now enjoy two-thirds majorities in nine (see Table 2, last column). Under these circumstances, legislatures are more likely to act as agents of powerful presidents than as checks on their authority.

Survival, Not Consolidation

Half a decade after founding elections reached a peak in Africa, many more countries have retained civilian rule than have succumbed to military intervention. These countries have begun to establish a pattern of relatively competitive and participatory contests for top political offices. As such, second elections have probably helped some democracies to survive on the African continent. Yet, wherever elections have revealed persistent disagreements about basic political rules—witness the increasing frequency of opposition boycotts since 1994—they have not helped to consolidate democracy.

On a purely formal level, presidential and legislative (though not municipal) elections are taking place in Africa's surviving civilian multiparty systems with acceptable punctuality. There is a growing sense among political elites that they cannot avoid going through at least the motions of competitive elections if they want to retain a semblance of legitimacy. Recent boycotts, moreover, have often led their proponents into the political wilderness, thus reinforcing the impression that elections are the principal game in town. And the intensity of postelection disputes in second elections serves to underscore the importance universally attached to elections.

By the same token, the quality of multiparty elections in Africa is far from perfect—and getting worse. Military dictators are devising ever more cynical formulas to avoid truly competitive founding elections. And in second elections, civilian presidents have not hesitated to use executive power to rig the rules. The more dominant the elected ruling party and the more secure its legislative majority, the greater its latitude in this regard. In contrast to electoral volatility and incumbent turnovers in second elections in Eastern Europe and Latin America, African dominant parties have usually reinforced their supremacy the second time around. After a period of turbulent transitions, African politics is returning to an institutional legacy of "big man" rule, and the electoral alternation of leaders is again becoming abnormal.

To assess the prospects of Africa's surviving electoral democracies, analysts must distinguish those that are slowly dying (like Zambia by 1997) from those that are gradually consolidating (like Ghana by 1997). And one should never underestimate the difficulty of democratic consolidation on the African continent. So far, among African countries, only Mauritius has satisfied even the most minimal (and excessively electoral) conditions for consolidation set by the "two-turnover test." It is not certain that countries like Benin and Madagascar, each of which has seen one post-transition turnover, will also tread this path. After all, the ruling parties of Africa's longest-surviving multiparty systems—Botswana, Senegal, and Zimbabwe—have never lost at the polls. In this regard, Zambia seems to represent a far more common trajectory. There, a dominant party, aided by an opposition boycott but checked by international criticism, obtained an imperfect renewal of its domestic mandate in a second election.

In all political regimes (including new democracies), the meaning of incumbent victories is more difficult to interpret than the meaning of historic voter realignments. Especially in a "big man" political culture, it is unclear whether the reelection of an incumbent constitutes the extension of a leader's legitimacy or the resignation of the electorate to his inevitable dominance. For these reasons, the meaning of Africa's second elections will necessarily be murkier than that of the watershed contests of the early 1990s. This round of elections poses special challenges to analysts, who must cut through the rhetorical appeals of both winners and losers. When all is said and done, however, the fact that intense political struggles are being waged over the convening, the conduct, and the meaning of second elections is proof positive that, in Africa, the institution of elections is beginning to matter.

NOTES

1. Samuel P. Huntington, *The Third Wave: Democratization in the Late Twentieth Century* (Norman: University of Oklahoma Press, 1991), 266–67. According to this standard, the consolidation of democracy occurs whenever the winners of a founding election are defeated in a subsequent contest, and the new winners themselves later abide an electoral turnover. Actually, the "two-turnover test" may be a misnomer since its fulfillment actually calls for three elections, potentially involving three alternations.

2. Terry Lynn Karl, "Imposing Consent: Electoralism and Democratization in El Salvador," in Paul W. Drake and Eduardo Silva, eds., *Elections and Democratization in Latin America, 1980–1985* (La Jolla, Calif.: University of California–San Diego, Center for International Studies, 1986), 9–36.

3. Fareed Zakaria, "The Rise of Illiberal Democracy," *Foreign Affairs* 76 (November–December 1997): 22–43.

4. Mitchell A. Seligson and John A. Booth, *Elections and Democracy in Central America, Revisited* (Chapel Hill: University of North Carolina Press, 1995), 18.

5. Michael Bratton and Nicolas van de Walle, *Democratic Experiments in Africa: Regime Transitions in Comparative Perspective* (New York: Cambridge University Press, 1997), 6.

6. "Sierra Leone: Falling Out Parade," *Africa Confidential,* 29 March 1996, 4.

7. "Gabon: Have Petrol, Will Travel," *Africa Confidential,* 4 October 1996, 6.

8. "Côte d'Ivoire: No Contest," *Africa Confidential,* 20 October 1995, 7.

9. "Low Turnout of Voters in Comoros Islands Poll," Reuters, 2 December 1996.

10. See Michael Bratton and Daniel Posner, "A First Look at Second Elections in Africa, with Illustrations from Zambia," in Richard Joseph, ed., *State, Conflict, and Democracy in Africa* (Boulder, Colo.: Lynne Rienner, 1998).

11. National Democratic Institute, "Preliminary Statement by the NDI International Observer Delegation to the December 7 Elections in Ghana" (Accra: NDI, 10 December 1996). See also "Interim Report of Domestic Election Observers" (Accra: Network of Domestic Election Observers [NEDEO], undated); and International Foundation for Election Systems, "Supporting the Electoral Process in Ghana: Results of the 1996 Presidential and Parliamentary Elections" (Washington, D.C.: IFES, January 1997).

12. In Comoros, a new head of government was elected, but under circumstances where the incumbent (Djohar) did not run again (see "Yes?" in Table 2, column 7).

13. "Benin's Ex-President Says His Loss Is a Win," *Christian Science Monitor,* 22 August 1996.

14. Of the 19.1 percent of Zambians who disputed the quality of the 1996 elections, just 16.4 percent (i.e., 3.1 percent of the national population) said they did so *because* of the exclusion of Kaunda from the presidential race. Most cited other reasons. See Michael Bratton, Philip Alderfer, and Neo Simutanyi, "Political Participation in Zambia, 1991–1996: Trends and Determinants" (Michigan State University Working Papers on Political Reform in Africa, No. 16, East Lansing, 1997), 7.

3

THE REBIRTH OF AFRICAN LIBERALISM

E. Gyimah-Boadi

E. Gyimah-Boadi teaches political science at the University of Ghana, Legon, and is executive director of the Center for Democracy and Development, a think tank for democratic development based in Accra, Ghana. He was a fellow at both the Woodrow Wilson Center and the International Forum for Democratic Studies in Washington, D.C.

Much of the recent expert commentary on democratization in Africa is awash in dismissiveness and pessimism. Skeptics describe the process as a public-relations exercise, "spin control" by African rulers intent on making their regimes more presentable to Western donors in the aftermath of the Cold War.[1] African democratization has also been regarded as premature, and thus as somewhat comparable to Lenin's effort to stage a Soviet revolution before the development of a full-fledged proletariat in Russia.[2] Multiparty elections—the most dramatic manifestation of the new politics in Africa—have been denigrated as permitting "voting" without "choosing," and their outcomes have been dismissed as leading to "choice-less democracies."[3] The most negative assessments have focused on the persistence and alleged resurgence of illiberalism.[4]

In fact, this grim characterization of governance in contemporary Africa is accurate to some degree, though it falls short of doing full justice to a highly complicated situation. To gain a better idea of the larger picture without bogging down in excessive detail, it may help to identify broad trends and movements in African democratization, highlighting some of the important ways in which the foundations for liberal government and democratic consolidation are being laid even as key obstacles remain and setbacks continue to occur.

If relatively free and fair multiparty elections can serve as even a partial standard, then Africa's democratic progress has been impressive. Before 1990, only Botswana and Mauritius had a record of holding regular multiparty elections. As a result of domestic and external pressures against authoritarian rule, the majority of African countries have gone through some sort of multiparty elections, and about one-third of them have become electoral democracies since 1990. Some have held or are about to hold their second consecutive set of free elections. In Ghana, for instance, neither of two previous returns to constitutional rule (in 1969 and 1979) had lasted more than 30 months. When a democratically elected government completed its full four-year term and held new elections in 1996, a milestone seemed to have been passed. In Benin and Madagascar, 1996 brought the peaceful transfer of power from one elected regime to another—an event that is still much too rare in Africa. Despite their failure to produce alternations in power, "second transitional" elections in Ghana in 1996 and Kenya in 1997 were marked by an increase in the competitiveness that bodes well for the future prospect of peaceful turnovers of power both in these two countries and elsewhere on the continent.

The diminution of censorship and official harassment since the early 1990s has permitted an independent press to emerge in parts of Africa that have never before had one. Independent FM-radio broadcasting is becoming commonplace. The media in general have been enthusiastic about exposing official wrongdoing, and some journalists (such as Fred M'embe of the *Zambian Post* and Kofi Coomson of the *Ghanaian Chronicle*) have displayed superhuman bravery while defending democracy and good government in their respective countries.

Yet Africa's democratization remains incomplete, and careful observers cannot fail to note that consolidation still faces uncertain prospects. Many elections have been marred by massive fraud and vote rigging (often in favor of incumbents); others, such as those in Nigeria and Algeria, have been annulled altogether for producing results displeasing to military powerholders. Political liberalization has too often triggered or intensified ethnoregional, sectarian, or other communal conflicts. In Algeria, Rwanda, and Burundi, downward-spiralling cycles of such strife have engulfed whole peoples in violence that is horrible beyond words. Even where more or less successful multiparty elections have been held, acrimony still dominates relations between the government and its opposition (whether the latter is primarily extraparliamentary, as in Kenya, or based in the national assembly, as in Benin). Moreover, mistrust between government and civil society often continues to run high.

Many of the governments brought to power by elections have resisted inclusiveness, preferring to operate through the blunt force of crude majoritarianism. Military coups (as in Niger) or executive arrogations of power (*à la* the one engineered by President Alberto Fujimori in Peru) remain distinct possibilities. Strongmen, having maneuvered their way through somewhat competitive elections, typically hedge their bets by refusing to disband their private armed forces. Fighting between such militias crushed democratic hopes in

Congo-Brazzaville in the spring of 1997 as rivals for the presidency
sought to eliminate one another before campaigning began.

Transitions from authoritarian rule in Africa have been convulsive,
beset as they are by reverses, inadequate results, and the stubborn
persistence of illiberalism. Yet this is not the whole story, for the
current political situation contains significant elements of hope. A
closer look at developments in three areas vital to democratic governance suggests a more complex and less gloomy picture of liberal
democracy's prospects in Africa. These areas are: 1) the renewed
interest in constitutionalism and constitutional government; 2) the
continued surge in civil society; and 3) the resurrection of parliaments.
Despite serious shortcomings, the overall trend of events in these areas
offers reason to think that the foundations of liberalism and democratic
consolidation are being laid, albeit gradually and unevenly.

The Rise of Constitutionalism

Generally neglected in the era of single- or no-party presidents,
military rulers, authoritarian strongmen, and charismatic politicians,
constitutionalism has assumed a new prominence in the Africa of the
1990s. The old postindependence constitutions—illiberal documents
that proscribed opposition parties, conferred permanent tenure on
presidents, and ignored *habeas corpus*—have been jettisoned, sometimes with considerable drama, by "sovereign" national conferences,
constituent assemblies, or constitutional commissions. A number of
countries have promulgated liberal democratic constitutions providing
formal checks and balances, independent courts, guarantees for human
rights and civil liberties, and limitations on the discretionary powers of
state officials. Recent amendments to existing constitutions, moreover,
have tended to strengthen rather than weaken their liberal democratic
content. This is in stark contrast to what happened in the 1960s and
1970s, when the amendment process was commonly used to push
through expansions of executive power. Finally, many of the new
constitutions provide significant protections for private property
(though the extent of actual protection will probably depend largely on
judicial interpretation).

Some of the new African constitutions boast highly innovative
features that attempt to marry aspects of existing political culture and
local experience with the practice of democratic government. The
radical federalism and ethnicized political parties of Ethiopia may well
be intended, as critics charge, to entrench Tigrean hegemony. Yet these
devices also represent an effort to confront that society's ethnosectional
problems within a multiparty framework. The consultative "councils of
traditional rulers" (as in South Africa and Namibia) and "councils of
elder statesmen" (as in Ghana and Benin) attempt to institutionalize the

participation of key social forces and fill something like the role of an upper house in a bicameral parliament. New constitutional courts in Benin and South Africa are proving useful in countering crude majoritarianism and claims of executive privilege.

In some cases (notably Côte d'Ivoire and Ghana), the processes of constitution making or amending could not be sufficiently liberated from the grip of incumbent autocrats. In Zambia and Côte d'Ivoire most notoriously, the new constitutions featured special clauses designed to help incumbents retain power by keeping their opponents off the ballot. In the former case, the amendment was meant to bar former president Kenneth Kaunda (the strongest rival to President Frederick Chiluba), from contesting the next election. And in Côte d'Ivoire, Henri Konan-Bédié resorted to a similar maneuver to ward off a potential challenge from former premier Alassane Ouattara. Aside from such flagrant examples, constitutional crises loom in many countries as the new, more liberal arrangements are put seriously to the test for the first time.

In a disturbing number of cases, constitutional change has done nothing to eliminate overly broad libel and sedition laws that powerholders have been using against their critics. Officials in "liberalized autocracies" comply with the laws and constitution only in the most minimal way and in disregard of the democratic spirit behind them. In addition, incumbent regimes are inclined to use their parliament majorities to push through amendments and legislation that run counter to the democratic ethos.

Efforts to foster the rule of law are impeded by the persistence of a culture of arbitrariness among security and law-enforcement agencies, especially at the local levels. The weakness of official commitment to the rule of law was further betrayed by the already-mentioned failure of governments in Ghana and Congo-Brazzaville fully to disband partisan security and paramilitary organs.

The Flourishing of Civil Society

The contribution that Africa's nascent civil society made to the anti-authoritarian struggles of the early 1990s has been widely recognized. The role of popular forces (trade unions, traders' associations), elite organizations (professional associations, academic unions), and religious groups and leaders in the prodemocratic agitation that brought down autocratic regimes is well known. African political lore now memorializes the part, both active and passive, that the "civvies" played in rendering apartheid-era South Africa ungovernable and opening the way for a democratic settlement, and extols the acuity, commitment, and even heroism that prominent Christian prelates such as Anglican archbishop Desmond Tutu of South Africa and the Roman Catholic bishops Isodore de Souza of Benin and Fanoko Kpodro of Togo made to democratic transition in their respective countries. More recent but no less stirring was the resolve that the Women's Forum of Sierra Leone showed in early 1996, when it thwarted the attempt by that country's military regime to prevent the return of democratic rule.

The civil societies of Africa face a myriad of formidable obstacles— including sustained campaigns of official intimidation and repression— as they work on behalf of democracy. In Zambia, the Chiluba administration clamped down heavily on domestic poll-watching groups such as the Zambian Independent Monitoring Team (ZIMIT) and the National Committee for Clean Campaign (NCCC) when they dared to criticize the manner in which the November 1996 elections were conducted. Branded as agents of foreign interests, the two groups had their offices raided by state-security agencies, their documents confiscated, and their leaders detained. Indeed, as nongovernmental organizations (NGOs) and prodemocracy civil associations have gained prominence in various countries, governments (including elected ones) have become determined to control them. Botswana, Ghana, Kenya, and Zimbabwe have proposed or enacted legislation, nominally aimed at developing a national regulatory framework for associations, that would have the effect of subjecting NGOs to a crippling degree of state control. For instance, an NGO Bill initiated by the elected Rawlings–National Democratic Congress government in the parliament of Ghana included pernicious provisions requiring mandatory registration of NGOs with a proposed National Advisory Council of NGOs over-whelmingly dominated by government appointees; it also required that NGOs be "willing and able to work in cooperation with any agency of state that the minister may direct."

In addition, African civil societies continue to suffer severe material and organizational deficiencies. Nearly all of the governance-promoting NGOs are run on soft money, usually from foreign donors. The implementation of locally initiated programs must often wait for external assistance. Thus in Ghana it had been impossible to mount the widely praised election monitoring activities of the Network of Domestic Election Observers (NEDEO) in 1996 until external funding became available. At the time of this writing, many of the innovative initiatives planned under the Network for Conflict Prevention of the Cotonou-based African Study and Research Group on Democracy and Social and Economic Development (GERDDES-Afrique) were on hold pending assistance from UNESCO and other external sources. The recent insistence of donors that NGOs become financially self-sustaining is posing an additional burden that diverts the attention of democracy and governance NGOs from their primary work.

Indeed, there has been a thinning of the ranks of NGOs, especially the "civic" subspecies that are more directly involved in democratic activism. Key leaders have taken posts in the newly elected governments or have plunged into partisan politics. Most disturbingly, some civil society groups have been seized by atavistic tendencies, even fracturing along ethnic, regional, or religious lines. Middle-class civic associations have not worked well with their working-class counterparts, and rural groups have rarely been included in the networks of civic activists. The credibility of civil society has been all but ruined by religious fundamentalism in Algeria and ethnic genocide in Rwanda and Burundi. Credibility has also been undermined by the personalistic tendencies of the charismatic leaders of the various civic organizations and NGOs, as well as lack of self-regulation, failure to adhere to an explicit code of ethics, and lack of attention to basic rules of corporate governance.

> **The 1990s have seen the emergence of independent, nonpartisan national and continental NGOs dedicated to the promotion of democratic governance and human rights.**

The good news is that, despite such travails, African civil societies have flourished during the present decade as never before. They have continued to play major roles during and after transitions. Despite the intensified repression brought to bear by the regime of General Sani Abacha, Nigeria's National Democratic Coalition (NADECO) persisted in its struggle to end military authoritarianism. The Swaziland Federation of Trade Unions and its leader Jani Sithole continue to stand in the forefront of the protracted agitation to constitutionalize that country's anachronistic absolute monarchy.

In those countries where the transition to democracy is relatively advanced, civil societies are keeping themselves busy in the service of democratic consolidation. They continue to act as watchdogs for citizens' rights. In Zambia, for instance, clergy condemned the Supreme Court's conviction and imprisonment on contempt charges of journalist Masautso Phiri, who had accused the justices of having been "bribed" by President Chiluba. Such an action, the clerics argued, violated "the rules of natural justice," for the justices in effect had acted as judges in their own case. Similarly, the Zambian Law Society has been an outspoken defender of such victims of postelectoral repression as ZIMIT and the NCCC.

The 1990s have also seen the emergence, under exceptionally energetic leadership, of independent, nonpartisan national and continental NGOs dedicated to the promotion of democratic governance and human rights. Notable examples include the Institute for Democracy in South Africa (Idasa), the Media Institute of South Africa,

GERDDES-Afrique, the Institute of Economic Affairs (IEA) in Ghana, and the Foundation for Democratic Process in Zambia (FODEP). This is yet another important indicator of the growing strength of civil society in Africa. These groups are playing crucial roles in the democratic development of their respective countries. Idasa played a major role in conceptualizing and modeling a Truth and Reconciliation Commission in South Africa consistent with that country's commitment to national unity in the post-apartheid era.[5] FODEP has been a key institution in the provision of civic education in Zambia. The IEA, the Ghana Legal Literacy Foundation, and other prominent NGOs have played active roles in election support, civic education, parliamentary capacity building, and the like. And GERDDES-Afrique has played a pioneering role among African NGOs in independent election monitoring and conflict mediation.

Moreover, African civil societies seem to be gaining a greater awareness of the pivotal role that they must play in fostering democratic governance. They are banding together to defend their interests and their rights; they are networking nationally, regionally, and even globally (witness the recently formed National Council of NGOs in Kenya, South Africa's National NGO Coalition, Afronet, and the like); they are becoming more sophisticated in general. Some are beginning to move away from the crudely confrontational style of their early years in favor of a focus on consensus, moderation, more thoughtful policy debate, and other modes of constructive engagement. Thus, it is becoming increasingly difficult for their detractors to brand them as "enemies of the state" or quislings. At the same time, they are gaining greater visibility and collective clout.

South Africa's NGOs and "civvies" are reorienting themselves to engage in the work of post-apartheid social and economic reconstruction. Idasa is working on a new generation of innovative programs designed to help reduce racial and ethnic prejudice among South Africans, to safeguard the rights of immigrants from other parts of Africa, and to support improvements in governance at both the national and provincial levels. Committed during the years of de facto single-party rule (1992–96) to providing a voice to Ghana's extraparliamentary opposition, the IEA is now focusing on improving the multiparty National Assembly's capacities for deliberation and representation.

Clearly, Africa's civil societies are among the chief engines driving the continent's political development. With their increased sophistication and mounting capabilities, they are helping to drive the shift from unalloyed state hegemony to nascent pluralism. Their growing self-awareness and determination to defend their autonomy against all efforts at suppression or cooptation (especially those originating from the state) are signs that they are here to stay. The first springtime of African civil society followed hard on the heels of decolonization, but soon faded before authoritarianism's onslaughts in country after country. The second springtime, which began in the Cold War's wake, shows promise of enduring far longer than its ill-fated predecessor.

Parliaments Make a Comeback

After years of marginalization, parliaments have began to emerge as key institutions in African governance. Many a new African democracy boasts a legislature that has been restored after a long hiatus. The new liberal constitutions have substantially improved the legal and political status of parliaments by equipping them with greater powers. As products of relatively competitive multiparty elections and with stronger popular roots than their counterparts of yesteryear, the new parliaments appear to enjoy greater prestige. They also seem to be exuding greater confidence as formally autonomous bodies and crucial venues for the making of policy.

Despite this progress, however, African parliaments will continue to face serious challenges to their attempts to foster better governance. The long hiatus has left them poorly developed as institutions. Few of them have been around long enough to accumulate much democratic capital. They often lack the traditions of tolerance, give and take, respect for minority opinion, and the like that make it easier to deal with such perennial issues of representative government as how to reconcile loyalty to one's party with loyalty to one's constituents, nation, or conscience.

Notwithstanding the resourcefulness of a few individual lawmakers, African parliaments are notoriously deficient in physical plant and equipment. MPs work out of cramped, poorly furnished offices (if they are lucky enough to *have* offices) with little or no secretarial support. Both the facilities and the skills necessary for public-policy research and analysis are strictly limited. So is money—a reflection of both the parlous state of many African economies and the desire of many African presidents to keep legislatures weak and subordinate. Low pay and scanty perquisites expose MPs to grave moral and political hazards.

Nonetheless, multipartism has made it possible for genuine parliamentary opposition to emerge; in time, it will no longer be possible to write off African parliaments as rubber stamps for the executive. There is some evidence of capacity building among African parliaments, especially in some of their specialized agencies. A number of international donors, including the Canadian International Develop-ment Agency (through the Canadian Parliamentary Center), the U.S. Agency for International Development (through the National Democratic Institute), the German party foundations, and the Economic Development Institute of the World Bank are assisting this process with a variety of programs.

Under the South Africa–Canada Legislative Cooperation Program of the Canadian Parliamentary Center (CPC), South African legislators at both the national and provincial levels are enjoying Internet information and discussion links with their Canadian counterparts; in Ethiopia, the CPC is working with Parliament to establish an Office of the Ombudsman and an independent Human Rights Commission; and in Ghana, the CPC has been running capacity building workshops focusing on the formulation, implementation, and monitoring of economic policy for the Finance and Public Accounts Committee of parliament. Under NDI, Westminster Foundation, and Hans Siedel Foundation programs, Ghanaian parliamentarians are picking up valuable skills in caucusing and lobbying. At the very least, these programs are helping to build confidence and to forge closer solidarity among Africa's new legislators.

At the most basic level, the weakness of African parliaments stems less from low capacities than from a persistent culture of authoritarianism. Whatever might be the letter of constitutional provisions, the prevailing political culture tends toward the de facto marginalization of legislatures. Presidents see them as rubber stamps or safety valves for the venting of popular anger and frustration, not as arenas for real policy making or serious counterweights to executive power. In Africa's new democracies, one finds a lingering penchant for strong leaders of the "man on horseback" type who take decisive steps to spur rapid social and economic transformation. Such leanings, embodied in a strong chief executive at the head of a centralized administration, are behind the preference for presidentialism over parliamentarism in the new democracies. Even where parliamentary government exists, most legislative initiatives come from the government rather than private members. Parliaments have also been marginalized by executives who evade legislative oversight and effective checks and balances through the use of "shadow governments," "kitchen cabinets," and other arrangements that inherently resist parliamentary oversight.

Even where out-and-out military rule is not present, highly contestable notions of "national security" and "the national interest," as well as attendant "official secrets" acts and criminal libel laws, inhibit the effective discharge of key parliamentary functions. Such laws and practices, for instance, are preventing the auditor general and the Public Accounts Committee of Ghana's National Assembly from subjecting the Rawlings administration's defense expenditures to full scrutiny.

On the whole, African parliamentary systems have yet to marry multipartism (which stresses the representative elements of liberal democracy) with the grassroots participation and engagement that all-inclusive single parties or mass movements sought to stimulate in an earlier era. The multiparty legislatures of Africa today suffer from inadequate links to rural society and inadequate citizen involvement in the period between general elections. But legislatures in no-party, single-party, or "movement"-based systems suffer from a crippling lack of engagement with city dwellers and the well-educated, including the professional classes.

In certain telling instances, the problems facing parliaments may best be described as "self-inflicted." It is hard to see how the interests of Niger's National Assembly in promoting good governance and public accountability were served by that body's 1997 decision to pass, with evident glee, a law imposing limits on press freedom tighter than those that prevailed under direct military rule. Similarly, it is difficult to appreciate how the heavy-handed manner in which the speaker of the Zambian parliament reportedly hounded an errant journalist in 1996 could advance the cause of transparency in that country.

As products of recent transitions, African parliaments tend to be "negative coalitions" cobbled together to dislodge—or to entrench—incumbents. As such, they are incapable of passing coherent legislation. In many of Africa's liberalized autocracies, the distinctions between the party on the one hand and the state, government, or regime on the other tend to be blurry at best. Amid such an atmosphere of fused interests and personnel, it comes as no surprise that exercising parliament's oversight function, checking the executive, and fostering transparency and accountability are daunting tasks indeed.

Laying the Foundations

African democratization in the 1990s is off to a good start if, as Larry Diamond contends, time is an important determinant of institutionalization.[6] In many an African country, the new democratic regime has already lasted longer than any previous such regime ever did. Most significantly, the renewed interest in constitutionalism and all that goes with it has opened the way for the establishment of rule-bound states and governments. Efforts are afoot to reduce official arbitrariness and to enforce human rights and civil liberties guarantees. Laws enshrining the writ of *habeas corpus* are being revived—a trend in keeping with the new constitutions' tendency to circumscribe government's power to curtail lawful rights and liberties. When a coup attempt failed in Zambia in late 1997 and a "state of emergency" was declared, the grounds for the declaration may have been rather flimsy, but the conditions limiting it were significant. Prior parliamentary approval had to be won, and the state of emergency was to have a fixed lifespan of three months that could only be extended by another explicit act of parliament. This compares favorably with the practices commonplace in preliberalization Africa, when indefinite states of emergency and official curfews were often imposed.

Again thanks in part to new constitutional provisions, judiciaries and independent commissions are beginning to assert their autonomy. In exercising its constitutionally mandated original jurisdiction over all matters pertaining to the 1992 Constitution, the Ghanaian Supreme Court has issued a number of landmark judgments directing the government to give the opposition equal access to the state-owned media; to cease using public funds to celebrate the 31 December 1981 coup that consolidated Rawlings's power; and to stop requiring that political demonstrators obtain police permits. In Benin, the Constitutional Court has called both the National Assembly and the president to account in major constitutional matters. The Court has also asserted its final authority over the declaration of election results, compelling then-incumbent Nicéphore Soglo to accept his electoral defeat at the hands of ex-president Mathieu Kérékou in 1996.

African governments continue to crave the chance to tame their courts. They do not appear to have given up on efforts to pack the bench with lackeys or to intimidate individual judges and, indeed, the judiciary as a whole. Yet the current situation represents a vast improvement over earlier times, when judges were routinely replaced for issuing opinions unfavorable to political authorities. It is also true that the rising spate of constitutional cases in Africa's new democracies could pose the threat of full-blown constitutional crisis. Such litigation is partly a reflection of poor constitutional design, but it also indicates that the new constitutions are being taken seriously and gradually becoming normative points of reference for politicians, institutions both public and private, and citizens at large. The recent significant drop in the number of arbitrary confiscations of private property by African governments may reflect a growing commitment to the private sector as the leader in development, but it also seems to bespeak a new level of respect for the property rights enshrined in the new constitutions.

Legislatures are gradually emerging as central institutions of democratic governance. They are increasingly playing important roles in making national policy and ratifying international agreements; and they are attempting to exercise unprecedented levels of oversight with respect to the other branches of government—especially the executive. Uganda's parliament, though organized on a no-party basis, has effectively confronted ministers over corruption. Zimbabwe's parliament, though dominated by the party of long-ruling President Robert Mugabe, has rejected tax proposals deemed unjust. The Ghanaian National Assembly's Public Accounts Committee is gradually becoming a force for proper auditing and transparency, especially since the augmentation of opposition representation that followed the 1996 elections.

Links between parliaments and civil societies remain weak but are gradually strengthening. Traditions of open formal lobbying are being cultivated to replace the custom of lobbying through personal and private channels and cutting deals in private. In Ghana, the Hans Siedel Foundation of Germany and the Ghana Legal Literacy Foundation, a local NGO, have been organizing lobbying-skills seminars for parliamentarians and civic groups.

Parliaments are gradually developing the skills and mechanisms to identify and align with nonstate institutions and the private sector. Legislators have become more receptive to hearing about the interests and views of social and civic groups. The IEA has arranged for various civic organizations and interest groups, as well as independent experts, to offer testimony and memoranda on proposed legislation before parliament. This new openness and collaboration has greatly expanded public participation in policy making and enriched the whole deliberative process.

The Trend Toward Liberalization

The career of African democratization in the 1990s is a checkered one. Elections have frequently been marred by fraud, and occasionally by force; the commitment of elected rulers to democratic governance has been weak; and the new constitutions, parliaments, civil societies, and other key institutions of democratic politics remain fragile. More important, successful multiparty elections have not been enough to overturn prevailing patterns of personal rule and neopatrimonial politics. In fact, neopatrimonialism has not only shown itself able to coexist comfortably with multiparty rule, but may even have derived a new intensity from it. Corruption, excessive patronage, and expensive perks for the political class—to say nothing of unjustifiably large cabinets, ministerial retinues, and costly presidential establishments— are common phenomena in Africa's young democracies.

Material and professional limitations, the persistence of perniciously harsh laws, and hostile courts continue to hamper the effectiveness of the press. Governments continue to enjoy near-monopolies over radio and television broadcasting, while restrictions on private stations (usually applied through regulatory machinations) impose additional limits on the media's ability to foster accountability and transparency. The task of the watchdog, whether undertaken by the press or other agencies, remains particularly difficult to discharge in the prevailing political culture of Africa, where high-level government operations are shrouded in excessive secrecy and a generalized "blackout" is imposed on official information.

Despite all this, there is also a perceptible countervailing trend toward liberalization and liberalism. Increasingly competitive multiparty elections, crusading journalists, increasingly assertive judicial bodies, livelier parliaments, and more-vibrant civil societies—all operating under new liberal constitutions—add strength to this current. Constitutionally grounded agencies of horizontal accountability, such as Ghana's Commission on Human Rights and Administrative Justice (CHRAJ), the Constitutional Courts in Benin and South Africa, and ombudsman's offices elsewhere on the continent, are enforcing human rights guarantees and imposing limits on governments as never before.

Illiberalism has persisted, but it is not on the rise. Authoritarianism is alive in Africa today, but it is not well.

This emerging liberalism is especially manifest in widespread concern for greater transparency and accountability, which are on the increase even in weak democracies such as Ethiopia, Ghana, Tanzania, and Uganda. Governmental transparency and accountability are also being boosted by the resumed publication of the Auditor General's reports in Ghana on a timely basis, and by the increasing activism of constitutionally mandated bodies such as Uganda's Office of the Inspector General.

The process remains largely unconsolidated, to be sure, and the institutions of liberalism enjoy only a tenuous hold. But their simultaneous emergence in the 1990s, in addition to the increasing support that they are attracting from bilateral and multilateral donors (including the international financial institutions), represents an unprecedented assault on the institutional redoubts of authoritarianism, official arbitrariness, corruption, and other manifestations of neo-patrimonial rule.

Comparing conditions today with those that prevailed in 1990, the worst that we can say is that, in spite of a democratizing trend, illiberalism has persisted. It may indeed have done so, but it is not on the rise. Authoritarianism is alive in Africa today, but it is not well. It is under siege thanks to the combined efforts of trade unions and other civic organizations, independent media organs, parliaments (especially their opposition contingents), and liberal constitutions, including the agencies grounded in those documents. This, of course, has not happened by chance. It reflects, at least in part, the retreat from the statism of the first three decades after independence, and the rebirth in the 1990s of African liberalism.[7]

NOTES

1. Achille Mbembe, "Democratization and Social Movements in Africa," *Africa Dēmos* 1 (November 1990): 4.

2. Marina Ottaway, "African Democratisation and the Leninist Option," *Journal of Modern African Studies* 35 (March 1997): 1–15.

3. Thandika Mkandawire, "Crisis Management and the Making of Choiceless Democracies in Africa" (Center for Development Research, Copenhagen, Denmark, no date, mimeograph); and Claude Ake, *Democracy and Development in Africa* (Washington, D.C.: Brookings Institution, 1996), 136.

4. Robert D. Kaplan, "Was Democracy Just a Moment?" *Atlantic Monthly,* December 1997, 55; and Fareed Zakaria, "The Rise of Illiberal Democracy," *Foreign Affairs* 76 (November–December 1997): 22–43.

5. The proceedings of two Idasa conferences crucial to the development of this model are published in Alex Boraine, Janet Levy, and Ronel Scheffer, eds., *Dealing with the Past: Truth and Reconciliation in South Africa* (Cape Town: Idasa, 1997); and Alex Boraine and Janet Levy eds., *The Healing of a Nation?* (Cape Town: Idasa, 1995).

6. Larry Diamond, *Prospects for Democratic Development in Africa* (Stanford, Calif.: Hoover Institution, Hoover Essays, 1997), 3.

7. For a useful and detailed discussion of African liberalism, see Naomi Chazan, "Between Liberalism and Statism in African Political Cultures and Democracy," in Larry Diamond, ed., *Political Culture and Democracy in Developing Countries* (Boulder, Colo.: Lynne Rienner, 1994), 59–98.

4

EIGHT PROBLEMS WITH AFRICAN POLITICS

Célestin Monga

Célestin Monga is a Country Economist at the World Bank in Washington, D.C. He has taught economics and political science at Boston University and the University of Bordeaux. His books include L'argent des autres (1997) and The Anthropology of Anger (1996). The views expressed in the following essay are entirely those of the author, and do not necessarily represent the views of the World Bank.

Since the early 1990s, most of sub-Saharan Africa's 48 countries have undergone major political and social changes. Two events, occurring almost simultaneously in early 1990, triggered these changes. The first was Nelson Mandela's release from a South African jail, and the second was the calling in Benin of what would become a widely copied National Conference designed to arrange the end of an authoritarian regime (in this case President Mathieu Kérékou's 17-year-old Marxist dictatorship). Within months, people across the continent were engaging in classic expressions of opposition to authoritarianism such as popular uprisings and civil disobedience, as well as exploring new forms in the collective quest for liberty. Single-party regimes found themselves forced to permit multiparty competition, constitutions and election laws were redesigned, and competitive elections of one sort or another went forward. Yet seven years after these historic events, the net results of the "third wave" of democratization in Africa remain unclear.

Most close observers agree that some countries have performed quite well. Besides Botswana and Mauritius, which have been continuously democratic since independence in the 1960s, Benin, Eritrea, Malawi, Mozambique, Namibia, South Africa, and even Mali seem to be following a "progressive" path to democratic transition.

Still, many caveats remain. Promises to give power to the people, to make new political and social institutions more effective, and to organize more balanced and stable systems of government have mostly been slow to be fulfilled. In Benin and Madagascar, old authoritarian rulers have returned to power through the ballot box, carried by rising discontent at the painful economic "shock therapy" implemented by the first freely elected governments and aided by the new leaders' poor political skills.

In the Central African Republic, Congo-Brazzaville, and Niger, democratically elected presidents have failed to meet the challenges of tolerance and creativity that are the hallmarks of true leadership, and have faced civil strife or military coups. In Cameroon, Kenya, and Togo, former authoritarian rulers have been able to retain power by circumventing the new rules of the game and keeping a grip on military power and the public fisc. In Nigeria and Sudan, the so-called democratization process has run into so much trouble that it is almost impossible to define the path that these countries are now following. Indeed, these numerous setbacks—joined by the protracted decline and fall of the Mobutu Sese Seko regime in Zaire—have reinforced the belief that it is hard, if not impossible, to persuade Africa's authoritarian leaders to accept democratic rules.

This essay examines the various outcomes of these struggles, assesses the results of the disjunction between increased demand for freedom and participation and the insufficient supply of these political goods, identifies the main impediments to democratic transition in the region, and sketches the techniques used by authoritarian regimes to sustain themselves. Our method of proceeding will be to discuss the eight phenomena that fuel collective skepticism about Africa's democratization.

1) The Weakness of Political Parties. In theory, political parties constitute the mechanism *par excellence* of democratic transition. According to political scientists, a modern party must meet four criteria. These are continuity (that is, a life span exceeding the dominance of the party's founders), a nationwide organization, the desire to exercise power, and consistent efforts to garner significant popular support.[1]

Many African political organizations do not even meet the first criterion. Quite often, a political party south of the Sahara is little more than a platform for a single individual, a structure whose rules can readily be changed to suit its founder, whose charisma and money are its main engines. As the vehicle of its leader, the party's life expectancy and prospects are tied to its founder's fate. Its program will often be limited in scope, and may not show much philosophical consistency.

African parties also often fall short of the mark on the second count. Not many of the continent's countries have political organizations with broad national bases. Very often, parties are tied to the home regions of their leaders.

African parties' desire to exercise power is also problematic. An examination of their actual strategies (as opposed to their rhetoric) reveals that the goals pursued by party leaders vary from grabbing a few crumbs of the "national pie" to gaining a role in the everyday operation of government (though not necessarily in the formulation of its objectives), receiving a say in the making of certain political decisions, keeping a rival group out of power, or even contributing to the political education of the next generation of African leaders.

As spotty as their performance may be according to the first three criteria, it is on the fourth—the effort to garner popular support at the ballot box— that African parties fall farthest from the mark. Few countries have the electoral infrastructure—including credible officials—needed to mount free elections on a regular basis. In some, such as Nigeria, undemocratic rulers have hampered parties' ability to compete by using threats, intimidation, or corruption to keep intellectuals and prominent politicians out of the opposition and in the ranks of the government and its state-managed "transition" process.[2]

Few countries have the electoral infrastructure— including credible officials—needed to mount free elections on a regular basis.

Indeed in most countries, mayors, prefects, deputy prefects, election officials, and judges feel that their own fates are tied to that of the current (authoritarian) regime. They need no instructions from on high to go about ensuring that the elections do not upset the status quo. Yet there are encouraging countertrends: The 1996 Ghanaian presidential elections were widely perceived to be an improvement over the 1992 voting, with a more independent electoral administration and extensive international and domestic electoral observation.[3]

Most of Africa's new opposition parties are fragile creations born of the need to compete in the electoral process. They typically lack the material, financial, and especially human resources to function effectively under the often unfair conditions imposed by the authoritarian regime. Fearing audits or other official reprisals, big and small businesses alike order their employees to avoid politics. Amid the resulting suspicion and vulnerability, where the mere public expression of a divergent view on any subject is enough to put an end to a career even in the private sector, few workers dare to display their political preferences.

In such an atmosphere, opposition parties have objective reasons for being in no rush to participate in elections. Their leaders often find themselves caught between the need to run and garner votes and the feeling that they are taking part in a charade. If the latter feeling dominates, they may order a boycott, but will be weakened in doing so by their lack of means of communication that would allow them clearly to explain the obstacles they face. The international community may misunderstand their situation and motives, and their own party activists, frustrated at having to suffer the humiliations of the battle for democracy without even being part of the electoral process, may disobey the boycott order.

2) Manipulation of the Electoral Process. The gap between the traditional functions of political parties and the reality in Africa today is not attributable to historical and cultural factors alone, but also and especially to political, judicial, and sociological ones. Indeed, the "aberrant" quality of African political parties is above all the result of deliberate actions taken by authoritarian governments, which are highly skilled at dominating the political game.

In many French-speaking countries, the entire electoral process falls within the purview of the Ministry of Territorial Administration or the Ministry of the Interior. Citing French tradition, such countries have always rejected the idea of an independent electoral commission.

In English-speaking countries, by contrast, such commissions are the rule rather than the exception. But governments interfere in the electoral process as much as necessary to assure a win. This might take the form of injustice toward prominent opposition candidates, such as occurred in Ghana in 1992 when President Jerry Rawlings pulled out all the stops against his adversaries, accelerating the electoral schedule in order to deny them adequate preparation time, banning meetings in specified localities, and deliberately using outdated voter rolls.[4]

Sometimes African autocrats prefer to take no chances, even when the electoral administration and the judicial system are under their thumb. They employ any means necessary to disqualify their adversaries, and may even assassinate them. Albeit increasingly rare, the second recourse still has its fans. In Togo in 1991, for example, there was an attempt on the life of Gilchrist Olympio, President Gnassingbé Eyadéma's main opponent, while Olympio was campaigning in the North. Investigators never clearly established the guilty party, but those who asked themselves *"Cui bono?"* thought of the head of state. Eyadéma's brutal methods of repression dated back to 1967, when he came to power by way of a military coup after the assassination of none other than Gilchrist's father, Sylvanius Olympio.

The milder technique, disqualification, is more common. Various stratagems can be used. Age requirements for office—always available for alteration—are a popular recourse. After the 1991 fall of Mali's dictator Moussa Traoré and before the National Conference met to review election rules, the charismatic student leader Mountaga Tall was eliminated from contention in this way.

The best-known discriminatory practice, however, remains the nebulous "nationality clause" requiring candidates to be native-born. The introduction of such a feature into the election laws allows for an attack on what opponents symbolically hold most dear—the authenticity of their love of country. Nationality clauses are meant to stoke the fires of popular nationalism at election time. Well-known and recent cases of the invocation of such a clause to stop a candidate include those of Alassane Ouattara in Côte d'Ivoire, Kenneth Kaunda in Zambia, and

Richard Leakey in Kenya. Each was the object of an intense governmental campaign designed to squelch his hopes of occupying the highest office in the land.

In June 1995, Laurent Dona-Fologo, secretary-general of the long-ruling Democratic Party of Côte d'Ivoire, publicly mocked critics of his country's nationality clause: "They would like it if people with dubious identities could rule the Ivory Coast!"[5] The main target of this remark, opposition presidential candidate Alassane Ouattara, was kept off the ballot even though he had served as prime minister for almost four years and was the candidate of a major party. Similar tactics were used against Zambia's former president Kenneth Kaunda because he struck the incumbent, Frederic Chiluba, as his most formidable rival. Kaunda found himself accused of being a Malawian who had illegally run Zambia for several decades. Only intense national and international pressure kept him out of prison. In Kenya, President Daniel arap Moi speaks of Richard Leakey, the noted paleontologist and former director of the Kenya Wildlife Service, as a "white who would like to recolonize the country." Leakey's Safina party has yet to be legally recognized.

> *Another recent innovation of African authoritarianism is the establishment of different levels of citizenship with correspondingly unequal political rights.*

Such campaigns can backfire, however. The explosive pseudo-patriotism they engender can lead to witch hunts and collective xenophobia. Thus in Côte d'Ivoire, President Henri Konan-Bédié has become the target of rumors, gleefully circulated by the opposition press, that his origins (never indisputably demonstrated to be indigenous) are actually Ghanaian.[6] In Zambia, President Chiluba has suffered a similar fate as his adversaries spread stories about his alleged Zairian roots.

Another recent innovation of African authoritarians is the establishment of different levels of citizenship with correspondingly unequal political rights. If one concurs with Thierry Michalon that political equality among citizens is the psychological foundation of democracy,[7] it is no surprise to see African dictatorships attempting to use such "adjustable-size" citizenship to drive wedges into their adversaries' popular support. The Constitution that Cameroon's National Assembly adopted in January 1996 at the urging of President Paul Biya provides for a distinction at the regional level between "autochthonous" Cameroonians and those who are not. The official goals, proclaimed in the preamble, are to take the sociological "representativeness" of the electorate into account and to protect "minorities." Yet neither the notion of "representativeness" nor that of "minority" has ever been defined—

this in a country where, according to official statistics, no ethnic group exceeds a quarter of the population. By introducing such vague ideas into the Constitution (which he submitted to a legislature under his control rather than to a popular referendum), Biya was seeking to divide opposition voters and return public debate to his favorite subject—the tribal question. His cynicism was on target, for tribal demands stirred up by the "autochthony" provision soon roiled the big port city of Douala and its environs, long an opposition bastion.

In addition to violence or the politics of ethnicity, sub-Saharan Africa's authoritarians also have ready to hand all the well-known financial means of weakening and dividing opponents and their organizations: bribery, the maintenance of intra-opposition rivalries, restrictions on opposition parties' funding, and the like.[8]

3) A Narrow Political Field. The upshot of these efforts is a political arena where the opposition has been custom-tailored to specifications dictated by the government in power. Even a cursory look at the players in the African political game reveals that incumbents and oppositionists often have similar profiles and agendas. Examining the transition in Benin, Tessy Bakary identifies the crucial problem as the dearth of new blood. "Benin's political arena," he observes, "thus appears as a sort of Jurassic Park, peopled with three species of 'professional' politicians: the dinosaurs, or has-beens, who dream of once again becoming what they were or what they could not be; the wannabes and the others, in between, who dream of becoming something; and the born-agains of democracy, who appeared after the National Conference."[9]

Providing a rough sketch of political trends in Cameroon, Cilas Kemedjio reaches the same conclusion:[10] Though political leaders on all sides make claims of originality, the national political landscape remains rather uniform, with actors implicitly basing their ideology on one of four different models. Kemedjio's inventory of these models has a wider application, for one finds similar patterns across most of Africa.

First there is the *nostalgic model,* which looks back to the mythic prosperity of a bygone age, a prosperity that certain opposition leaders promise to restore if elected. Belief in a better past is kindled by the chaos and penury that current leaders have brought or perpetuated. In some countries, former presidents who have been out of power for a while have become exalted victims and rallying points for numerous businesspeople, bureaucrats, and others susceptible to illusion. The best illustration of this is the case of the late Jean-Bédel Bokassa, who ruled the Central African Republic from 1966 to 1979, and for the last three years of his regime was its self-styled "emperor." Today, many citizens seem to have forgotten the extraordinary human rights violations for which he was responsible, remembering only that civil servants got paid on time. This model's appeal in Zambia explains why President Chiluba is so afraid of competition from former autocrat Kenneth Kaunda.

Next there is the *self-justifying dictatorial model* that oscillates between naked and brutal uses of power reminiscent of colonialism at its most high-handed and the practice of enlightened despotism African-style, informed by effulgent and elaborate propaganda. Robert Mugabe's Zimbabwe and Omar Bongo's Gabon typify this model.

Third is the *charismatic and symbolic model*. This represents one of the oldest oppositional currents, advocated by groups of intellectuals faithful to the history of the independence movement. Emblematic and charismatic resistance leaders from the 1950s and 1960s are the central figures here. Appealing to a prophetic political past and decrying the takeover of independence movements by small and closed elites shaped by neocolonialism, this model's supporters (who revere assassinated heroes like Thomas Sankara in Burkina Faso or Patrice Lumumba in Zaire) reinforce their own sense of moral legitimacy.

Finally, there is the *model of intellectual insubordination,* which envisions intellectuals not as political actors per se, but as the revealers of the truth of everyday life and as the architects of a precise agenda that political parties must take into account if the alternation of power is to have any real meaning. The group behind this model is perhaps best personified by historian Laurent Gbagbo, the former college professor who founded the Ivorian Popular Front, Côte d'Ivoire's main opposition party. Gbagbo challenged the powerful President Félix Houphouët-Boigny (d. 1993) in the 1980s, and spent years in exile after escaping from jail.

This outline allows us to identify ideological parallels in the strategies and everyday actions of various actors. It likewise points to the existence of a common "political imaginary" or mental landscape that reveals itself, above all, in the shared desire of African leaders to narrow the political field.

4) A Constrained Civil Society. It may seem surprising that in several countries rollbacks of the process of democratic reform imposed by soldiers or politicians have met with public indifference or even approval. This was the case in the Gambia and Niger in 1996, and might easily have been the case in both Congo (1993–94) and the Central African Republic (1996–97), where numerous citizens sympathized with army factions that rebelled against democratically elected governments. One could be led to conclude that political disenchantment in these countries has become so massive as to doom democratization to failure, that the pursuit of freedom did not stem from a real desire for change on the part of the people, and that calling for democracy was merely the pastime of a frustrated elite.

In truth, African peoples show relatively little interest in politics largely because so many social groups are denied access to the benefits of political change. In many countries, the democratic transition is being held hostage by a few urban and rural elites who are eager to see the continued marginalization of leaders from the more active organizations within civil society. The desire of the few to deny the dreams of the many is tangible in politicians' efforts to manipulate or else exclude groups and organizations that wish to take part in the political process. Whether manipulated or excluded, civil society is effectively suppressed. In Cameroon, for instance, legal changes in December 1990 opened up the political space to opposition parties, but left trade unions as such still unrecognized. The Biya administration took refuge in semantics, claiming that the new law provided only for the recognition of "organizations," not *"syndicats"* (the French word for unions). To the surprise of outside observers, many opposition leaders declined to challenge this interpretation. Perhaps this should not have been such a shock, for in most African countries, politicians still feel comfortable excluding trade-union, women's, and students' groups from politics, since their absence makes it much easier to cut deals across party lines.

> *The desire of the few to deny the dreams of the many is tangible in politicians' efforts to manipulate or else exclude groups and organizations that wish to take part in the political process.*

The ambition that politicians on all sides harbor to annihilate civil society can also be glimpsed in their reluctance to adjust the age of majority to demographic and sociological realities. In those many African countries where people under 30 compose about 70 percent of the population and where the average life expectancy is around 55, there is no good reason to keep the age of majority at 20 or 21. Yet politicians refuse to lower it, for they want to keep the overly demanding young— who, according to a number of surveys, possess a good understanding of political problems and issues—out of the political "marketplace" and curb any activist impulses among the people at large.

Adding to the gravity of the problem is the sophistication of the techniques available for stifling the new discursive spaces that have opened up in African societies. The German political theorist Jürgen Habermas has elaborated a concept of the public sphere that is useful for understanding what is occurring in Africa today, even though the application of his ideas to different historical and geographical settings is subject to debate.[11] Indeed, if the emergence of public spaces where members of different social groups can freely discuss the issues of the day is the best evidence for democratic transition, then the boom in the number of places where people are talking deserves attention.

Brazzaville's open-air eateries, bars and bistros in Douala, cafés in Abidjan, soccer stadiums in Accra, tennis clubs in Dakar, Rotary Clubs in Nairobi, the weekly *tontine* meetings of women in Cotonou, *khat* rooms in Djibouti—all of these falsely labeled "exotic" places are venues where discussion has become the vehicle for questioning the social order. They are public spaces in full transformation.

In some countries, the party in power has tried to hijack this transformation. Asked on national television in 1987 to name his proudest accomplishments, Cameroon's President Biya said they were the easing of restrictions on the sale of alcohol and the reduction of the paperwork needed to open a bar or bistro. His opponents saw in this only a cynical plan to "intoxicate" the citizenry. What his statement in fact betrayed was that he could win votes by providing Cameroonians with other places of recreation, other public spheres with which the "poor" ought to content themselves. In Gabon, President Bongo's wife has organized some powerful women's groups behind new charity initiatives. These, while worthy of respect, also represent attempts to improve the image of the Gabonese ruling class, to compete with "popular" nongovernmental organizations whose leaders are critical of that class, and to build up counternarratives amid the prevailing atmosphere of collective anger against the political system.

5) A Controlled Press. The quality and availability of information in a society have always been key factors in the production of political power. During the 1960s and 1970s, Africa's authoritarian governments stopped at nothing to control speech and information, executing numerous dissidents for challenging the official line. Toward the end of the 1980s, however, a softening set in nearly everywhere. Independent media were increasingly tolerated, and certain countries, such as Senegal, even licensed private radio stations owned by staunch government foes. Yet to say that brutality and censorship have disappeared would be an exaggeration. What the authorities have given with one hand in the area of freedom of expression, they have taken back with the other in that of information availability. Privately owned newspapers have been allowed to go to press throughout most of Africa, but official pressure on commercial distributors and retailers has remained heavy. Given that the typical country's distribution network dates back to colonial times and by and large remains in the hands of foreign news organizations, it is easy to see how a strong government can determine which newspapers appear nationally. In the former Zaire, no distribution service even exists to guarantee that papers reach the back country, where every publication is on its own.

Authoritarian governments have also been counting increasingly on compliant courts to make accommodating rulings against critical publications and journalists. In recent years, the continent has seen a legion of journalists go on trial for their reporting, while newspapers have faced official lawsuits designed to ruin them financially. In Côte d'Ivoire, journalists have been jailed for suggesting that President Henri Konan-Bédié's presence at an international soccer match held in Abidjan had brought bad luck to the home team.

Relentlessly subjected to the government's wrath, some of the newly created media, which greatly helped set the democratic transition in motion, have become excessively partisan and polemical. Articles and editorials too often exude anger and other violent passions, which neither help to clarify public debate nor inform citizens regarding key issues.

6) The Absence of Civility. The politics of fear pervades the rhetoric and governing styles of politicians. Cameroon's President Biya refuses to use his adversaries' names, referring to them only as "thugs," "vandals," and "outlaws." Gabon's President Bongo is subtler: "The opposition doesn't make me lose any sleep. Those folks run the streets, I run the country."[12] Zaire's Mobutu Sese Seko spoke contemptuously of his opponents as "Kinshasa loud-mouths out of touch with the Zairian heartland."[13] His recent downfall seems to show that more than a few "Kinshasa loud-mouths" chafed at his kleptocratic rule.

During campaigns and elections, the already low level of civility in the public debate reaches its nadir. For example, when asked about challenger Paul Ssemogerere's chances of winning the 1996 presidential election, Uganda's President Yoweri Museveni declared: "How can that idiot win? . . . I cannot surrender my army to an idiot who is campaigning in churches trying to convince Catholics to vote for a fellow Catholic."[14] On radio and television, Ghana's Jerry Rawlings characterized his 1992 opponents as "punks," "disgruntled politicians," and "thieves."[15] Following the 1995 legislative elections in Benin, an opposition figure referred to the wife of then-President Nicéphore Soglo as "a piece of horse manure."[16]

This violence in speech reflects the violence of the political game itself, which leaders view as a "winner-takes-all" fight to the finish where defeat means a loss not only of the emoluments and status that office brings, but sometimes of life itself. The game is for keeps. One must win—by any means necessary. The modern state, as Max Weber said, holds a monopoly on the legitimate use of force; the transition, in the eyes of many African politicians, is a battle for control over the state's coercive apparatus. In this frenetic Darwinian struggle, soldiers have a comparative advantage that the more ambitious among them have often exploited in countries where the new political class lacks the skill to curb the power of the military.

7) Privatized Violence and Politicized Armies. Nearly everywhere in sub-Saharan Africa, the armed forces remain a threat to hijack or halt democratization. To make matters worse, what passes for the national armed services in many countries are actually tribal armies that have been assembled by political leaders not to defend the nation, but to maintain themselves in power and put down internal insurrections. With rare exceptions, these armies are idle corps with almost nothing to do when there is no repression to carry out. Similarly, in some countries the army functions as a kind of armed jobs program, a place where young men from the president's home region can draw a paycheck.

In those countries where the army's ranks do contain a cross-section of the populace, sitting heads of state frequently create special "Presidential" or "Republican" units that are nothing more than praetorian guards, armed to the teeth and recruited mostly from the president's own tribe. These "supersoldiers," whose senior officers are usually trained in Morocco or Israel, are the real military power. The means at their disposal are generally impressive, and their budgets do not always appear on the government's official books.

Some heads of state do not even bother to try and disguise this praetorianism, openly recruiting soldiers from their own tribes or forming tribal militias to do dirty work that the regular army might balk at, such as political assassinations, terrorist acts meant to cow the populace, money laundering, and the like. Congo's President Pascal Lissouba freely admits that the massive military recruitment of 1995 primarily benefited his own tribe. He has also implicitly acknowledged that each of the three private militias that paralyzed the army and brought about the bloody civil strife of 1993–94 had at least the sponsorship of one of Congo's three leading political figures: former president Denis Sassou-Nguesso, Brazzaville mayor and deputy Bernard Kolelas, and Lissouba himself. In Côte d'Ivoire, Gabon, Kenya, Togo, Zambia, and Zimbabwe, the ruling party uses the regular army to hold past and potential foes of the regime in check.

When a regular army is marginalized, ambitious factions in its ranks may soon begin planning to seize power. Unsuccessful coup attempts have occurred in recent years in the Central African Republic, Guinea, and São Tomé and Príncipe. A successful putsch took place in Niger in early 1996. Following a model with certain features that originated in Latin America, ambitious army officers appear to have found a recipe for legitimating takeovers: decry deteriorating economic and social conditions; stack the courts with your cronies; resign from the army to soften your image; pretend to be above the fray of factions and clans; and arrange a rigged presidential election so that you can claim the people's mandate and show the world how up-to-date and democratic you are. With a few variations, this script has been followed by former Captain Blaise Compaoré (Burkina Faso), former Colonel Lansana Conté (Guinea), former Flight Lieutenant Jerry Rawlings (Ghana), former Captain Yahya Jammeh (the Gambia), former Colonel Ibrahim Baré

Mad'nassara (Niger); and by former warlords Idriss Deby (Chad), Yoweri Museveni (Uganda), and Meles Zenawi (Ethiopia). Nigerian General Sani Abacha is widely believed to be working along the same lines.

8) International Support for Dictatorship. One need not be a proponent of dependency theory to recognize the degree of Western contempt for the sociopolitical transformations taking shape in Africa. It is perceptible in the statements of some European and U.S. politicians concerning the continent and in the place assigned to sub-Saharan Africa on the diplomatic agenda since the end of the Cold War. If it were only a matter of contempt, one might chalk it up to the rules of the international-relations game. But in the case of Africa, this contempt is regularly transformed into political and economic actions deliberately designed to disrupt or delay the democratic transition. Thus while political reforms have gone forward in Eastern Europe and Latin America *with* the blessing of both the former Soviet Union and the United States (each of which exercised at least informal control over local dictatorships in its sphere of influence), democratization in Africa has occurred *against* the wishes of France and has met with indifference from the other major Western powers who have commercial, financial, and military interests there.

Antoine Glaser and Stephen Smith have drawn up an impressive list of "players" from France who work behind the scenes and wield tremendous political and economic influence over Francophone Africa.[17] High-ranking civil servants at the Elysée Palace and the Quai d'Orsay in Paris; members of the Senate and National Assembly with personal interests in lucrative industries like oil, diamonds, gold, or logging; and businessmen who are linked to political networks in France and French-speaking African countries have been able to create a very powerful informal world where major economic decisions (on privatization, trade policy, tax reform, and the like) are made.

One cannot imagine Western countries acting in such a way in other parts of the world. More recently, in the wake of the execution of the Ogoni leader and environmental activist Ken Saro-Wiwa in Nigeria by the Abacha regime, the nefarious role that Western oil companies play in propping up African dictatorships has received extensive international press coverage.

It sometimes happens that outside forces opposed to political reform south of the Sahara are more open about their support of dictatorships. France has defense agreements containing what can only be described as deliberately ambiguous wording with the Central African Republic, the Comoros, Côte d'Ivoire, Djibouti, Gabon, Senegal, and Togo. This allows it to keep about eight thousand men stationed in these seven countries—not counting the ones sent under ad hoc military agreements to protect the existing regimes in Cameroon and Chad.[18] Under cover of mutual-aid pacts with former colonies, French troops occasionally intervene in the internal affairs of sovereign nations, propping up corrupt regimes threatened by domestic discontent over their poor governance and disregard for human rights. Asked about the intervention of French troops against Central African soldiers who had taken to the streets to demand their back pay, President Ange-Félix Patassé declared: "But I'm French! The fact that I've become a Central African doesn't mean I have to renounce France! I'm a Gaullist. The Central African Republic is a Gaullist country. . . . As an institution of the Republic, the French army had to protect me."[19] Asking the likes of Cameroon's Paul Biya or Togo's Gnassingbé Eyadéma to implement democratic reforms is tantamount to thinking that the USSR or Poland could have been democratized under Brezhnev or Gomulka. Yet some Western countries continue to expect the very men who plunged their countries into chaos to bring about change, raising doubts about the West's good faith.

Imperatives for Consolidation

More than the rigors of macroeconomic structural adjustment programs, it is the factors outlined above that explain the problematic nature of the democratic transition south of the Sahara. These factors have given rise not only to alternative networks but to veritable political black markets in most African nations. Setting the true pulse of the nation, they have their own rhythms, secret institutions, functioning mechanisms, and market systems that affect political supply and demand and impose a "premium" on those who are fighting to expand participation and improve the quality of citizenship.

How can African democracies become consolidated? Depending on the place and time, various tasks must be accomplished to orchestrate the quest for a sustainable democracy. With respect to sub-Saharan Africa today, beyond the necessary espousal of pluralism, I would propose the following imperatives:

1) Settling past grievances. There must be a resolution of human rights violations stemming from the years just before and during the early phase of the transition. The mass murders and continuing conflicts in Rwanda and Burundi remind us of the importance of collective memories in lands where innocent blood has been shed. The remarks of Burundi's former president Sylvestre Ntibantunganya must be understood in this way: "What is now necessary is for Burundians to be honest with themselves. . . . We must come to grips with our history even though it is nauseating."[20]

2) Restoring legitimacy. Political scientists have yet to reach a consensus on the usefulness of the concept of political legitimacy, especially when it is defined in terms as vague as "the right to govern." But Rodney Barker's definition of legitimacy—"the belief in the rightfulness of a state, in its authority to issue commands, so that the commands are obeyed not simply out of fear or self-interest, but because they are believed to have moral authority, because subjects believe that they ought to obey"—at once helps clarify and underscore the importance of the concept within the African context.[21] In a world where populations have cultivated unruliness as a means of surviving under authoritarianism, the "ought to obey" entailed in legitimacy has too often been transformed into "ought not to obey."

3) Showing solidarity and compassion. It is never easy to move out of authoritarianism, especially in a climate of economic austerity. Economic violence feeds political violence, and vice versa. The framers of Africa's new political institutions must not fail to address the multiple aspects of the current social crisis.

4) Expanding the political market. As we have seen time and again, African leaders wish to keep political participation as low as possible. By limiting the number of their interlocutors, they have an easier time repressing the democratic movement or co-opting into their ranks the hungriest of their "opponents" to help put a modern veneer on the status quo. The effectiveness of the new political systems will be closely linked to their ability to build formal and informal bridges between the government and society at large.

5) Ensuring military neutrality. The places where the army has disrupted democratization at a fairly advanced stage of the process (the Central African Republic, Congo-Brazzaville, Niger, and São Tomé and Príncipe) tend to be countries where the elected leaders failed to take concrete measures to alleviate crisis, and where mechanisms to resolve conflicts between the executive and legislative branches were either wholly lacking or poorly conceived. Better leadership and better-conceived political systems can reduce the probability of military uprisings.

The prospects of the democratic transition in Africa will depend on how well these five critical tasks are addressed. It is encouraging to observe that some of the emerging democracies have already taken them into account.

NOTES

1. See Joseph LaPalombara and Myron Weiner, "The Origin and Development of Political Parties," in LaPalombara and Weiner, eds., *Political Parties and Political Development* (Princeton: Princeton University Press, 1966).

2. Julius O. Ihonvbere, "Are Things Falling Apart? The Military and the Crisis of Democratization in Nigeria," *Journal of Modern African Studies* 34 (June 1996): 193–225.

3. See Terrence Lyons, "Ghana's Encouraging Elections: A Major Step Forward," *Journal of Democracy* 8 (April 1997): 65–77; and E. Gyimah-Boadi, "Ghana's Encouraging Elections: The Challenges Ahead," *Journal of Democracy* 8 (April 1997): 78–91.

4. The voter rolls that Ghana used in 1992 dated to 1987. They covered an electorate of 5.9 million voters; 1992 estimates placed the real number at around 8.4 million. According to some observers, the failure to update them resulted in the presence of many deceased persons on the lists, whereas many people of voting age had not been registered.

5. Quoted in *Jeune Afrique Economie,* April 1995, 71.

6. He is rumored to be the illegitimate son of former Ivorian president Félix Houphouët-Boigny and a Ghanaian woman. Asked about this by the press, Konan-Bédié has claimed to be amused but provided no information about his real father's identity. See his interview with *Jeune Afrique Economie,* January 1993, 20–33.

7. See Thierry Michalon, "L'état inutile?" in A. Sedjari, ed., *Etat-nation et dynamique des territoires,* forthcoming.

8. See Célestin Monga, "Dollars, francs CFA et démocratisation: Symbolisme politique et fonctions économiques de l'argent en Afrique francophone" (paper presented at a conference on "Retour du pluralisme et consolidation de la démocratie en Afrique," Université Laval, Quebec City, Canada, 5–6 May 1995).

9. Tessy Bakary, "Faut-il craindre le retour de Kérékou?" *Jeune Afrique Economie,* April 1996, 10–14.

10. Cilas Kemedjio, "Mutations camerounaises: Essai d'une cartographie politique" (unpubl. ms., University of Rochester, Department of Modern Languages, 1996).

11. Habermas himself has asserted that the bourgeois public sphere is "a category that is typical of an epoch. It cannot be abstracted from the unique developmental history of 'civil society' (*bürgerliche Gesellschaft*) originating in the European High Middle Ages; nor can it be transferred, ideal typically generalized, to any number of historical situations that represent formally similar constellations." Habermas, *The Structural Transformation of the Public Sphere: An Inquiry into a Category of Bourgeois Society* (Cambridge: MIT Press, 1989), xvii. I disagree with Habermas here, since I think that he is positing an unrealistic conceptual idealization.

12. Interview with Bongo in *Jeune Afrique Economie,* August 1994, 12.

13. Interview with Mobutu in *Jeune Afrique Economie,* June 1994, 17.

14. Museveni quoted in *New African,* April 1996, 10.

15. Quoted by Mike Oquaye in "The Ghanaian Elections of 1992—A Dissenting View," *African Affairs* 94 (April 1995): 264.

16. Interview with Soglo in *Jeune Afrique Economie,* May 1995, 58–65.

17. Antoine Glaser and Stephen Smith, *Ces messieurs Afrique: Le Paris-village du continent noir* (Paris: Calmann-Lévy, 1992).

18. *Marchés tropicaux* (Paris), 30 August 1996, 1868.

19. Interview with Patassé in *Jeune Afrique Economie,* May 1996, 16.

20. Interview with Ntibantunganya in *Jeune Afrique Economie,* April 1996, 61.

21. Rodney Barker, *Political Legitimacy and the State* (Oxford: Clarendon Press, 1990), 11.

5

AFRICA: AN INTERIM BALANCE SHEET

Crawford Young

Crawford Young is professor of political science at the University of Wisconsin–Madison. He has taught in Uganda, Zaire, and Senegal. His books include Ideology and Development in Africa *(1982),* The Rise and Decline of the Zairian State *(coauthored, 1985), and* The African Colonial State in Comparative Perspective *(1994).*

When the global "third wave" of democratization began to lap the shores of Africa in 1989, even the most sanguine observers expected that transitions from the continent's dominant mode of governance—patrimonial autocracy—would be rife with contradictions.[1] Recent events have proved them right: astonishingly high participation in Algerian presidential elections despite violence and threats from some Islamist extremists; a show of elections, with minimal participation, put on by the integralist military autocracy in Sudan; the promulgation of yet another constitution for military-ruled Nigeria, with further prolongation of that country's "permanent transition"; a political impasse leading to a coup in Niger, followed by promises that democracy would be restored within months; the return, via the ballot box, of former strongman Mathieu Kérékou to the presidency of Benin, birthplace of the national conference; elections in Sierra Leone held amid such widespread insecurity that voting was impossible in many regions; elections in the island republic of Mauritius in which (for the second time in 13 years) the ruling coalition stepped down after losing every one of the 60 seats at stake. The crosscurrents evident in these strikingly divergent events, occurring within months of each other, showed both the vitality and the fragility of the liberalization process.

A preliminary inventory of outcomes shows that only Libya and Sudan have held out resolutely against the third wave, with even the latter eventually feeling compelled to make a token gesture in the form of the above-mentioned nonparty elections. The other holdout, Colonel Muammar Qadhafi's contrarian regime in Libya, has used defiance of conventional norms as a source of legitimacy for nearly three decades.

Elsewhere in Africa, the tides of political opening have almost always brought changes. Transitions have ranged from the abortive (Nigeria) or denatured (Cameroon, Zaire) to the profound (South Africa). But even where incumbents have manipulated democratization to preserve their power, some of the parameters of politics have changed.

Most of the early scholarship on liberalization in Africa centered on the dynamics of transition.[2] Now, as many countries begin to undergo their second set of postliberalization elections, it is time to shift focus and begin evaluating the breadth and depth of democratic consolidation in various countries and the sustainability of the new practices.[3]

Independence and Its Aftermath

Borrowing Samuel P. Huntington's imagery, one might say that Africa has experienced its own three waves of democratization. The first consisted of constitutional changes, following models provided by the outgoing colonial powers, that laid down the ground rules for decolonization in the late 1950s and early 1960s. The second wave, feeble and short-lived, affected scattered locales in the late 1970s and early 1980s.

Powerful international and domestic forces propelled both these earlier waves. As anticolonialism intensified both in colonies and in the world at large following World War II, beleaguered metropolitan powers began to open once-exclusionary institutions of rule to indigenous participation as part of an apprenticeship in democratic self-government. Giving the colonies constitutional structures modeled on those of the metropole became a key step in the dignified retreat from empire. Local nationalists cooperated because they saw elections as a means of hastening independence and boosting their own claim to rule. Communist and Third World dictatorships supported democratization as part of the fight against imperialism. The West, meanwhile, viewed democratization as the natural endpoint of the transition to self-rule.

As soon as independence was won, however, support for democratic governance largely ceased. The doctrine of the mass single party as the vanguard of African progress soon took root, planted by the most charismatic leaders of the independence generation (Habib Bourguiba of Tunisia, Kwame Nkrumah of Ghana, Sékou Touré of Guinea, Julius Nyerere of Tanzania), and nurtured by persuasive academic commentators.[4] There was little public resistance to the destruction of the fragile constitutional structures created as part of the decolonization process, nor, a little later, to the epidemic of military coups.

African leaders' overriding goals became rapid development and the liberation of their economies from neocolonial control. Democracy, argued the new leaders, was a luxury that poor countries could not afford. Political competition and debate would divert energies from the urgent task of mounting a united assault on underdevelopment. Pluralism would allow fissiparous tendencies to emerge, threatening the consolidation of nationhood. The concentration of authority, not its dispersion, would be best for development and economic sovereignty.

At the time, the Soviet bloc and Maoist China seemed to offer the most impressive examples of swift economic transformation. Few Western observers were questioning Soviet claims of double-digit growth, and China's "great leap forward" of 1958–60 was viewed by many as a stunning achievement. Only years later did many realize that there were fatal contradictions in the Soviet economic model, and that the "great leap forward" was a catastrophe that had cost the lives of as many as 30 million people. Although the advent of full-fledged Afro-Marxism was years away, the late 1950s and early 1960s saw many an African leader adopt a Soviet-style emphasis on central planning, the capacity of the state to organize and direct development, the urgency of industrialization, large state-run enterprises, and so on.

Neither state socialism nor radical Third World nationalism saw much of value in postindependence constitutional democracy, and vocal defenders of democracy for Africa were scarce in the West as well. Development economists were sympathetic to state-led development, and dominant "modernization" theories readily acknowledged that economic development came first with democratization expected to follow later, a perspective that could easily rationalize military rule.[5] Former colonial powers were less interested in democracy than in preserving their economic advantages and privileged connections in their former colonies. Global strategists wanted reliable clients in the great game of the Cold War. The human rights movement was still weak and scattered, and gave scant attention to Africa. International backing for democracy in Africa vanished almost as soon as the independence celebrations ended. Indigenous nationalists had seen democracy primarily as a weapon in their struggle for independence; once that was won, democratic arrangements introduced under late colonialism seemed superfluous.

Africa's Second Wave

The second wave, when it came in the 1970s, was no *tsunami* but a discernible stirring, though apparent mainly in retrospect. The single-party regimes and military dictatorships that had dominated the continent since the morrow of independence were visibly fraying and had few intellectual defenders left. Three of the bloodiest and most notorious tyrants—Idi Amin of Uganda, Jean-Bédel Bokassa of the Central African Republic, and Francisco Macias Nguema of Equatorial Guinea—were overthrown in 1979. The destruction of the public realm by unchecked personal tyranny in each country bore witness to the perils of what

Richard Sklar calls "developmental dictatorship."[6] Several single-party regimes sought renewed legitimation by copying the Tanzanian practice of allowing competitive contests for parliamentary seats within the ruling party. These elections invariably led to the displacement of roughly half the incumbents and provided some outlet for public discontent.

Other significant democratic openings included Senegal's 1976 decision to begin phasing out the single-party model. By 1983, the country had multipartism, albeit with dominant-party control. Burkina Faso in the late 1970s experienced a period of competitive democracy. The Gambia and Botswana remained throughout moderately democratic, though without political alternation. Mauritius in the Indian Ocean, which is perhaps only ambiguously an African state, was the sole example in the second wave where greater political opening produced a change of rulers. In the 1982 elections, the ruling party lost all 60 directly elected seats in the National Assembly.

The second wave's two defining cases were Ghana and Nigeria; their simultaneous political openings in 1979 were the high-water mark, and with their failure the tide of liberalization receded. After taking over Ghana in 1972 and indulging in a brief initial period of reformism, the military regime of General Ignatius Acheampong had descended into unrestrained corruption, much of it involving cocoa, the country's leading export. By 1979, pressures for transition were becoming irresistible. After failing to win support for a military-civilian diarchy, the military agreed to full democratization.

Nigeria's was the single most important transition in the second wave. It began in earnest in 1975 with the coup that brought General Murtala Muhammad to power. Murtala was assassinated within a few months, but not before he had set up the transition that would be faithfully executed by his successor, General Olusegun Obasanjo. As with the first Nigerian transition in the 1950s, the process unfolded amid exceptionally favorable economic circumstances thanks to soaring world oil prices.

Although its results proved ephemeral, the extensive and broad-based process of public reflection and debate that produced the Second Nigerian Republic stands out as an innovative exercise in constitutional engineering. It showed groundbreaking candor by proposing institutions that explicitly took into account the country's cultural diversity, abandoning illusory notions that it could be coercively contained, marginalized by "national integration," or dissipated by "modernization."

In the event, it was not cultural pluralism but colossal financial and political corruption, culminating in the rigging of the 1983 elections, that destroyed the legitimacy of the Second Republic. The popular welcome that greeted the Nigerian military intervention of late 1983 marked the end of the second wave. Across most of Africa, democracy faded into the background for the time being.

On the whole, the global conjuncture remained unfavorable to democratization. The Soviet strategy of promoting a "socialist orientation" in Africa crested in the late 1970s with the emergence of seven states professing a Marxist-Leninist doctrinal commitment and the radicalization of populist-socialist regimes in Algeria and Tanzania. In response, Western powers bestowed more favors upon governments willing to resist this trend. For the most part, aside from the cases of Ghana and Nigeria, the political openings of the second wave liberalized autocratic formulas, rather than introducing fully democratic regimes.

The Crisis of the Autocratic State

Yet even as Africa's second wave was petering out, the worldwide third wave of democratization was gathering force, especially in Latin America. In Asia as well, entrenched autocracies in South Korea, Taiwan, Pakistan, and the Philippines gave way to more polyarchic regimes. African patrimonial autocracy began to seem outside the Third World mainstream.

At about the same time came a radical change in the terms under which African states engaged the international community. It began in the area of economic policy. The 1970s had been a time of aggressively asserted economic nationalism, a decade peppered with nationalizations and sweeping indigenization programs. In dramatic contrast, the beginning of the 1980s found Africa at a developmental impasse. In 1981, the World Bank offered a blistering critique of African development performance.[7] A widespread debt crisis became evident at the same time, and African states found themselves facing a phalanx of public and private international creditors. The World Bank ventured into "policy-based lending" for the first time, teaming up with the International Monetary Fund and Western donor countries to propose rigorous economic liberalization programs as the ransom for debt rescheduling and further development aid. "Neoliberalism" and "structural adjustment" entered the lexicon of political economy.

Meanwhile, the alternative of recourse to the "camp of socialism," so valuable to African states as a source of political leverage and room for international maneuver, progressively vanished. By the 1980s, the Soviet Union was reassessing its commitments and cutting its financial obligations in the Third World. The turning points for Africa were Moscow's 1981 rejection of Mozambique's attempt to join COMECON, and its 1982 rebuff of a Ghanaian delegation seeking support for a radical approach to the economic crisis. In the mid-1980s, a pattern of Soviet disengagement from Africa was becoming clear; by the end of the decade, the USSR would be in full retreat.

In the West, Keynesian economics and the social democratic ethos, which had colored much of the thinking about development in the 1960s and 1970s, came under fierce attack from doctrinaire advocates of free-market policies. At this time there arose the "Washington consensus" on development policy, which favored making external assistance conditional on economic liberalization. The progressive discrediting of state socialism during the 1980s, well before the fall of the Berlin Wall, made "economic reform" the only game in town. Africa had little choice but to accept at least the discourse of reform.

The failure of structural adjustment programs to bring about early recovery . . . intensified the mood of the crisis.

The failure of structural adjustment programs to bring about early recovery (their sponsors had predicted positive results within three to five years) intensified the mood of crisis. Influential voices both inside and outside Africa began to argue that political reform was a necessary concomitant of economic liberalization. The African state itself, as historical agent of development, came under challenge.[8] The argument ran that the thorough prebendalization of the public realm had created a state incapable of effective macroeconomic management.[9] Without a remoralization of public institutions, plus minimal accountability, economic liberalization could never endure.

Along with economic buffeting, dwindling state legitimacy was also helping to create a favorable climate for political change. For the citizens of many lands, the state had become a predator. Silent disengagement from the state became increasingly evident. Obstacles mounted to the patrimonial management of power. The resources needed to oil the gears of clientelism were drying up and becoming subject to tighter monitoring by international financial institutions intent upon structural adjustment. The stage was set for the third wave of African democratization. The 1988 Algerian riots were an early sign, shredding the three-decade-old revolutionary mystique of the National Liberation Front (FLN) and opening the way to political competition. The army aborted the transition in 1992, when it seemed that elections would bring the Islamic Salvation Front (FIS) to power, but the FLN's 1989 abandonment of its claim to political monopoly resonated.

Also in that year, longtime Beninese ruler Mathieu Kérékou, one of the deans of Afro-Marxism, found himself at bay. His government could not meet the state payroll or obtain external credits; he was abandoned by his former clientele and faced rising street protests as well as a barrage of denunciations from intellectuals, teachers, civil servants, unions, and students. There seemed no way out except to accede to their demand for a "national conference" of the so-called *forces vives* of the nation. Once assembled, the conference declared itself sovereign, and proceeded to create transitional institutions; Kérékou, isolated, could not resist this seizure of power by "civil society." The contagion soon spread throughout French-speaking Africa, whose people saw in Benin's national conference, as one admirer put it, "the beauty of something unique, incomparable."[10] National conferences drove incumbents from power in Mali, Niger, Congo, and Madagascar; they failed to do so in Gabon, Zaire, and Togo, but still changed the "rules of the game."

In Zambia, the support system sustaining the three-decade-long political monopoly of the United National Independence Party collapsed. Possibly overconfident of his capacity to survive multiparty competition, President Kenneth Kaunda permitted an honest election in 1991 and was swept from power. Even more potent in their continental impact were events in South Africa, where the unexpected release from prison of Nelson Mandela and the legalization of the African National Congress set in motion a process that led to the end of apartheid and then to genuine majority rule in 1994. In 1990, Nigeria—Africa's most populous polity— was in the midst of what looked like a credible, if slow, transition back to constitutional rule. Thus currents of change seemed to run strongly throughout the continent; democratization appeared to be mantled in the same cloak of inevitability that had clad the independence movements of the 1950s.

Equally important was the international conjuncture. The completely unexpected demolition of the Berlin Wall, and then the collapse of state socialism and of the Soviet Union itself, echoed powerfully throughout the world. By 1990, U.S. policy was aggressively promoting democratization, aided by the efforts of unusually outspoken ambassadors in Cameroon, the Central African Republic, Zaire, and Kenya. Even France—long indulgent toward its African partners—warned that the pré carré was not exempt from democratization. Within the World Bank, influential voices called for political reform as a necessary companion to economic liberalization.[11] "Governance"—including such polyarchic features as citizen influence and oversight, responsible and responsive leadership, and meaningful accountability and transparency—became a regular theme in the discourse of structural adjustment.[12] Political conditionality was far less systematic than the economic variety, but nonetheless was in the air.

Yet another factor driving democratization was the need for elections as part of accords settling longstanding crises. In Angola and Mozambique, some mechanism for gauging the relative constituencies of the internationally recognized regimes and their insurgent challengers was indispensable. In Namibia, recognition from the Organization of African Unity (OAU) was not enough to install the South West African People's Organization (SWAPO) in power; the sanction of an internationally supervised election was crucial. In war-torn Sierra Leone and Liberia, elections—however problematic—seem essential to any settlement pact.

These last two instances, along with Somalia and Rwanda, suggest another conjunctural factor of increasing, even frightening, weight: the collapsed state, an outcome as unanticipated as the disappearance of socialism. Before Charles Taylor and his insurgents sparked a chain reaction of disintegration in Liberia in 1989, and before factional combat following the ouster of President Mohamed Siad Barre triggered a similar process in Somalia two years later, analysts of African politics had never considered state collapse a likely prospect. Although the weakness and declining authority of African states was widely acknowledged, the international system was expected to sustain at least the shell of what Robert H. Jackson has termed the "quasi-state" by shoring up sovereignty through a variety of external means. Yet the "collapsed state" goes beyond the "quasi-state," for the international system is not easily capable of bringing the former back to life.[13]

Uneven Progress

Africa's third wave of democratization is now well into its second half-decade. However uneven its progress, democracy now sets the terms of political discourse in Africa; in this sense, the third wave has already proved more durable than the first two. Yet the euphoria that accompanied the arrival of the third wave in Africa has long since evaporated; even the most optimistic advocates of democratization would join Larry Diamond in cautioning that democratization is "bound to be gradual, messy, fitful, and slow, with many imperfections along the way."[14]

In no other region of the world has the global third wave encountered such a hostile economic and political environment. African economic difficulties are far more debilitating than those found elsewhere. Prolonged state decline and attendant corrosion of the effectiveness and legitimacy of the public realm have exacerbated cleavages of ethnicity, religion, and race. Not even in the post-Soviet world—the closest parallel, where wrenching economic adjustment, scarce social capital, and unsupportive political cultures impede the consolidation of democratic regimes—does the path seem so thorny.

Despite all this, many countries have made it beyond the initial phase of transition and are now wrestling with the more complex problems of consolidation and institutionalization. In some other cases, initially promising transitions have become sidetracked, without necessarily being entirely compromised or abandoned. In other countries, such as Nigeria and Zaire, incumbents have strung out and manipulated the transition process so much that democratization has lost its initial credibility and degenerated into a permanent charade.

In only a handful of instances can one speak with reasonable confidence of a beginning of consolidation, as measured by at least a second set of reasonably fair, open, and competitive elections (Benin, Cape Verde, Mauritius, Botswana, and Namibia are plausible candidates, although the latter two have yet to see any alternation in power). In a number of countries, longtime incumbents were evicted in the first transitional elections (Central African Republic, Congo-Brazzavile, Madagascar, Malawi, São Tomé and Príncipe, South Africa, and Zambia). The journal *Africa Dēmos* provides the most extensive classification of degrees of democratization.[15] Its 1995 findings list just three states as irretrievably authoritarian: Libya, Nigeria, and Sudan; after the shameful fiasco of the 1996 elections, many would add Equatorial Guinea. Seven others were unclassifiable because sovereignty was contested (Algeria, Angola, Burundi, Liberia, Rwanda, Sierra Leone, and Somalia). Each of the 42 remaining countries had some form of partial or substantial democracy.

In a significant number of cases, incumbents won elections, often by encouraging the proliferation of opposition parties, exploiting control over regional administrations, and wringing out whatever political mileage remained in the old ruling party. Some observers conclude that such outcomes reveal a deep flaw in the entire third wave. Claude Ake writes of "the crude simplicity of multiparty elections," which allows "some of the world's most notorious autocrats . . . to parade democratic credentials without reforming their repressive regimes." This observation leads Ake to a broader dismissal of the whole process as a form of democracy "whose relevance to Africa is problematic at best and at worst prone to engender contradictions that tend to derail or trivialize democratization in Africa."[16]

Elections like Kenya's in 1992 have shown how determined autocratic cliques are to cling to power, at considerable cost to the polity. Intent on discrediting the very notion of political competition, key individuals in President Daniel arap Moi's inner circle fomented ethnic clashes in the Rift Valley that drove 350,000 from their homes and killed 1,500. It also came to light that Moi and his clique had illicitly acquired almost $400 million in campaign-related funds.[17] Despite all this, however, Kenyan civil society is breathing easier after partial liberalization, and the political climate is less fear-ridden and closed than it was in the late 1980s.

Chicanery by incumbents can backfire, for denatured elections lose much of their legitimating value. Opposition protests and boycotts, whether of tainted elections themselves or of the institutions that result from them, can make an impact. Cases that might fit this pattern include Burkina Faso, Cameroon, Egypt, Ethiopia, Equatorial Guinea, Gabon, Ghana, Guinea, Guinea-Bissau, Côte d'Ivoire, Kenya, Mauritania, Togo, Tunisia, and Zimbabwe. Opposition protest was most vehement in Cameroon and Kenya. At the other end of the spectrum, complaints about the electoral process were relatively muted in Burkina Faso, Ghana, Tunisia, and Zimbabwe.

The occupants of Africa's presidential palaces have learned from experience in the half-decade since political liberalization began affecting the parameters of politics in their various countries. Such adaptive behavior is not new. After the epidemic of military coups in 1965–66, autocrats began constructing protective devices that helped to keep a number of them in power for three decades: scrambled command lines, ethnic-security maps, presidential-guard forces staffed by foreign mercenaries, multiple security forces. Tunisia's Zine al-Abidine Ben Ali, Gabon's Omar Bongo, Zimbabwe's Robert Mugabe, and Egypt's Hosni Mubarak are still in power because they have been agile enough to retain the initiative under changed rules.

The global conjuncture has changed significantly since the early 1990s. The international community today is less united and compelling in its pressures. And in Africa, since political liberalization has not produced the "second independence" initially imagined, citizen skepticism concerning the process is several shades deeper. Internationally, the competing imperatives of neorealism and what one recent commentator stigmatized as "Mother Teresa" diplomacy have become more evident.[18] Within a year, France had retreated from the commitment to African democratization that it made at the 1990 La Baule meeting with French-speaking African heads of state. Britain and Japan were never enthusiastic partisans of a high priority for political liberalization. In the case of the United States, contradictions soon became apparent. Pressure for democratization has not been applied in situations (such as those of Egypt and Algeria) where security and strategic—or Huntingtonian "clash of civilizations"—preoccupations have ranked high.[19] States like Uganda and Ghana, which receive high marks for economic liberalization, feel less pressure for democratization. The talk about "governance" that comes out of the international financial institutions is confined to the institutional requisites for "sound macroeconomic management" and an "enabling environment" for freer markets.

The Politics of Identity

Skeptics have advanced two main arguments challenging the therapeutic value of democratization for African states. First, they charge that competitive multipartism and open elections necessarily bring regional, ethnic, religious, and racial identities into play, intensifying disintegrative pressures on fragile states without contributing to either stability or legitimacy. Second, pointing to what Thomas M. Callaghy calls the "high historical correlation in the contemporary era between authoritarian rule and the ability to engage in major economic restructuring in the Third World," the skeptics note the severity of Africa's economic crisis, and claim that the intrinsic difficulty of convincing electorates of the need for painful austerity measures renders recovery impossible, and ensures another turn of the downward spiral.[20]

Few would deny that electoral competition readily flows along societal fault lines of ethnicity, religion, or race, in the world at large as well as Africa. Such identities serve as tempting vote banks for party organizers. With the perhaps momentary eclipse of ideological divisions, in an epoch where all forms of socialism remain blighted by the stigma of the failed Soviet version, political challengers have great difficulty in defining an alternative vision of society. Electoral discourse is thus limited to vague slogans expressing desire for change and opposition to incumbents. One finds few cases (Senegal is one) where political alignments are not significantly affected by communal solidarities.

Of the many transitions now in process, however, only four have seen escalating communal violence: Rwanda, Burundi, Algeria, and Congo. The endemic intercommunal strife in Sudan and Somalia has nothing to do with democratization, which on the contrary appears necessary if there is to be any hope for peace. Of the four cases, only in Congo did the ethnic violence involve armed factions directly issuing from electoral politics. The violence unleashed by the ethnic youth militias that terrorized Brazzaville for several months in 1993 and provoked large-scale ethnic cleansing of the capital's neighborhoods finally subsided at the end of that year when the party leaders who had fomented it reverted to more civil forms of rivalry under prodding from the OAU. The militias, however, are still at large, and Congo remains a cautionary tale in the drama of political liberalization.

In Algeria, the violence broke out when the military intervened to suspend an election process that would have produced a victory for the FIS. It cannot be known whether the FIS would have followed the Iranian path of political exclusion of those not sharing its vision of the Islamic state. What is certain is that an armed uprising by FIS elements, and later by far more extreme factions of the Groupe Islamique Armé, began soon after, and brought the country to the brink of civil war. Also clear is that the successful political opening begun by President Liamine Zeroual with the November 1995 elections created new opportunities for isolating the extremists and reincorporating most of the religious currents within civil society into the political process.

In Burundi, after the searing experiences of ethnic massacres in 1965, 1972, and 1988, the Tutsi-dominated military regime of Pierre Buyoya took meaningful steps toward national reconciliation. Buyoya expected his Union pour le Progrès National to reap electoral victory from this, and indeed, its main challenger, the Hutu-dominated Front Démocratique Burundais (FRODEBU), won only 60 percent of the vote even though the country was 85 percent Hutu. Buyoya accepted defeat graciously, and ceded power to the FRODEBU presidential candidate, Melchior Ndadaye. There was hope for ethnic accommodation through power-sharing and liberalization. The fatal flaw in the transitional arrangements was Tutsi control over the security forces. Tutsi officers assassinated

Ndadaye and several other FRODEBU leaders in October 1993, unleashing ethnic violence that has brought Burundi to the brink of a genocidal dissolution of state and society.[21]

As for the holocaust in neighboring Rwanda, which horrified the world in the spring of 1994, the evidence is even clearer that only some formula for power-sharing accompanied by political opening could have averted armageddon. Power had long been in the hands of a Hutu ethnarchy that later recast itself as a single-party military autocracy under Juvenal Habyarimana, who seized power in 1973. For more than a decade, the regime enjoyed a reasonable quotient of legitimacy with the Hutu majority, bolstered by a moderately competent development record and substantial external assistance. By the late 1980s, however, decline had set in amid increasing venality, growing regional favoritism, and decreasing governmental effectiveness. In 1990 came the invasion by the Rwandan Patriotic Front (FPR), an insurgent group consisting mostly of Tutsi exiles long resident in Uganda. Although contained with French, Belgian, and Zairian military assistance, the insurgency triggered a political crisis that led to the abandonment of single-party rule in 1991. Multipartism did not completely cure the deepening disaffection of civil society, but at least offered hope for political compromise and the containment of ethnic and regional tensions.

Hope vanished when the April 1994 assassination of Habyarimana became the occasion for genocidal massacres instigated and executed by extremist Hutu bands linked to the former ruling party. At least half a million people (mostly Tutsis) were killed, and two million Hutus later became refugees in neighboring countries. (Rwanda's total population before the massacres had been about eight million.) The FPR successor regime is unlikely to enjoy peace or stability until the country can come to terms with its past through a negotiated settlement that provides security to all citizens. Given the depth of the trauma, democracy will probably be off the national agenda for a long time.

Democratic responses to the problem of ethnicity can take many institutional forms. Consider the Ethiopian and Ugandan cases. In Ethiopia, the Shoan Amharic hegemony that lay at the core of both the imperial regime and its Afro-Marxist successor provoked a spate of rebellions around the ethnic and regional periphery. The 1991 military defeat of the Afro-Marxist regime at the hands of the Eritrean People's Liberation Front and the Tigrean People's Liberation Front (TPLF) compelled a far-reaching redefinition of the polity. Eritrea became independent, and ethnicity became the basis for a redrawing of Ethiopia's provincial boundaries. The new Ethiopian constitution goes farther than any other existing in the world today toward enshrining the principle of ethnic self-determination, up to and including the right to secession.

The actual exercise of ethnic self-determination, however, is constrained by the residue of Leninism that still affects the ruling

Ethiopian People's Revolutionary Democratic Front (EPRDF), which is essentially a creature of the TPLF. So far, the EPRDF leadership has handled the ethnic question by creating client parties in the various regions; full acceptance of the new political order by major ethnic groups such as the Oromo or Somali—to say nothing of the once-dominant Amhara—has yet to be demonstrated. Still, many Ethiopians regard the present limited political opening as an improvement upon the authoritarian regimes of the past.

In Uganda, President Yoweri Museveni is maneuvering to preserve the rule of his National Resistance Movement (NRM) under the ostensible constitutional sanction of a no-party democratic order. Large sectors of Ugandan opinion view this arrangement with an acquiescence that is at best temporary and uneasy. Yet the remarkable recovery that Uganda has enjoyed under his leadership has earned Museveni substantial room for maneuver. Enthusiasm for a return to political parties is tempered by the prospect of a return to prominence of the Uganda People's Congress and the Democratic Party, whose intense and partly religion-based rivalry dating to the 1960s is blamed for many of the misfortunes that followed. But the 1994 Constitution provided only a five-year delay for introduction of party politics, not a permanent mandate for NRM rule under the disguise of a no-party system.

The evidence to date does not permit the conclusion that identity politics offers an insuperable obstacle to political liberalization. The saliency of cultural diversity in most African states, however, poses clear challenges to sustainable democratization. There is need for thoughtful statecraft to devise constitutional formulas that can accommodate ethnic, religious, or racial differences. Evidence from around the world suggests that cultural pluralism should be acknowledged rather than ignored, through arrangements that induce inclusionary politics and create structural incentives for intercommunal cooperation.[22]

Economic Performance

Less clear is the critical issue of whether a politically liberalized state can sustain the rigorous macroeconomic management that is needed to restore economic health. The evidence on African economic performance since 1960 shows beyond doubt that patrimonial autocracy has failed. There is no need to review the dismal statistics through the 1980s; it suffices to note that while Ghanaian per-capita income comfortably exceeded that of South Korea in 1957, by 1993 per-capita income in South Korea was nearly 18 times what it was in Ghana.[23]

However strong the general case that can be made for the sequencing of reform on the East Asian model, with political opening coming after economic development, the applicability of this model to Africa is doubtful. Only Tunisia, with its highly effective and cohesive state apparatus, remotely resembles East Asia's "little tigers," yet Tunisian per-capita income grew by an average of only 1.2 percent a year from 1980 to 1993.[24] The logic of sequencing operates in reverse in Africa: Partial or substantial *political* transitions or liberalizations have occurred in most states, and the present international environment is hostile to overt authoritarian restoration. Although large states such as Nigeria and Sudan, or a maverick rentier state like Libya, can withstand external pressures, smaller and weaker African states are far more vulnerable. One may recollect the speed with which forcible coups have been reversed in the last three years in São Tomé and Príncipe, Lesotho, and Comoros; the authors of the January 1996 coup in Niger, though they could point to a debilitating institutional impasse and poorly designed "national conference" constitution to justify their actions, were soon compelled to agree to new elections (now slated for September 1996).

> *It is also worth noting that the two most impressive sustained economic-development records among Africa's 53 states belong to a pair of continuously democratic polities, Botswana and Mauritius.*

Relatively effective economic liberalization can earn some breathing space. Ghana and Uganda experienced far less international pressure for further political liberalization than did Kenya and Cameroon. But the conscious construction of a regime modeled on the Taiwan or South Korea of the 1960s and 1970s is impossible to imagine, even if internal societal and political circumstances permitted.

It is also worth noting that the two most impressive sustained economic-development records among Africa's 53 states belong to a pair of continuously democratic polities, Botswana and Mauritius. Botswana enjoyed average annual growth of 14.5 percent from 1970 to 1980, and 9.6 percent from 1980 to 1993. Over the same quarter-century, Mauritius maintained a steady growth rate of over 6 percent. Mauritius, little more than a huge sugar plantation at the time of its independence in 1968, has since the mid-1980s doubled its per-capita GDP to more than $3,000 per year. Its now-diversified economy has an unemployment rate of only 2 percent. And yet, in 1982 and again in 1995, fairly conducted elections resulted in ruling parties' losing all the contested seats, with peaceful turnover of power ensuing in both instances. Some special factors operate in both cases, but the indisputable success of Botswana and Mauritius is not just luck. Effective, cohesive bureaucracies, relatively high levels of public integrity, and careful economic management have played a large role. An expanding economy has in turn doubtless made democratic governance more sustainable.

Thus the question of the relationship between regime type and economic performance in Africa remains open. World Bank figures and other country-level statistical indicators yield no definitive answers. Indeed, it would be naive to expect causal pathways to stand out with much clarity when there are so many intervening variables involved. Stephan Haggard and Robert R. Kaufman, in their study of the political economy of democratic transitions in Latin America and Asia (but not Africa), conclude that the challenge of building state capacity in the poorer developing countries is forbidding, especially given the enormous debts and acute economic distress that many suffer. Winning political support for economic reform is hard at best, and becomes harder when its gains are intangible to constituents.[25] Electoral imperatives can spur profligate spending by incumbents: the Tanzanian government borrowed 33 billion Tanzanian shillings before the flawed 1995 elections.

The interim balance sheet on democratization in Africa is mixed but mildly positive. Not all experiments will survive, yet many countries have experienced important changes beyond the most visible one of multiparty elections: a freer and more vocal press, better respect for human rights, some headway toward achieving the rule of law. The more visionary forms of integral populist democracy are unlikely to be attained. The democratizing reforms that have occurred so far fall far short of consolidated democracy by any reasonably rigorous criteria, such as those proposed in a seminal 1996 article by Juan J. Linz and Alfred Stepan.[26] Nevertheless, slow, halting, uneven, yet continuing movement toward polyarchy is possible. There is no plausible and preferable alternative on the horizon.

NOTES

1. Samuel P. Huntington, *The Third Wave: Democratization in the Late Twentieth Century* (Norman: University of Oklahoma Press, 1991).

2. For example, Jennifer A. Widner, ed., *Economic Change and Political Liberalization in Sub-Saharan Africa* (Baltimore: Johns Hopkins University Press, 1994); Goran Hyden and Michael Bratton, eds., *Governance and Politics in Africa* (Boulder, Colo.: Lynne Rienner, 1992); John W. Harbeson, Donald Rothchild, and Naomi Chazan, eds., *Civil Society and the State in Africa* (Boulder, Colo.: Lynne Rienner, 1994); Larry Diamond, Juan J. Linz, and Seymour Martin Lipset, *Democracy in Developing Countries: Africa* (Boulder, Colo.: Lynne Rienner, 1988).

3. By liberalization, I mean such measures as acceptance of freer media, particularly the press, more respect for human rights, the ending of politically motivated incarceration, and the widening of freedom of association, as well as formally democratic measures such as competitive elections. Thus liberalization moves the polity toward a democratic opening, and as such is closely akin to democratization.

4. See, for example, the well-reasoned arguments in Government of Tanzania, *Report of the Presidential Commission on the Establishment of a Democratic One-Party State* (Dar-es-Salaam: Government Printer, 1965). For influential academic briefs for the single party, see Ruth Schachter Morganthau, *Political Parties in French-Speaking West Africa*

(Oxford: Clarendon, 1964); Immanuel Wallerstein, *Africa: The Politics of Independence* (New York: Vintage, 1961); Thomas Hodgkin, *African Political Parties: An Introductory Guide* (Harmondsworth: Penguin, 1961).

5. One may recollect the (in retrospect) surprisingly indulgent appraisals of the military as equipped with the integrity, nation-building commitment, and discipline to direct the early stages of development, in such influential works as Morris Janowitz, *The Military in the Political Development of New Nations: An Essay in Comparative Analysis* (Chicago: University of Chicago Press, 1964) and John J. Johnson, ed., *The Role of the Military in Underdeveloped Countries* (Princeton: Princeton University Press, 1962).

6. Richard Sklar, "Democracy in Africa," in Patrick Chabal, ed., *Political Domination in Africa: Reflections on the Limits of Power* (Cambridge: Cambridge University Press, 1986), 17–29.

7. *Accelerated Development in Sub-Saharan Africa: An Agenda for Action* (Washington, D.C.: World Bank, 1981).

8. See Richard Sandbrook, *The Politics of Africa's Economic Stagnation* (Cambridge: Cambridge University Press, 1985); Donald Rothchild and Naomi Chazan, *The Precarious Balance: State and Society in Africa* (Boulder, Colo.: Westview, 1988); John Ravenhill, ed., *Africa in Economic Crisis* (New York: Columbia University Press, 1986).

9. Richard Joseph, *Democracy and Prebendal Politics in Nigeria* (Cambridge: Cambridge University Press, 1987).

10. F. Eboussi Boulaga, *Les conférences nationales en Afrique Noire: Une affaire à suivre* (Paris: Karthala, 1993).

11. See, for example, the article by World Bank official Pierre Landell-Mills, "Governance, Cultural Change, and Empowerment," *Journal of Modern African Studies* 30 (December 1992): 543–67.

12. Goran Hyden has most systematically advanced and defended this concept; see his "Governance and the Study of Politics," in Hyden and Michael Bratton, *Governance and Politics in Africa* (Boulder, Colo.: Lynne Rienner, 1992), 1–26.

13. I. William Zartman, ed., *Collapsed States: The Disintegration and Restoration of Legitimate Authority* (Boulder, Colo.: Lynne Rienner, 1995); Robert H. Jackson, *Quasi-States: Sovereignty, International Relations, and the Third World* (Cambridge: Cambridge University Press, 1990).

14. *West Africa* (London), 4–10 March 1996, 328.

15. *Africa Dēmos* (Atlanta) 3 (March 1995): 35.

16. Claude Ake, *Democracy and Development in Africa* (Washington, D.C.: Brookings Institution, 1996), 130–31. To replace the "impoverished liberal democracy which prevails in the industrial countries" (p. 129), Ake proposes a resolutely utopian, integral-populist version.

17. *Africa Confidential,* 2 December 1994, 4–5.

18. Michael Mandelbaum, "Foreign Policy as Social Work," *Foreign Affairs* 75 (January–February 1996): 16–32.

19. Samuel P. Huntington, "The Clash of Civilizations?" *Foreign Affairs* 72 (Summer 1993): 22–49.

20. Thomas M. Callaghy and John Ravenhill, eds., *Hemmed In: Responses to Africa's Economic Decline* (New York: Columbia University Press, 1993), 467. See also the more pessimistic reading in Callaghy, "Africa: Back to the Future?" *Journal of Democracy* 5 (October 1994): 133–45. In these two arguments, we may note, one encounters a reprise of the brief for the single-party regime, circa 1960: the overriding urgency of nation-building, and the imperative of centralized, unchallenged state developmental authority.

21. For illuminating background, see René Lemarchand, *Burundi: Ethnocide as Discourse and Practice* (Washington, D.C.: Woodrow Wilson Center Press, 1994); Filip Reyntjens, "The Proof of the Pudding Is in the Eating: The June 1993 Elections in Burundi," *Journal of Modern African Studies* 31 (December 1993): 563–84.

22. I agree with Donald L. Horowitz on the primacy of incentives for cooperation; see his *A Democratic South Africa? Constitutional Engineering in a Divided Society* (Berkeley: University of California Press, 1991). Cf. Arend Lijphart, *Power-Sharing in South Africa* (Berkeley: Institute of International Studies, University of California–Berkeley, 1985), and *Democracy in Plural Societies* (Berkeley: University of California Press, 1977).

23. World Bank, *Workers in an Integrating World: World Development Report 1995* (New York: Oxford University Press, 1995), 162–63.

24. Ibid., 162.

25. Stephan Haggard and Robert R. Kaufman, *The Political Economy of Democratic Transitions* (Princeton: Princeton University Press, 1995), 377–79.

26. Juan J. Linz and Alfred Stepan, "Toward Consolidated Democracies," *Journal of Democracy* 7 (April 1996): 14–32.

II

South Africa: An African Success?

6

THE NEW SOUTH AFRICA: RENEWING CIVIL SOCIETY

Wilmot G. James & Daria Caliguire

Wilmot G. James is professor and dean of humanities at the University of Cape Town. Between 1994 and 1998 he was executive director of the Institute for Democracy in South Africa (Idasa). Daria Caliguire, a graduate of the John F. Kennedy School of Government at Harvard University, is a consultant at the Ford Foundation and is currently developing a project integrating human rights and development.

South Africa is fast approaching the beginning of its third year of democratic rule. Against a background of intractable conflict spawned by apartheid and the uncertainty and fragility of the preelection negotiation period, the democratic transition that the country has undergone over the past two years has been remarkable—even miraculous. The 1995 edition of the *Human Rights Watch World Report* refers to South Africa's transition to democratic rule as "the magnificent outcome of [a] long and costly struggle."[1] Indeed, the end of apartheid and the installation of Nelson Mandela as president of a new government led by the African National Congress (ANC) was one of the great historic moments of the twentieth century. For South Africans of all races, the nationwide balloting of April 1994 was more than an election; it was a celebration.

Although the party is not quite over, South Africa has already settled sufficiently into a new pattern of politics to permit us to ask some important questions: What kind of democracy is it that South Africans have crafted? And what are the long-term prospects for the new political arrangements? These are difficult questions to answer, both because the process of democratization remains relatively open and undefined and because there is little agreement in the analytic community as to the necessary conditions for democratic sustainability.

Accounting for much of the uncertainty is the absence of a permanent constitution. South Africans went to the polls in April 1994 with the understanding that the elected government would form a Constituent Assembly, one of whose tasks would be to fine-tune the interim constitution adopted by the outgoing parliament at the end of 1993. Still unsettled are several major issues of institutional design, such as the degree of federalism that will characterize South Africa and the nature of the country's electoral system.

There are also deeper questions. For example, what kinds of strains will the country's inherited social and economic conditions place on the political system? To what extent will the nation's vibrant—and, in some respects, uniquely configured—civil society, which was shaped by the antiapartheid struggle, be able to meet the numerous challenges it now faces and help institutionalize the new democratic regime?

Terms of the Transition

South Africa's transition to democracy was not a revolution in the classic, radical sense in which the term is used by Theda Skocpol—that is, a transformation of the structures of both state and society.[2] Rather, it was a negotiated settlement among opposing parties that resulted in representative government based on universal franchise. Such an agreement had come to be perceived by all parties as the only viable exit from a situation of stalemate.

Under the terms of the settlement, some key institutions of the state—including the military, the police, and the civil service—were left intact, but the legislative and executive branches of government were redesigned so that those who governed South Africa would represent the entire citizenry. New institutions, such as a Constitutional Court, were created in order to complete the separation of powers. Preexisting patterns of ownership and control of property were protected, so that the racial composition of the different socioeconomic classes remained unchanged.

A government of national unity would emerge as the institutional manifestation of the settlement among the parties. An extremely inclusive system of proportional representation was adopted for the national elections, with no minimum threshold required for entry into parliament. In addition, all parties that received more than 5 percent of the national vote gained representation in the executive cabinet; the threshold required for representation in the nine provincial cabinets was 10 percent. In the April 1994 elections, the ANC received 62.6 percent of the national vote, the National Party (NP), 20.4 percent, and the Inkatha Freedom Party (IFP), 10.5 percent. All the other parties, including the Pan-Africanist Congress (PAC), received less than the minimum threshold both nationally and in each province and are therefore without representation in national and provincial cabinets. In the spirit of accommodation and inclusiveness, Mandela has appointed representatives from marginal parties to other political offices, such as ambassadorships. The sharing of power embodied in the government of national unity promotes the reconciliation of the interests of different parties as the principal feature of South African politics. The settlement, in turn, sets limits on the government's freedom to transform state and society, in terms of both scale and timing.

The design of the institutions of governance is regulated by the interim constitution adopted at the end of 1993. The agreement among the parties was that the Constituent Assembly—made up of the National Assembly and the Senate—would draft a final constitution over a period of two years. Any changes to the interim constitution would require approval by a two-thirds majority, which no single party commands. Constitutional deliberations have involved an elaborate process of public consultation while also suffering delays caused by the parties' having to campaign for the local-government elections of 1 November 1995.

A perhaps more significant problem is that the IFP has been boycotting the Assembly's proceedings since April 1995, although it does make written submissions to the various parliamentary committees. The supposed reason for the boycott is a dispute about procedure: The IFP claims that the ANC has reneged on a preelection agreement to allow for some form of international mediation of the major conflicts among the parties in the realm of constitutional design. There are many areas of disagreement, but the primary issue is the extent of federalism and, in particular, the amount of control that the province of KwaZulu-Natal (the IFP's stronghold) will have over what the interim constitution defines as national functions, such as law enforcement and education.

That the IFP nevertheless prepares and makes submissions to the Constituent Assembly gives its boycott a somewhat ambiguous character. Clearly, however, there are serious problems to be addressed. In KwaZulu-Natal, the IFP-led provincial government limps from one crisis to another, the most recent one produced by allegations that one of the provincial ministers has been a party to political violence. These difficulties stand against the backdrop of an ongoing civil war. In 1993, the worst year of the conflict, more than two thousand individuals were killed for political reasons. The mortality figure for 1994 was 1,600, with the death rate declining sharply in the months after the election—perhaps indicating the positive impact of democratic governance.[3] Nevertheless, a total of 674 people were killed for political reasons between January and September of 1995, suggesting that the problems are still unresolved and that democracy has not brought about a fundamental change in the way people attempt to settle their differences.

The IFP is also keeping a secessionist agenda alive. It has begun to develop its own provincial constitution, and refers to KwaZulu-Natal as a "kingdom." The combination of the IFP's boycott of the Constituent Assembly, the difficulties that the IFP and the ANC are experiencing in developing an effective system of provincial government, and the IFP's drive for autonomy poses a grave danger to the legitimacy of the future South African constitution, and to South African democracy. Without a legitimate constitution, there would be little agreement on the basic rules of the political game, and virtually no moral constraints on secessionism.

Levels of Government

Although the April 1994 balloting put in place a national legislature and nine provincial legislatures, local governments were left unaffected. In accordance with the interim constitution, local governments inherited from the previous regime were made more representative by the addition of individuals from formerly disenfranchised communities, with elections for genuinely representative bodies scheduled to take place on 1 November 1995.

The local elections were critical for South Africa's transition to democracy, for they constituted the first true test of nonracial rule. Also, a great deal had been invested in local governments as vehicles of the Reconstruction and Development Programme (RDP), the ANC's master plan of political and economic reform, which to that point had not made much headway in yielding tangible benefits to poor South Africans.

Preparations for the November 1 elections were marred by problems. Whereas the 1994 national elections were administered by an Independent Electoral Commission, local elections were the responsibility of the provinces, whose efforts were coordinated by a task force that ultimately reported to the minister of provincial affairs and constitutional development, Roelf Meyer. A number of jurisdictions were unable to make the necessary administrative preparations in time, largely as a result of delays caused by constitutional battles over the demarcation of municipal boundaries. Thus, the balloting had to be postponed in KwaZulu-Natal, metropolitian Cape Town, and some rural areas in Gauteng, Eastern Cape, Western Cape, Northern Province, and Mpumalanga. However, the bulk of the country voted on November 1 in what could be considered, on balance, to be very successful elections.

The outcome gave the ANC an even bigger majority than it obtained in the April 1994 elections. Setting aside for now KwaZulu-Natal and metropolitan Cape Town—both areas where the ANC is not strong—it garnered 72 percent of the popular vote (compared with 62.6 percent in the April 1994 elections). With the electoral system working in its favor owing to the institution of a rule intended to safeguard "minority" participation in government at the local level, the ANC took control of local governments in many areas of the Western Cape that had previously been NP strongholds. While the NP suffered some setbacks, smaller parties like the black nationalist PAC, the white conservative Freedom Front (FF), and the liberal centrist Democratic Party (DP) were marginalized to an even greater extent. The poor performance of the FF is especially noteworthy, for it revealed how little enthusiasm there remains for the promised *Volkstaat* (white-separatist state).

The outcome of the local-government elections is revealing in two respects. First, the ANC—despite a less-than-stellar record on the implementation of its economic reform policies—has succeeded in consolidating and expanding its base of support. This raises the question whether South Africa is becoming a country with a permanent majority, with no turnover in government on the horizon. Second, the IFP and the NP may be in more trouble than they think. With the bulk of the elections out of the way, the ANC can now concentrate its campaign efforts on KwaZulu-Natal and metropolitan Cape Town. Moreover, voters in these areas will go to the polls knowing the preferences of their fellow citizens.

The local-government elections represented the successful completion of the plan for democratic representation in the three tiers of government—national, provincial, and local—spelled out in the interim constitution. In terms of formal institutional design, transitional arrangements—with the exception of the constitution itself, of course—have been converted into more durable ones.

The Nongovernmental Sector and Civil Society

After South Africa has held the remaining local-government elections and adopted a final constitution, the institutional picture will be complete. The question that is already beginning to emerge is how well these mechanisms will stand up to the social and economic pressures generated by the country's unique historical legacy. Economically, South Africa is much better endowed than most developing countries. Yet its economic potential is largely unknown, and its extreme racial inequality will place considerable demands on the system.

In the January 1996 issue of the *Journal of Democracy,* Adam Przeworski and his coauthors identify a number of variables that are critical to the sustainability of democratic regimes.[4] One is the choice of parliamentarism versus presidentialism; the former is alleged to be superior, because it is less likely to result in governmental paralysis. Another is the economy's potential to generate at least US$5,000 in earned income per capita. A third is the external political environment; obviously, new democracies are more likely to flourish in regional, continental, and global environments that are themselves democratic.

To these one could add a fourth variable: the extent to which there is a well-organized and vibrant civil society that is able to check the power of government, hold the leadership accountable, and promote a strong sense of citizenship among the public. Civil society is admittedly a nebulous notion. Broadly, however, it refers to the space between the family and the state in which citizens can initiate independent action to uphold civil liberties, a bill of rights, freedom, and justice.

In South Africa, nongovernmental organizations (NGOs) and community-based organizations (CBOs), along with churches, trade unions, and voluntary associations, have created and filled in the outlines of civil society. (In the present discussion, "NGOs" refers to both NGOs and CBOs; both are defined by a broader public purpose than voluntary associations.) They were originally formed as a response to apartheid, making up a political force that stood in opposition to an unjust and oppressive regime. With the support of foreign donors, NGOs and CBOs proliferated, providing humane anchors and safe havens to a people victimized by apartheid. Immediately preceding the April 1994 elections, the sector was probably at its peak, with approximately 54,000 NGOs and CBOs, of which about 20,000 could be considered to be development-oriented.[5] These organizations provided a broad range of services, from educational support and training (particularly for blacks) to rural development and media services; many were involved in the promotion of human rights.

Since the elections, a significant number of NGOs, including many that had existed for a long time, have closed or drastically curtailed their operations. This has given rise to a general perception that the sector is shrinking. Theoretically, it stands to reason that as the new government takes on the delivery of certain services to the entire population, including segments that were denied benefits in the past, the role of the NGO community should diminish. The organizational changes that are required before the government can fulfill its new functions, however, are costly in terms of both time and resources. Thus during this transitional period, NGOs are needed to assist the government in the delivery of services. Their technical expertise, administrative capacity, and existing networks within currently underserved communities make them especially well placed to play this role.

The NGO community is also important to the new South Africa in the broader sense mentioned above. It is generally agreed that a healthy democratic society requires a vibrant, pluralistic, and participatory civil society, of which NGOs constitute an important part. Thus a decrease in the size and scope of the sector could have a negative effect on the process of democratization. During this transitional stage, the drive to build South Africa's first legitimate democratic government—particularly the overzealous approach of some actors—may lead to a tendency to overcentralize state power, at the cost of weakening civil society.

The political transition in South Africa has destabilized the NGO community in a number of ways. The most fundamental change has been a loss of focus. The April 1994 elections formally eliminated the struggle against apartheid as the NGO community's *raison d' être*. With the loss of such a clear enemy, NGOs throughout the country are struggling to redefine their mission under the more ambiguous rubrics of development and democratization.

The NGO sector has also seen a restructuring of its funding base since 1994, giving rise to a severe financial crisis. Most affected has been foreign funding, on which NGOs had been heavily dependent. It does not appear that the total amount of foreign aid to South Africa has decreased; in fact, it may even have increased, although aggregate figures are unavailable. In many cases, however, donors have changed their eligibility requirements for recipients, shifted their funding priorities, or simply suspended operations for a period long enough to threaten the survival of their beneficiaries.

Significant portions of the NGO community currently face serious financial difficulties.

With the emergence of a legitimate South African government, the donor community has opted for a less fragmented approach to giving aid. Instead of funding a diverse array of individual NGOs and projects scattered across the country, foreign donors are now channeling funds directly to the national government through bilateral agreements for disbursement under the umbrella of the RDP. The RDP office, however, suffers from a weak administrative structure and low organizational capacity, causing the flow of funds to grassroots NGOs to dry up.

A June 1995 survey of NGOs confirms that significant portions of the NGO community currently face serious financial difficulties.[6] The survey concluded that funding of 41 development-oriented NGOs from foreign sources dropped more than 40 percent between 1994 and 1995 (from a total of R10.1 million to R6 million [US$1=R3.65]).[7] For the 1995 fiscal year, the NGOs surveyed face a total operating deficit equal to one-third of their combined budgets, with no prospects for alternative sources of funding. This situation seriously threatens the delivery of basic services such as health care and education to residents of outlying rural areas, where government infrastructure is virtually nonexistent.

The financial drought has become so severe that in August 1995 a cross-section of NGOs petitioned Jay Naidoo, the minister in charge of the RDP, to approach donors on behalf of the NGO community and ask them to consider a multipronged funding strategy that would not divert essential funds away from NGOs to the RDP.[8] The government granted the NGOs' request, thereby relinquishing its role as gatekeeper of all development funding. Its willingness to throw a lifeline to the NGO community not only showed that it recognized the seriousness of the financial crisis, but also constituted an acknowledgment of the structural failures of the RDP and the dangers inherent in a centralized system of funding and, by extension, programmatic authorization.

A third and final factor contributing to the destabilization of the NGO sector has been a loss of leadership. Many of the new political leaders and members of the state bureaucracy were the old South Africa's

activists and dissidents, large numbers of whom were members of the
NGO community. A depletion of leadership endangers the viability of
the sector just as surely as does a loss of funding. A case in point is the
July 1995 closing of HAP (Human Awareness Programme) Organisational Development Services, an NGO formed in 1977 that focused
on "strengthening the organizations of civil society" against the apartheid
state. In HAP's final publication—a directory of South African NGOs—
the group cites as its primary reason for closing the "bleed[ing] of skills
to government and the private sector."[9]

Now in evidence is a growing tendency to structure the relationship
between NGOs and the state in a more corporatist way. The impetus for
a coordinated, streamlined, and centralized approach to government-
NGO relations has come from both sides. From the government's vantage
point, and specifically that of the RDP office, the construction of central
channels of communication and interaction would presumably translate
into a system of decision making and delivery that is more efficient and
easier to administer. From the perspective of the NGO community, which
by its very nature is atomistic and unorganized as a sector, a coordinated
approach to dealing with the government would allow NGOs to speak
with one voice and thus have a greater chance of being heard.

Several developments over the past 18 months reveal this tendency
toward a corporatist model of relations between state and civil society.
In November 1994, a National Economic, Development, and Labour
Council (NEDLAC) was created to replace the old National Manpower
Commission as the primary policy-making body for the promotion of
economic growth and social equity. Whereas the original body had a
tripartite structure allowing for representation of government, business,
and labor, the explicit aim of NEDLAC is to bring "civil society" into
the decision-making process through the addition of a fourth chamber—
a development chamber. In accordance with this objective, the government conducted a national selection process to determine which NGOs
would represent civil society. The selection criteria turned out to be so
stringent and inappropriate, however, that only three NGOs qualified.[10]

A second development has been the formation of a national coalition
of NGOs. In August 1995, the National Non-Governmental Organisation
Coalition was launched in Johannesburg as the culmination of a series
of studies, new regional coalitions, and national summits involving the
RDP office and various representatives of the NGO community.
Although the idea that NGOs should organize themselves into one
representative body originated with the government as a means of
facilitating the implementation of the RDP, the main impetus has come
from within the NGO community itself. The sector sees the formation
of the national coalition as a means of attaining more input into policy
making and as a way to put NGOs on a more equal footing with
government institutions in a new "social partnership."

A third and related development has been the NGO community's petitioning of the government for the creation of an "enabling environment" for NGOs. An independent study was undertaken by a group of NGOs (which later formed the National NGO Coalition) to assess the legal and policy framework within which NGOs operate and form the basis of recommendations to government on how to improve it. The study found that NGOs are hindered by a myriad of repressive policies, laws, and structures inherited from the old regime. For example, strict controls had been placed on fundraising—the lifeline of NGOs. In order to raise funds, NGOs must obtain a permit from the government-appointed director of fundraising. Yet there are no set guidelines or criteria governing the granting of permits, leaving it subject to the discretion of the director and therefore open to abuse. Moreover, NGOs that are declared "affected"—that is, deemed to be involved in politics—are prohibited from receiving foreign funding.[11]

With the change in government, the NGO community has requested at the very least the elimination of controls, and preferably the development of legislation that specifically supports the work of NGOs. Together with interested parties, the national coalition of NGOs is drafting a Non-Profit Organisations Bill that calls for the creation of a commission, independent of both government and the NGO sector, to oversee the changes. Specifically, it calls for a review of six major pieces of existing legislation that negatively affect the operations of NGOs. It also calls for the creation of a Registry Secretariat that, among other duties, would make available to the public the annual reports and statutory documents of NGOs. The overall aim is to facilitate the flow of information about NGOs and promote transparency within the sector.

Finally, a fourth development is the establishment in November 1995 of the Transitional National Development Trust, through which all foreign, government, and private-sector funding to NGOs is to be channeled. The government was in favor of such a centralized funding mechanism, as it can be used to ensure that NGOs meet the delivery goals of the RDP. Clearly, however, the tying of NGO funding to compliance with government policies raises serious questions about the autonomy of the nonprofit sector.

A Democratic Culture?

Prospects for the consolidation of democracy in South Africa depend on the ability of its citizens to uphold principles of democratic behavior. It is certainly true that the various liberation movements campaigned against apartheid on a democratic platform and that many South Africans have embraced democratic attitudes and values in their day-to-day lives. It is also the case that even in longstanding and mature democracies, political intolerance and undemocratic behavior are not uncommon.

It is nevertheless troubling that contemporary South African society exhibits a strikingly low level of political tolerance. Of course, the worst expression of this intolerance is the violence in KwaZulu-Natal, where differences of opinion are all too frequently settled by murder. Even on a broader level of attitudes and values, however, South Africans are not inclined to tolerate difference. A national survey conducted by Idasa found that over 60 percent of South Africans would prefer not to allow a member of the political party they most opposed to engage in political activities, ranging from staging a public protest to holding a meeting in their neighborhood.

The horror of the situation in KwaZulu-Natal notwithstanding, there is room for optimism that democratic attitudes will eventually take root. The local-government elections took place largely without incident, although it must be said that campaigns were conducted within rather than across known constituencies, so that, for example, the FF did not dare venture into ANC territory, and vice versa.

Another hopeful sign is that the vast majority of politically active South Africans express their views through the more peaceable and accepted forms of protest, rather than more aggressive, "illegitimate" means. The Idasa survey revealed that when all forms of activity are taken into account—petitioning, public demonstrations, boycotts, strikes, sit-ins and occupations, property damage, and political violence—the black community is by far the most politically active segment of the population. Blacks are twice as active as the Coloured community, with whites showing little political activity other than petitioning. In all groups, however, the rate of participation in the more accepted forms of activity is significantly higher than in the more controversial forms.

A third hopeful sign is that churches, which are well placed to foster peace and goodwill, remain the most important organizations in the lives of South Africans of all races. The Idasa survey found that, by almost 2 to 1, South Africans ranked their church ahead of their political party as the institution with which they most closely identified. As primary components of civil society, churches are uniquely situated to bring about positive change in people's attitudes, beliefs, and behavior.

None of these positive factors should stop us from promoting the education of the public in the fundamentals of democracy and human rights as one of the highest priorities for the new South Africa. The first target should be the nation's youth, for they represent the future. Formal and informal efforts are needed to prepare them for the many demands, expectations, and responsibilities associated with democratic citizenship.

In July 1995, we asked Kader Asmal, the minister of water affairs and forestry in the government of national unity, to give us his assessment of the new democratic regime and what it had accomplished. His answer was instructive: Not only did democracy put an abrupt halt to the iniquities of the past, he said, but it restored the basic dignity, honor, and respect to which all South Africans are entitled. Although material improvement of people's lives is required and will be an important criterion of South Africans' overall satisfaction with the new regime, this fundamental dignity that can be bestowed only by a fair and just democratic order is even more crucial, and is part of the chemistry that links people to political parties and their leaders.

Despite these achievements, South Africa still faces several daunting challenges. The new government must work to solve the major problems of institutional design so that a permanent constitution can be ratified. It must establish the conditions for peace in KwaZulu-Natal. It must resist the tendency toward overcentralization of state power, which threatens the autonomy of civil society. Finally, if it is to underwrite the necessary improvements in the lives of the people, it must create the conditions for sustainable economic growth in a competitive and changing global environment. If South Africa can make significant progress on all these fronts, it stands an excellent chance of seeing its precious new regime take root and flourish.

NOTES

1. *Human Rights Watch World Report 1995* (New York: Human Rights Watch, 1994), 5.

2. Theda Skocpol, *States and Social Revolutions* (Cambridge: Cambridge University Press, 1979).

3. Statistics supplied by the Human Rights Committee of South Africa.

4. Adam Przeworski, Michael Alvarez, José Antonio Cheibub, and Fernando Limongi, "What Makes Democracies Endure?" in *Journal of Democracy* 7 (January 1996): 39–55.

5. Development Resources Center, "Independent Study into an Enabling Environment for NGOs" (draft discussion paper, 1993), 9.

6. Independent Development Trust, "Survey of the Financial State of 128 South African Non-Governmental Organisations (NGOs) and Community Based Organisations (CBOs)" (Cape Town, 1995), 7.

7. Ibid., 10.

8. Clair Bisseker, *The Cape Times* (Cape Town), 9 August 1995.

9. HAP Organisational Development Services, *1995 Bridge Directory* (Johannesburg: HAP Organisational Development Services, 1995), 1.

10. Interview with Obit Zimande, coordinator of the NEDLAC development chamber, May 1995.

11. Development Resources Center, "Independent Study into an Enabling Environment for NGOs," 6.

7

THE NEW SOUTH AFRICA: A SEASON FOR POWER-SHARING

Vincent T. Maphai

Vincent T. Maphai, currently corporate affairs director at the South African Breweries, was executive director of the Program on Social Dynamics at the Human Sciences Research Council of South Africa. This essay is part of a larger research project funded jointly by CISAC and the Research and Writing Program of the John D. and Catherine T. MacArthur Foundation.

Constitutional engineers commonly overlook a significant factor in democratization—time. Some institutions that may be workable or even necessary in the short term may undermine the long-term process of democratic consolidation. This is true of several elements of Arend Lijphart's well-known model of consociational democracy. Lijphart's consociationalism has four basic components: the sharing of executive power by all significant groups (government by "grand coalition"); such groups' retention of a high degree of cultural or regional autonomy; proportionality in the distribution of civil-service positions, public funds, and legislative seats (the latter through proportional representation, or PR); and a minority veto on most vital issues.[1]

This essay assesses the changing value of power-sharing for South African democracy over time. In particular, it will be shown that while government by grand coalition was necessary to bring about South Africa's transition to democratic rule, its continuation would hinder the institutionalization of the new regime. An examination of the intellectual debate reveals that both proponents and opponents of consociationalism follow a similar logic. For example, Lijphart and two of his South African critics, Janet Cherry and Steven Friedman, proceed from a specific conception of democracy, focusing on its virtues and understating its costs. They fail to recognize that each version of democracy contains features that other reasonable people would find undemocratic. Furthermore, none of the three sufficiently distinguishes between democracy and democratization.

South Africa's 1993 interim constitution provided both for PR (with the election of parliament from national and regional party lists) and a government of national unity (GNU). Any party with at least 5 percent of the national vote was guaranteed representation in the executive cabinet. Moreover, any party with at least 20 percent of the vote became entitled to a deputy presidency. In the April 1994 national elections, the National Party (NP) garnered 20.4 percent of the vote, thereby securing a deputy presidency (filled by former president F.W. de Klerk) and six cabinet portfolios. The Inkatha Freedom Party (IFP), with 10.5 percent of the national vote, obtained three cabinet positions. (In the permanent constitution adopted in May 1996 by the House and Senate, sitting as a Constituent Assembly, PR was retained but the provision for the GNU was dropped.)

The government thus formed under the interim constitution is clearly an example of a power-sharing system. Whether the South African settlement fully exemplifies Lijphart's consociationalism, however, is open to debate. Lijphart's own conclusion was that the "newly founded [South African] democracy . . . embodies all of [consociationalism's] basic principles" and represents "optimal power-sharing."[2] Yet at least one component of the model—an explicit minority veto—is missing. More important, the constitution does not contain a single group-based provision, focusing instead on the rights of the individual. Indeed, the general consensus is that the South African constitution is not a consociational document but takes the individual as the basic unit of reference, as do the constitutions of most liberal democracies.[3]

It may be too early to say whether the South African experience vindicates consociationalism, or even just some of its power-sharing features. Lijphart celebrated the success of South African consociationalism within little more than two months of the April 1994 elections. Critics of power-sharing in South Africa were almost as quick to condemn it. Any serious assessment will require a much longer view.

An Essential Precondition

There is no doubt that power-sharing was an essential precondition of democratization in South Africa. Indeed, it was the minimum that the NP would have been willing to settle for. For the African National Congress (ANC) it was, at worst, an irritant. In fact, it served as a confidence-building device for all concerned. Broadly, it was the minimum requirement for stability. There were also specific payoffs for the various actors. For the ANC, it guaranteed continued and essential support from whites. For the NP, it provided a means of monitoring and limiting the power of the ANC. For the international community, it met a combination of objectives: It brought political legitimacy through the ANC, as well as the promise of pressure for free-market policies from the NP and the IFP.

Within a year of the April 1994 elections, there were signs of success.

South Africa was a functioning democracy. President Nelson Mandela had managed to hold together two extremely heterogeneous constituencies—South Africa as a whole, and his own party, the ANC. Moreover, he had divided the white right wing by adopting a conciliatory tone toward the moderate right. He had prevented the reluctant IFP from withdrawing from the GNU. Clearly, the four-year period (1990–94) of problem-solving that preceded the elections had bridged the gap between former enemies. Fears that power-sharing would lead to a government hobbled by conflict also proved to be unfounded. The level of strife that has characterized the GNU would probably have been matched in a government consisting of the ANC alone. To date, no major crisis emerged that could be attributed to the GNU.

Certainly, government by grand coalition has its costs. According to J.E. Spence, examples of such costs in South Africa include the tension that the GNU has experienced between high expectations for improvement in material conditions and demands for fiscal discipline from both internal and external sources.[4] Furthermore, in their eagerness to convey an impression of unity, coalition participants have tended to postpone difficult but crucial decisions. Unresolved issues that came to haunt the GNU included the powers of the provinces and the constitutional role of racial or ethnic minorities.

Spence's examples, however, do not negate the fundamental value of power-sharing in South Africa. The GNU adopted the ANC's Reconstruction and Development Programme (RDP) without crippling political conflict. In bringing political stability and legitimacy to the country, it has created the conditions that have enabled the process of democratization to go forward. Deferring decisions in the face of unresolved differences is not, after all, an uncommon feature of governments, parties, and organizations of all types. Nor is it necessarily inappropriate, especially when it clears the way for progress on areas of agreement. Furthermore, certain tensions that are evident within the GNU are not necessarily direct consequences of power-sharing, but could easily have arisen in any event. The conflict between the demands of neoliberal market policies and the pressure for the redistribution of wealth exerted by the ANC's constituency is a case in point. Even without its two core partners, the South African Communist Party (SACP) and the Congress of South African Trade Unions (COSATU), the ANC is itself a coalition. The organization is racially, ethnically, and ideologically diverse; its membership includes liberals, socialists, capitalists, communists, Christian revivalists, gay-rights activists, pro-choice advocates, and both hunters and animal-rights activists. Given this heterogeneity, there is no guarantee that the alternative to the GNU would have been any more effectual.

Still, the benefits of consociationalism should not be exaggerated. The IFP's general demeanor and the postelection experience in the province of KwaZulu-Natal undermine claims that power-sharing guarantees stability in divided societies. At the center, power-sharing did not prevent walkouts or repeated threats of secession by the IFP. This is not to suggest that an alternative system would have succeeded in doing so; indeed, the consequences of the IFP's exclusion from government would no doubt have been worse. In KwaZulu-Natal, where the IFP and the ANC uneasily share power following a bitter, violent electoral contest and a narrow IFP victory, political violence shows no sign of abatement. Neither the ANC forces in KwaZulu-Natal nor the IFP seems to consider power-sharing a viable mechanism for the management of conflict or for governance of the province. Rather, each party is intent on consolidating its own power and reducing the other's political effectiveness.

Although South Africa exhibits a measure of racial and ethnic tolerance, it should not be attributed exclusively, or even largely, to power-sharing. Consociationalism was not the cause of tolerance, but the result. Power-sharing was the mechanism adopted to give expression to the parties' prior readiness to eschew racially exclusive politics in the interest of mutually beneficial outcomes. Similarly, PR had the effect of greatly diversifying representation in parliament, making possible the election of ethnic minorities, ANC exiles, women, labor activists, students, and others who could not have won seats in such great numbers under a single-member-district system. Yet it was precisely the desire to diversify its own parliamentary representation in this way that was a major motivation behind the ANC's endorsement of PR.

If this analysis is correct, then consociationalism faces a theoretical difficulty. Consociationalism is designed to minimize conflict in "deeply divided" societies. Yet it would appear that such societies would not adopt consociationalist measures in the first place until levels of hostility had diminished substantially. In South Africa, power-sharing was adopted at both the national and regional levels. At the national level— the level of racial and linguistic diversity—it was reasonably successful, with political violence all but disappearing. In one province, KwaZulu-Natal—a linguistically homogeneous region—it was a disaster.

Indeed, the concept of "deeply divided" societies seems superfluous.[5] A modified version of Lijphart's consociationalism could apply to any society "in conflict," regardless of its level of ethnic heterogeneity. For example, in any society, PR seems to produce a fairer distribution of votes and a stronger inducement to the formation of coalitions than other electoral systems. Similarly, government by broad (if not grand) coalition is not uncommon in a wide range of democracies. The same is true of the minority veto, or the rule that the constitution can be amended only by special majorities. No serious democrat would want majorities to have a totally free hand in legislation. Finally, group autonomy — especially in the realm of education, as evidenced by the prevalence of private religious schools—and regional autonomy through devolution of power from the center are also common in democracies of all types. In other words, conflict-regulation mechanisms in "deeply divided" societies need not differ *intrinsically* from those in more ethnically homogeneous societies.

Finally, consociationalism fails to explain certain features of the April 1994 elections and their broader implications. For one thing, the level of racial and ethnic campaigning was very low. At the regional level, only the NP employed a racist campaign (in the Western Cape). There are other ambiguities as well. Is the NP, for example, still a "white" party? Is the ANC an "African" party? In fact, these major parties no longer coincide neatly with a specific ethnicity, even though in the 1994 elections the ANC was supported largely by Africans while the NP drew enormous white support. The apparent engagement of voters in a "census vote" has other possible and rational explanations. In any event, the assumption that ethnicity was an overriding factor leaves a number of electoral behaviors unexplained. In the first place, why did Africans vote overwhelmingly for the moderate, nonracial ANC rather than the militant Pan-Africanist Congress (PAC)? Second, where were the Coloured and Indian parties, which according to consociational theory should have emerged to represent the interests of these minority groups in the government?

For these and other reasons, the long-term value of consociationalism in South Africa has been questioned. Such skepticism is reinforced by a look at the dynamics of power within the GNU. A useful starting point is a consideration of why the ANC, which was virtually guaranteed a solid majority in the national elections of April 1994, accepted the consociational principle of the sharing of executive power.

The Balance of Power

For Lijphart, power-sharing is a moral and political imperative. In contrast, the ANC—which has always professed a commitment to a nonracial society, in which rights inhere in individuals rather than in ethnic groups—seems to have turned to power-sharing primarily for strategic reasons. The late Joe Slovo, the ANC's former strategist, argued that majority rule did not offer a practical solution to South Africa's problems, at least in the short term. Instead, it was "necessary to share power for a while and meet de Klerk halfway." Compromise was appropriate and necessary, provided it did not "block permanently any future advance towards a nonracial society." Clearly, Slovo regarded power-sharing measures as temporary provisions with "sunset clauses." He was also emphatic that the ANC was not responding to a moral demand.[6]

The position of the NP was no different. Insisting that a "Damascus conversion" before February 1990 did not explain his liberalization program, de Klerk maintained that his decision to participate in the democratization process "was not a question of morality . . . but of practical politics."[7] Evidently, the parties' commitment to power-sharing was motivated by a sense of mutual weakness. If that is the sole explanation, then it is at least conceivable that shifts in the balance of power might bring changes in the parties' attitudes.

Political power is made up of several elements: economic resources (wealth, skills, productive capacity), coercive power (control of the army and other security forces), control of the public sector, international standing, and political legitimacy as evidenced by electoral support. The ANC has always enjoyed overwhelming popular support, as the elections confirmed. Through its alliance with COSATU it had acquired a certain degree of economic power. Because the bulk of the COSATU membership is unskilled, however, this power was largely negative: Unions had the capacity to disrupt the economy. Internationally, the ANC's stature was far greater than that of the NP. Yet NP supporters dominated the top echelons of both the private and public sectors, even in the four nominally independent "homelands" of Transkei, Bophuthatswana, Venda, and Ciskei. Moreover, both domestic business and the international community remained uneasy about the ANC's links with the SACP, fears that were exacerbated by the ANC's frequent threats of nationalization. Business also worried that, under pressure from an impatient mass constituency, the ANC could turn to unsustainable macroeconomic populism, resulting in economic disaster. De Klerk was considered a sufficiently strong counter to the radical economic policies suspected of the ANC. This perception did not escape the ANC's attention, which explains why NP member Derek Keys retained the key finance portfolio in the new government after the 1994 elections. When Keys resigned unexpectedly in mid-1994, the local stock markets reacted. President Mandela went so far as to amend the constitution so that he could reach outside of parliament to appoint as Keys's replacement another highly respected businessperson, banker Chris Liebenberg, thereby retaining the confidence of the business community.

The ANC also lacked coercive power. The police were even more sympathetic to the right-wing Conservative Party than to the center-right NP. The security forces in South Africa have always been openly hostile to the ANC. The ANC, for its part, never intended its military wing, Umkhonto we Sizwe (Spear of the Nation, or MK), to be a serious match for the South African Defence Force (SADF). Referring to the MK's formation, Mandela remarked, "I never had any illusions that we could win a military victory; its purpose was to focus attention on the resistance movement."[8] As a liberation movement, the ANC had perfected the art of making the country ungovernable. Yet as a ruling party, like the NP, it could not exercise political power unilaterally. Following the April 1994 elections, the ANC acquired de jure authority, but the NP still monopolized de facto authority through its control of the practical instruments of power. Thus neither side could govern the country without the assistance of the other. By its very nature, however, a political stalemate is a watershed—a fact that constitutional engineers typically overlook. Not long after the elections, the balance of power had already begun to shift.

Changing Fortunes

The first indication of a waning of the NP's power was its loss of the key portfolios of defense and law and order, which were taken over by Joe Modise and Sydney Mafumadi of the ANC. The government then embarked on a plan to reduce the ranks of the renamed South African National Defence Force (SANDF) from 135,000 to 75,000 by 1999. The ANC made it clear that the government intended to alter the military's racial and political composition. By 1995, 11 former MK members had been appointed generals in the new integrated army. In addition, one out of every five army officers came from the ANC.

As Friedman notes, the NP also lost its "gatekeeper" status as a representative of various interests, which no longer relied on the NP to provide them with access to power. Significantly, de Klerk has kept a low profile in the GNU. He has been hurt by reports of illegal attempts by security forces to undermine the ANC during the negotiation process, and additional revelations could further diminish his standing. On numerous occasions, the leaders of the white right wing indicated publicly that Mandela took them much more seriously than de Klerk had ever done. This is hardly surprising, for de Klerk had no interest in supporting a group that had denounced him as a traitor. His party also has to compete with the right wing for support from whites.

The NP became redundant in the GNU in still other respects. First, domestic and international businesses gained direct access to ANC ministers and policy makers and became increasingly comfortable with the ANC's policies. Only the ANC had the international credibility to call off economic sanctions. It also had the legitimacy to help local entrepreneurs expand their businesses to other African countries, where South African companies have yet to fully exploit investment opportunities. Furthermore, from the perspective of business, the ANC had shifted significantly toward "responsible, investor-friendly policies." Second, the NP took a low-key and half-hearted approach to the several policy forums that were established (beginning in 1990) to deal with such key issues as the economy and housing. These forums were largely consultative. Nevertheless, they became important routes by which many organs of civil society—especially labor unions, business groups, and civic organizations—could exert an influence on the policy-making process.

Third, a "personal chemistry" seems to have developed between the white military and police generals and their ANC ministers. Moreover, the police and army became disenchanted with the NP after parliament passed the Promotion of National Unity and Reconciliation Bill in June 1995. The bill paved the way for the formation of a Truth Commission, whose role it is to investigate crimes and politically motivated murders, mostly by members of the security forces. The ultraconservative Afrikaner Freedom Front (FF) had opposed the bill, with the NP and ANC supporting it and the IFP abstaining. The security forces and NP supporters were displeased by what they viewed as the NP's excessive closeness to, or lack of assertiveness with, the ANC.

If the NP's role in the GNU has become merely symbolic, what of the third partner, the IFP? Its leader, Chief Mangosuthu Buthelezi, had several sources of leverage at the negotiating table. Aside from exerting political control over the KwaZulu people, he also controlled the key police and economic-affairs portfolios in the KwaZulu region. Furthermore, with the assistance of the South African security forces, the IFP had unleashed violence, especially in Natal and the Gauteng region, which includes Johannesburg. Another source of Buthelezi's power was his relationship with the Zulu monarchy, an important institution in the region's culture. The business community supported him because of his commitment to free-market principles. His intolerance of militant labor unions was an added attraction.

A great deal changed after the elections. Once the ANC adopted both the rhetoric and the substance of the free-market philosophy, the IFP's value to both the white and international communities diminished. Buthelezi also began to lose the support of the business community, which became increasingly concerned about his image as a war-mongering secessionist. His relationship with the Zulu monarch, King Goodwill Zwelithini, also deteriorated. With the central government assuming responsibility for the payment of traditional leaders, a pivotal power base for Buthelezi in KwaZulu-Natal, his support could only wither. He also stood to lose the secret funding and military support that he traditionally received from the security services. The ANC has still not fully exercised its power to weaken the IFP. Given the longstanding allegations that the army trained IFP assassins to eliminate ANC leaders during the apartheid era, revelations of the Truth Commission could easily hurt the party and its leader. Ultimately, the IFP's role in the GNU was subject to two structural limitations. First, the IFP is a regional party. Second, Buthelezi prefers to remain a regional leader of a strong province rather than assume the role of junior member in a national government. This might explain why his participation in the GNU has generally been disruptive.

Since the 1994 elections, the ANC's fortunes have not been wholly positive. The organization has yet to gain effective political control over the entire country. There are still "no-go" areas for Mandela in the IFP strongholds. Moreover, the president had to be hustled out of the 1995 May Day rally in Durban after some IFP supporters fired shots. There was a twist of irony here: "In the run-up to April's election, many of its opponents feared that an ANC government would fiercely assert its power and silence its foes. Nelson Mandela repeatedly described President F.W. de Klerk as a 'political weakling' and accused him of 'indecision.' Today Mr. Mandela's government faces that charge. Fears of tyranny are giving way to fears of anarchy."[9]

The ANC also came to discover that the very strategies and qualities that are essential to the success of a liberation movement often become liabilities once the struggle is over. During the antiapartheid struggle, the ANC's backbone consisted of militant workers, youth, and defiant urban-dwellers. Once in power, however, the ANC found that its constituency had diversified overnight to include rural, unemployed, and white people. The demands of these varied constituencies could not always be reconciled. An increase in the incidence of strikes during the postelection period and the ANC's failure to call off the rent boycott that had begun in the mid-1980s revealed the organization's vulnerability.

Unlike the NP and the IFP, however, the ANC is poised to become stronger as it gains effective control of the state apparatus. It faces no immediate electoral challenge from rival parties, as the local elections of 1 November 1995 confirmed. The PAC and the Black Consciousness Movement of Azania have yet to earn credibility among the electorate. In the short term, at least, the unravelling of the historic tripartite alliance (ANC-SACP-COSATU) is nothing more than a theoretical possibility.

Above all, government by grand coalition serves a symbolic function. Although symbolism in politics is not unimportant, the costs that consociationalism imposes on democracy should not be ignored. Within months of the installation of South Africa's GNU, voices of criticism were beginning to be heard.

Arguments Against Power-Sharing

A number of theoretical arguments against power-sharing have recently emerged. Cherry criticizes PR and South Africa's GNU on several grounds. She disputes the view that the "constitutional solution which accommodates minority interests (usually defined in racial, ethnic or religious terms) is a requisite for stability," arguing that ethnicity, while an indisputable factor, is not a "driving force" in South African politics. The basic issue is the "political and economic incorporation, not of minorities, but of majorities." In other words, the central imperative is not ethnic accommodation but "the implementation of development programs." Finally, she argues, ethnic accommodation is not always productive, as concessions to the IFP on the constitutional position of the Zulu monarchy have shown. Instead of being reciprocated, such concessions merely generated additional demands from Buthelezi.[10]

Friedman, too, doubts the value of the GNU. For him, "the durability of the postapartheid polity is likely to depend not on strengthening power-sharing between political parties but on corporatist accommodation between the majority in the new government, and key constituencies in its own and the minority camp."[11] As mentioned above, Friedman notes that the NP has lost its preelection status as a representative of various constituencies. Furthermore, he claims, the ANC cannot afford to ignore existing extraparliamentary interests, but should deal directly with them. Aside from the ANC, the partners in the GNU are "heads without bodies," so that the system cannot even guarantee stability.[12] Friedman recommends a corporatist solution, arguing that "prospects for South African stability would not be greatly altered were the polity to revert to that consociational nightmare, simple majority rule."[13]

Courtney Jung and Ian Shapiro criticize the GNU largely on conventional grounds. First, they argue, "there are doubts whether negotiated settlements lead to democracy in the medium term." Second, the system lacks effective opposition, "which every healthy society needs." Third, it offers no opportunities for a turnover of political elites. This situation is aggravated by the constitutional stipulation that prevents parliamentarians from crossing the floor to the opposition. Thus Jung and Shapiro recommend that the GNU be replaced with a majoritarian government. In addition, they argue, party backbenchers should be at liberty to cross the floor.[14]

Jung and Shapiro's concern about the weakness of opposition in South Africa is not misplaced, but this issue has little to do with the power-sharing model itself. Power-sharing is not compulsory; it is an option available to parties that meet certain thresholds of support. Further, the problem of "floor-crossing" may have been overstated. In fact, this limitation may have worked to the advantage of smaller parties. The chances of ANC or NP parliamentarians' crossing over to small parties like the PAC or the FF are negligible. Rather, movement tends to be from the opposition to the governing parties. Furthermore, floor-crossing would seem to undermine the very accountability that Jung and Shapiro are at pains to protect.

Missing in the debate over the GNU is a consideration of its temporal context. Arguments against the GNU can be boiled down to three main criticisms. First, it does not solve all problems. Power-sharing certainly fails on this ground, but so would any other system. Second, it contains some contradictions. This, too, would be true of any other arrangement. For example, a majoritarian system would violate some important democratic tenets, such as inclusiveness. Third, it has some negative side effects. The shortcomings of power-sharing have been amply demonstrated. Yet most remedies, including the best, have negative side effects.

In order to make their case against the GNU, the critics would have to demonstrate that the system has not achieved what it was intended to achieve and cannot be improved. Yet no such argument has, so far, been proffered. Even the sternest critics of power-sharing acknowledge its positive features. Alternatively, they would have to show that the GNU has achieved its goals only at enormous cost (or at costs that exceed the benefits), when there were other viable alternatives. This would certainly be the strongest argument against power-sharing.

Cherry and Friedman have assessed the cost of power-sharing, but not the cost of its absence at the time it was adopted. Furthermore, Friedman assumes—wrongly—that because the IFP and NP are toothless tigers within the GNU, they would also have been benign if they had been excluded. Finally, Friedman has not explored sufficiently why the NP and its leader became marginalized within the GNU. If it has something to do with the towering stature of Mandela, then the situation need not be permanent.

Cherry attaches great significance to accountability, popular participation, and economic development. The inclusion of economic development is important here, because this is an issue on which consociationalism is silent. Throughout the African continent, however, the anticipated fruits of the liberation struggle have always been the same: respect for human rights and improvement in material conditions. Still, while group-based inequality can cause or exacerbate ethnic mobilization, it does not follow that egalitarianism or development will end ethnic conflict. Cherry acknowledges the importance of inclusiveness, but she underplays its significance, especially at the beginning of the transition, when the legitimation of the new dispensation is essential.

Friedman's faith in corporatism is based on his perception that South Africa's culture of power-sharing is overshadowed by a deal-making culture that pervades the country, both at the national and local levels of politics.[15] Since the mid-1980s, local disputes such as rent and consumer boycotts have been resolved largely through negotiations involving civic associations, business communities, and local-government officials. Yet Friedman, like Lijphart and Cherry, also remains fixated on a particular conception of democracy, viewing it as a corporatist, consultative process involving state and civil society, or government and autonomous interest groups. Like consociationalism, however, corporatism may solve one problem only to generate others. Friedman is not unaware of these dangers, acknowledging that "if crucial pacts are made outside, then democracy may rest on shaky grounds." He concludes, however, that because corporatism is subject to public scrutiny, it is not inimical to democracy.[16] Whether such a corporatist pattern of interest representation helps or hinders democracy depends

in part on the source of funding of the consultative forums and the extent
to which they manifest democratic norms and procedures—issues that
Friedman has not explored sufficiently.

Cherry draws attention to other limitations of corporatism. One of its
fundamental requirements is powerful organs of civil society. In South
Africa, these are of three kinds: a white-dominated business lobby and,
within the black community, the labor movement and the civic
associations. As a result, "those who are most in need of development,
and those most in need of independent organs of civil society to
pressurize on their behalf, are those who do not have them. . . . Those
who are best organized—industrial workers, urban homeowners, or those
renting formal housing—are the most likely to be successfully
incorporated into such a 'corporatist' scenario."[17]

Finally, as Cherry notes, corporatism shifts the locus of decision
making from parliament to the corporatist negotiating forums. The Labor
Relations Act of 1995 is illustrative. Unions, business, and government
(the minister of labor) carefully negotiated the bill's details before it
was submitted to parliament. Yet members of parliament refused to be
rushed into its adoption, finally passing a modified version. Many
potential institutional participants in a corporatist system—notable
exceptions being business and labor—are too fragile to warrant their
endorsement as substitutes for other mechanisms, including power-
sharing. Some interests, such as rural workers, are simply not sufficiently
organized to be able to play the corporatist game effectively.

A Dynamic Process

Both the consociationalists and some of their critics focus on
democracy as a fixed destination. Yet the essence of democratization is
change. A country that is democratizing is likely to exhibit nondemocratic features, no matter which electoral system is adopted.
Consociationalism, corporatism, and liberal, participatory democracy
(which gives a prominent role to the civic associations) should each be
evaluated within a framework that views democratization as a dynamic,
ongoing process. As Crawford Young has argued,

> If we have learned anything about identity politics in recent decades, it is
> the importance of flux and change. No formulas are permanent. If we
> assume that democratization in Africa will be slow, uneven, and uncertain,
> yet will remain a defining element on the agenda of change and recovery,
> then constitutional formulas that embody these aspirations will need to
> remain open-ended, experimental, and responsive to evolving cultural
> realities.[18]

At the beginning of South Africa's transition to democracy, there
was no viable alternative to power-sharing. It was the only system

acceptable to all sides. Yet the institutions required to initiate a change are seldom appropriate for sustaining the new arrangements over the long term. In important respects—such as its devaluation of individual political preferences and its constraints on opposition and alternation in power— consociationalism is inherently undemocratic. In the long run, South Africa will be best served by a hybrid system. One element of this system should be a variant of PR along the lines suggested by Andrew Reynolds, in which the principle of proportionality is applied in smaller multimember constituencies that allow for more geographical representativeness and accountability.[19] By the time of the next election, however, the GNU will probably have outlived its usefulness. It should cease to be a constitutional prescription and become a political option.

In the long term, what South Africa needs least is consociationalism.

In South Africa, power-sharing served two essential functions at the dawn of democracy: It provided a mechanism for jointly drafting the rules of the game, and it acted as a confidence-building device. By 1995, both objectives had been largely achieved, and two other proposed roles appeared superfluous. As Cherry emphasizes, ethnic accommodation may turn out to be the least troublesome challenge facing South Africa. And as Friedman notes, whites (owing to their independent economic power) need the state less than blacks.

One should avoid the assumption that because ethnicity has been politically insignificant in the past few years, it will not become a major factor in the future. Few anticipated the extent to which the Western Cape, long a bastion of liberalism, would become a hotbed of Coloured-African tension beginning with the 1994 election campaign. Still, this does not mean that power-sharing must be a permanent feature of government.

Lijphart's consociational model envisions power-sharing among ethnic or communal groups (and their respective political parties). As South Africa's rulers sought to reform apartheid in the 1980s and ultimately to negotiate its termination, this was the model toward which they were moving as a means of protecting white-minority rights. But this is only one possible framework for power-sharing; there are at least three others.

Power-sharing can also occur among political parties as implicit, rather than explicit, representatives of groups. This was the real logic behind South Africa's 1993 interim constitution, which resulted in a weaker and more fluid correspondence between party and ethnicity than consociationalism envisioned. (Coloureds and Indians, for example, gave their votes to the two major parties, not their own ethnic parties, and the ANC in particular sent a broadly multiracial slate to parliament and the cabinet.) Third, power-sharing can occur between a majority ruling party and powerful organs of civil society. This is the corporatist option recommended by Friedman. Finally, there can be vertical and horizontal forms of power-sharing among levels and branches of government, respectively.

This fourth principle of power-sharing is currently accepted, with many variations, in numerous liberal democracies that distribute power among central, regional (state or provincial), and local tiers of government, and, at the center, among a (bicameral) legislature, an independent judiciary, and (in some cases) an executive presidency. As Lijphart's own work makes apparent, the issues of institutional design posed by the consociational model are better considered within the broader framework of variation between consensual and majoritarian forms of government.[20]

The future for all South Africans lies in the fourth model of power-sharing. This requires the strengthening of public institutions and their respect by political leaders. In particular, the impartiality of the judiciary, police, and civil service will be crucial. Two notable events that took place in 1995 provide grounds for optimism. In both cases, the president was constrained by the judiciary. In the first instance, Winnie Mandela, a junior minister in the government, was dismissed from her post by the president. The Supreme Court found that the president had acted unconstitutionally and reversed the decision. In September 1995, the Constitutional Court ruled in favor of the Western Cape government in the province's dispute with the central government over the demarcation of new nonracial jurisdictions. By a majority of 9 to 2, the court found that President Mandela's proclamations overriding decisions by the provincial government were invalid.

In the long term, what South Africa needs least is consociationalism. The cornerstones of its democracy will be a bill of rights, public servants of integrity, an independent judiciary, and the general legitimacy of public institutions. The GNU was a necessary device for initiating the transition to democratic rule. As a long-term arrangement, it would be a disaster.

NOTES

1. Arend Lijphart, *Power-Sharing in South Africa* (Berkeley: Institute of International Studies, University of California, 1985), 6. A general theory of consociationalism is given in greater detail in Lijphart, *Democracy in Plural Societies: A Comparative Exploration* (New Haven: Yale University Press, 1977).

2. Arend Lijphart, "Prospects for Power-Sharing in the New South Africa," in Andrew Reynolds, ed., *Election '94 South Africa: The Campaigns, Results and Future Prospects* (New York: St. Martin's, 1994), 222.

3. See Robert Mattes, "The Road to Democracy: From 2 February 1990 to 27 April 1994," in Reynolds, ed., *Election '94 South Africa*, 1–22.

4. J.E. Spence, "Everybody Has Won, So All Must Have Prizes: Reflections on the South African General Election," *Government and Opposition* 29 (Autumn 1994): 434–35.

5. For a comprehensive critique of the concept of "divided society" as it is employed by both Arend Lijphart and Donald Horowitz to characterize societies rent by enduring, polarized ethnic cleavage, see Vincent T. Maphai, "Is South Africa a Divided Society?" (paper presented to a faculty seminar on democratization, Stanford University, 16 November 1995). For Horowitz's perspective, see, for example, *A Democratic South Africa? Constitutional Engineering in a Divided Society* (Berkeley: University of California Press, 1991), and "Democracy in Divided Societies," *Journal of Democracy* 4 (October 1993): 18–38.

6. "ANC Radical Softens His Line," *The Independent* (London), 30 October 1992.

7. Cited in Allister Sparks, *Tomorrow Is Another Country: The Inside Story of South Africa's Road to Change* (New York: Hill and Wang, 1994), 91.

8. Ibid., 26.

9. "Who Exactly Is in Command?" *The Economist,* 19 November 1994, 48–49.

10. Janet Cherry, "Development, Conflict and the Politics of Ethnicity in South Africa's Transition to Democracy," *Third World Quarterly* 15 (December 1994): 613, 624.

11. Steven Friedman, "Yesterday's Pact: Power Sharing and Legitimate Governance in Post-Settlement South Africa," Centre for Policy Studies, Johannesburg, September 1994, 2.

12. This is my own expression, not Friedman's.

13. Friedman, "Yesterday's Pact," 15.

14. Courtney Jung and Ian Shapiro, "South Africa's Negotiated Transition: Democracy, Opposition, and the New Constitutional Order," *Politics and Society* 23 (September 1995): 269–308 (quotations are from 270).

15. Friedman, "Yesterday's Pact," 16.

16. Ibid., 20.

17. Cherry, "Development, Conflict and the Politics of Ethnicity," 624.

18. Crawford Young, "Democracy and the Ethnic Question," *Africa Dēmos* 3 (March 1995): 24–25.

19. The same "temporal" argument applies to the question of which electoral system is most appropriate: the system that was conducive to the initial transition to democracy—namely, a highly proportional system with very large constituencies—will not serve equally well for the purpose of the consolidation of democracy. For Reynolds's views, see his "Constitutional Engineering in Southern Africa," *Journal of Democracy* 6 (April 1995): 86–100; and "The Case for Proportionality," *Journal of Democracy* 6 (October 1995): 117–24. For a rebuttal, see Joel D. Barkan, "Elections in Agrarian Societies," *Journal of Democracy* 6 (October 1995): 106–16.

20. Arend Lijphart, *Democracies: Patterns of Majoritarian and Consensus Government in Twenty-one Countries* (New Haven: Yale University Press, 1984).

8

THE NEW SOUTH AFRICA: PROBLEMS OF RECONSTRUCTION

Charles Simkins

Charles Simkins is Helen Suzman Professor of Political Economy at the University of the Witwatersrand in Johannesburg. He is the author of Reconstructing South African Liberalism *(1986) and coeditor of* The Awkward Embrace *(1998), a study of dominant parties in middle-income democracies. Since 1994, he has advised the government on various issues of social and economic policy. He also serves as a member of the Statistics Council, a statutory body overseeing the statistical work of the South African government.*

When political parties were unbanned in South Africa and Nelson Mandela walked out of prison in February 1990, more than just a new political dynamic was unleashed. Within weeks, an intense debate about economic policy was also under way. New economic thinking was required from both the establishment and the African National Congress (ANC). The establishment had to confront the fact that the economy had become very inefficient. Per-capita GNP had been declining since the mid-1970s (with the exception of a blip caused by the gold-price boom of the early 1980s). The ANC had to confront the implications of the collapse of the communist system in Eastern Europe and the Soviet Union, especially as its own economic thinking had become radicalized over the course of 30 years in exile.

A degree of disorientation followed. Some intellectuals on the left transferred their allegiance from the authoritarian socialism of Moscow to the authoritarian capitalism of Seoul. Some intellectuals on the right, meanwhile, found themselves supporting popular calls for the transfer of local-government housing to tenants at nominal prices. International experts from academia and the global financial institutions made their appearance and contributed new perspectives, marking an end to South Africa's long period of intellectual isolation. South African business leaders were actively involved in the debate from the start, and sponsored a large number of meetings and conferences. One businessman, Derek Keys, became minister of finance in 1992 and continued to hold office through the first few months of President Mandela's government of national unity.

As it became clear that the third round of formal negotiations would lead to elections in 1994, the ANC came under increasing pressure to declare its economic policies in some detail. The old habit of referring to the Freedom Charter of 1955 was no longer enough, so in late 1993 it produced several drafts of a new plan, entitled the Reconstruction and Development Programme (RDP). A final version published in early 1994 was used as an election manifesto. The claim made for the program in the first paragraph of the document was all-encompassing: "The RDP is an integrated, coherent socioeconomic policy framework. It seeks to mobilise all our people and our country's resources toward the final eradication of apartheid and the building of a democratic, non-racial and non-sexist future."[1] In the run-up to the April 1994 elections, the ANC leadership asked to be judged by its performance on the RDP, which soon came to be regarded as the major statement of ANC policy. The ANC has continually stressed the transforming nature of the RDP, asking people to consider it not simply as a collection of projects, but rather as the embodiment of a set of values.

Few in South Africa would now deny that some sort of economic development program is needed. Apartheid has left a legacy of unemployment, unmet infrastructural needs, deficits in human capital, and great inequality in the distribution of income. Using a strict definition of unemployment, which requires that the unemployed individual be actively looking for work, the October Household Survey (an annual demographic and labor-market survey conducted by the state) found that 17 percent of "economically active" men and 25 percent of women were unemployed in 1994. An additional 9 percent of men and 16 percent of women are involuntarily unemployed but not actively seeking work. In the early 1990s, average class size in schools attended by blacks was twice that of schools attended by other groups, and blacks succeeded in passing the final examination given at the end of the last year of secondary school at only half the rate of other groups. The average per-capita income of blacks is about one-eighth that of whites. While the suburbs enjoy excellent public services, those in the townships are substandard and subject to frequent disruption. These gaps must be closed if democracy is to have a real impact on economic opportunity in South Africa.

It is essential that the RDP enjoy support beyond the adherents of the ANC. Although the ANC has three times as many seats in parliament as the next-largest party, the National Party (NP), it does not command the two-thirds majority needed to pass constitutional amendments by itself. More important, the interim constitution guarantees parties with more than 5 percent of the vote participation in government until 1999, so the NP and the Inkatha Freedom Party (IFP), headed by Chief Mangosuthu Buthelezi, are also part of the government of national unity.

The ANC of 1996 is far more aware than it was four years ago of the need to maintain the confidence of the business community. Business, in turn, is well aware that the ANC's constituents—a majority of all South Africans—must see some real improvement in their lot. The chief executive of the Council of South African Bankers, Piet Liebenberg, is reported as having said: "We can't imagine what would happen if the RDP is a failure."[2] Industrialist Anton Rupert had put it more bluntly back in 1976 when he warned that "if they don't eat, we don't sleep."

Adoption of the RDP as the policy of the government of national unity was signaled by the 15 November 1994 publication of a parliamentary white paper emphasizing three new themes. The first was the government's commitment to macroeconomic stability. This was one of a series of signals sent out to reassure domestic and foreign investors. Other signals have included the retention of Chris Stals (a firm defender of orthodox principles in monetary policy) as governor of the Reserve Bank and the appointment of a second businessman, Chris Liebenberg, as minister of finance upon the resignation of Keys. Emphasis on macroeconomic stability was deemed necessary because the projected state budget deficit for 1994–95 was 6.6 percent of GDP— an unusually high figure for South Africa. The 1995–96 budget projects a deficit of 5.8 percent; the government's stated intention is to bring it down to 4 percent by the 1997–98 fiscal year. Government debt as a proportion of GDP has been rising and is now nearly 60 percent, demanding that officials guard closely against falling into a debt trap. As it is, interest payments are expected to constitute almost 19 percent of government spending in 1995–96.

The second new factor was the establishment by act of parliament of a Reconstruction and Development Fund, which receives grants from the National Revenue Account as well as from international donors. The July 1995 *RDP Monitor* (a privately funded publication) estimated foreign-aid commitments to the RDP by 13 countries plus the European Union at R3.8 billion (US$1=R3.65).[3] Interest on monies held accrues to the Fund. The 1994–95 budget allocated R2.5 billion to the Fund, and an additional R5 billion was allocated in the 1995–96 budget. Total public expenditure for 1995–96 is estimated at R153 billion, so the RDP's share is quite small. According to the white paper, the government's intention is to increase the annual contribution by R2.5 billion per year until it reaches R12.5 billion, and to stabilize it at this level. This incremental approach is tied to a policy of maintaining the rest of government spending constant in real terms for the time being.

Clearly, the government intends to use RDP funding to lever changes in the spending patterns of all government departments. Traditionally, the role of the Ministry of Finance has been to ensure, through a year-long preparatory process, that the departmental budgets are consistent with overall spending goals. This sort of financial control will continue; what is new is interaction between the Office of the President (where the minister for reconstruction and development serves) and the spending departments to promote the developmental goals of government spending.

The third new element was the undertaking of about two dozen "presidential lead projects"—special projects that, it was thought, would enjoy high visibility and begin to achieve results rapidly. Most of these projects were in the fields of land reform and rural development, urban housing and infrastructure, education, and health.

A review of progress was issued by the RDP office on the first anniversary of the new government. The report called for an accelerated transfer of resources to support RDP projects and for a five-year spending plan that would get all parts of government to focus on the goals of the RDP. This does not necessarily reflect a new policy in relation to the Reconstruction and Development Fund, but it does indicate a realization that, in the end, the special funding devices connected with the RDP are a means to an end, rather than ends in themselves.

Indeed, the whole rationale for the Fund has come under attack. University of Cape Town economist Nicoli Nattrass has argued that it is "a costly and ultimately unnecessary piece of bureaucratic musical chairs."[4] Instead, he argues, the major reallocation decisions need to be addressed in cabinet committees and in the Ministry of Finance. Clearly, political battles for control of the pattern of state expenditure lie ahead.

State Incapacity

What progress has been made? The *RDP Monitor* of August 1995 reported that more than R1.7 billion of the R2.5 billion allocated to the Reconstruction and Development Fund in 1994–95 had not been spent in that fiscal year, and estimated that at least 20 percent of the 1995–96 allocation would not be spent.[5] The major reason is lack of state capacity. This has more than one dimension.

First, there is program incapacity: For instance, land-reform projects have to grope their way along in a policy environment that is frequently unclear. Nothing like the RDP has ever been attempted before in South Africa. Second, there is the problem of reconstruction of the civil service at both the second (provincial) and third (local) levels of government. Most of the new provinces have had to be cobbled together from fragments of the old provincial and homeland systems. Local-government elections were not held until 1 November 1995, and they will be held later in the Western Cape and KwaZulu-Natal because of an inability to agree on the demarcation of new nonracial jurisdictions. New local-government structures will also have to be built up from an inheritance of racially segregated institutions. Full consolidation of the services of provincial and local government is likely to take several more years. Third, establishment of the controls essential to good governance takes time and is not always adequate: One of the RDP's lead projects—the provision of free meals to schoolchildren—has collapsed in the Eastern Cape owing to poor administration and corruption.

The RDP could have been quicker to utilize the capacity of nongovernmental organizations (NGOs). This sector developed rapidly during the late 1980s and early 1990s. Governments in other countries wanted to assist South Africa, but could not give money to the South African government before 1994, so they gave it to NGOs instead. Now they have reverted to the standard pattern of government-to-government transfers, giving rise to an NGO funding crisis. The ANC has traditionally been suspicious of NGOs not directly under its influence; in 1994, there even surfaced a proposal (not acted on) that NGOs be required to have a government license in order to operate. More recently, the RDP office has realized that NGO capacity is a useful asset and is trying to harness it, but too late to prevent the dissipation of much of it. The two largest NGOs—the Kagiso Trust and the Independent Development Trust, which have worked together on a number of development projects, including in the areas of education, housing, and health—have proposed the formation of a National Development Agency through which RDP funds could be channeled to NGOs; a transitional body, the Transitional National Development Trust, has already been established.[6]

The RDP also needs the assistance of the private, for-profit sector. Urban infrastructure was very unequally developed under apartheid, and studies suggest that between R45 billion and R60 billion needs to be spent on additional construction. This sum cannot possibly be raised in any reasonable period of time through the Reconstruction and Development Fund, and the government is looking to the life-insurance companies and pension funds for help. Active behind-the-scenes work is going on, but it has not yet come to fruition. Both government and business must come to realize that mobilization of funds is not the only— indeed, not even the largest—problem in relation to urban infrastructure. Viable local-government systems must be in place, and there must be a consensus about the extent of the recovery of costs from township residents and cross-subsidization from rich to poor. Without these preconditions, large amounts of capital will be wasted and new conflicts will emerge. Still, huge sums of money will have to be found. Parliamentary appropriations to the Reconstruction and Development Fund will not suffice. Instead, the state will have to alter its portfolio of assets: Urban infrastructural development will inevitably be linked with privatization.

In this respect, the experience of the upgrading of Alexandra (a black township near Johannesburg) in the late 1980s is instructive. The government wanted the project undertaken as a means of deradicalizing the community, and the Development Bank of Southern Africa (DBSA) financed part of the work. The project was, of course, in political trouble from the start. Also, the Alexandra City Council had no engineers to administer the new infrastructure, which rapidly deteriorated for lack of maintenance. The purpose of redevelopment was to decrease the population of the township, but in fact population densities increased because people had nowhere better to go and immigrants were attracted by the promise of improved infrastructure. Because garbage disposal was erratic, people used the new sewage system for the purpose, severely damaging it within a short period of time. The new user charges formulated in 1988 were lower in nominal terms than those set in 1984, and were not introduced until 1992 (all this during a period characterized by an annual inflation rate of 15 percent). The DBSA continued to regard its financing as a loan, when there was clearly no possibility of its ever being repaid. Some of these negative circumstances surrounding the development of urban infrastructure have disappeared, but by no means all of them. In short, the Alexandra disaster should serve as a cautionary tale.

The other way to raise funds for capital development is through privatization. The term is not popular with the ANC, for three reasons: Employment in publicly owned enterprises is a potent form of patronage; there are fears that privatization will lead to a contraction in employment (in an economy that saw formal employment shrink from 5.3 million in 1988 to 4.96 million in 1993); and privatization makes pricing structures that redistribute wealth from rich to poor more difficult. Nonetheless, the pressure to privatize is on, because it makes sense for the state to restructure its portfolio of assets. One halfway measure is "restructuring" and "commercialization" with a view to attracting private shareholders as minority owners of enterprises that would still be controlled by the state as majority shareholder. What success that approach will have remains to be seen; it is certain that there will be new developments in this sphere in the next year or two.

Housing, Health, and Education

Another factor hindering implementation of the RDP is policy ambiguity. It is one thing to enunciate a list of desires, quite another to optimize within stringent budget constraints and sell the resulting policies to a constituency with high expectations. Housing policy provides the best example of this problem. Approaches to housing development in low-income and middle-income countries have changed a great deal in the last 15 years. Now out of favor is the mass state-housing approach, because it never reaches more than a fraction of the people in need and it creates irresistible pressures for ongoing subsidies. An alternative is the capital-subsidy approach, whereby targeted households receive a onetime government grant to assist them in the purchase of shelter. The application of the capital-subsidy policy to South African conditions was worked on extensively in the late 1980s, and the Independent Development Trust implemented a program creating 100,000 new units in the early 1990s, each with a subsidy of R7,500.

The ANC's instincts have always been in favor of mass state housing. By the time the election-manifesto version of the RDP was published, the capital-subsidy approach had made some, but not tremendous, headway in ANC circles, resulting in a rather confused section on housing policy. After the election, the veteran South African Communist Party leader Joe Slovo became minister of housing. He decided to promote the capital-subsidy approach, largely because of the unaffordability of the alternative. He had then to convince the provincial authorities (whose responsibility it is to actually deliver housing within the framework of national policy). Although some provincial housing authorities (especially those in Gauteng Province) were resistant, they eventually acquiesced, albeit reluctantly. After Slovo's death in early 1995, the picture became more confused. A new minister without the personal reputation of Slovo, or much experience in housing, declared openly that she felt uncomfortable with the capital-subsidy concept. This reopened the housing-policy debate and sent confusing signals to the private sector, whose cooperation in the capital-subsidy scheme is essential. Little is happening on the ground, and a process of apportioning blame has now begun.

Similar problems may emerge in the health and education sectors. The health debate took a lively turn with the publication of a report by an Australian advisor keen on extensive nationalization of the health system. The Department of Health has since revised these recommendations substantially, but the proposal of compulsory and universal "core health insurance" remains, with little information about how such a program could be financed. When that is worked out and announced, further controversy is likely.

The minister of education, Sibusiso Bhengu, has built up a reputation for inactivity, so policy fights have taken a while to emerge. But they are now beginning to occur. The minister introduced an education bill into parliament in early September; the bill was referred to the Constitutional Court after a petition was signed by one-third of the members of the National Assembly. Non-ANC parties argued that it contravenes the constitution by concentrating too much power at the central-government level. An education bill introduced in the Gauteng provincial legislature was also placed under court interdict on a technicality. There is particular tension over the Model C system introduced in 1991, whereby school buildings were handed over to elected school-governing bodies. After teacher salaries were paid (according to a fixed formula), the governing bodies were free to raise more money for maintenance, materials, further teaching services, and the like. The governing bodies were also free to set their own admissions policies. The ANC wants to end the Model C system and reestablish state ownership of school assets.

Another particularly difficult issue will be the governance and financing of the tertiary-education system. The number of students attaining secondary-school certificates is about to explode, having increased at a rate of 9 percent annually for the last decade. There will be insistent calls for a wider range of tertiary-education opportunities than exists at present, with corresponding demands on state resources. These demands will have to be balanced against the need for improvements in the quality of the school system.

There are two further potential threats to the RDP. The first is low economic growth. Although the growth rate has improved since the April 1994 elections, it is far from spectacular. The economy grew by 2.5 percent in 1994 and is set to grow by 2.5 to 3 percent in 1995. This rate is only a bit higher than the rate of population growth, and is clearly inadequate to bring about marked improvement in living standards within a reasonable time period. A cabinet committee is currently investigating ways of accelerating the RDP, but the real issues are much more fundamental. Gold mining is in decline, and much of South Africa's industrial structure is inefficient, with wages out of line with productivity by international standards. Rapid economic growth will not come easily until good policy (or good fortune) alters some of these basic conditions.

The second danger is that civil-service wages and salaries will swallow up any improved flow of revenue to the state, making it impossible to keep non-RDP government spending constant in real terms. This happened during the gold-price boom of the early 1980s. Criticized for allowing large civil-service pay hikes, then-President P.W. Botha was in no doubt as to where National Party interests lay. "But what is this?" he asked rhetorically at an NP congress. "It affects your husbands, your wives, your children. We shall certainly grant salary increases if the money is there." Holding the line will be as difficult for the ANC as it was for the NP, and for the same reason—a large and influential part of its constituency will be employed by the state. Adding to the difficulties is the primitive state of policy modeling within the civil service; usually there is no attempt at all to assess the consequences of decisions about remuneration.

Teacher pay is a case in point. The removal of race, then gender, discrimination in pay scales meant that the whole structure moved up to the level of the formerly most privileged—white males. Moreover, to encourage the acquisition of qualifications, salaries were linked to them.

The upshot was that between 1988 and 1992, average teacher pay increased by 30 percent in real terms, while manufacturing wages increased by only 3 percent and per-capita GNP fell. Not surprisingly, the resources available for hiring new teachers declined, and the national student-teacher ratio deteriorated from 30:1 to 33:1 over the same period. Teacher remuneration now accounts for a dangerously high proportion of total education spending in many parts of the system, limiting opportunities to improve the quality of education through purchases of new textbooks, equipment, and the like.

In September 1995, nurses abandoned their hospitals in a series of wildcat strikes to press their pay claims. Dispute over pay for police officers simmers just below the surface. The deputy minister of finance, Alec Erwin, recently told the Economics Society that there is a crisis in civil-service pay. Indeed there is, and on the manner of its resolution will depend the extent to which RDP goals can be attained.

The Development Context

How is the RDP to be viewed against the broader sweep of South African development? It is instructive to compare the transformation of South Africa to the French Revolution.

While older histories of the French Revolution stressed the static, extractive nature of the *ancien régime* and the misery of the peasantry and urban poor, more recent studies—for example, Simon Schama's *Citizens*[7]—have found mid-eighteenth-century French society to have been in a ferment of economic and social change. On the newer account, the monarchy fell because it could not manage the political consequences of this dynamism, rather than because of an explosion of wretchedness.

There are parallels in the South African experience. Heribert Adam saw as early as 1970 that the NP, far from being locked in a seventeenth-century worldview (as earlier liberals had sometimes averred), was intent on "modernizing racial domination."[8] More recently, John Kane-Berman's *South Africa's Silent Revolution* chronicled the many ways in which South Africa adapted to the coming political transition years before it took place.[9]

An example: Soon after then-Minister of Native Affairs Hendrik Verwoerd stood up in parliament in 1953 to enunciate the principle that education for blacks must match their situation under apartheid, funding for black education was fixed at Ł6.5 million (the rand was not introduced until 1961) plus 80 percent of the poll tax then levied on black people. This formula lasted for 15 years. Then it was blown apart by the long economic expansion of the 1960s, toward the end of which shortages of semiskilled and skilled labor became apparent. Educational expansion, once unleashed, was unstoppable and had proceeded so far by the early 1990s that the retention rates for the years 1992 to 1994 imply that the average black pupil spends 12 years in school (with two of these spent repeating grades). The ANC's schooling goals (10 years of compulsory education) had essentially already been attained—even surpassed— before the party ever took office. Verwoerd, incidentally, had a more accurate view than many of his NP successors of the political implications of the expansion of black education. But the line he drew simply could not be held.

Or take industrial relations. The largely black South African Congress of Trade Unions was banned in 1961, having been marginalized by the Industrial Conciliation Act of 1956, which denied black or racially mixed unions access to the formal industrial-bargaining system. At that time and well into the 1970s, much of the communication between management and labor was conducted through a paternalistic system of "boss boys" (in the mines) and *indunas* or headmen (in manufacturing concerns employing migrant labor). Essentially, this system incorporated black authority figures into enterprise command chains. Following the political repression of the early 1960s, there was quiescence for 12 years, until the strikes in Durban in 1973 reactivated black trade unions. It took only six years for the government to decide to recognize black trade unions and incorporate them into the formal structures.

Or, again, consider measures of occupational and income distribution. Formal employment has become increasingly skill-intensive, and all racial groups have participated in the change since the beginning of 1970s. The black middle class tripled in size between 1971 and 1989. Racial shares of personal income, which had been constant for 50 years (70 percent for whites, 30 percent for all other groups), started to shift after 1970. By 1985, the white share had dropped to 59 percent. In 1995, the white share stood at only 52 percent, with the black share at 34 percent and Coloureds and Asians accounting for the remaining 14 percent. The change was partly due to the shift of population shares during the period from 1985 to 1995; even so, blacks' average per-capita income rose by 10 percent in real terms, Coloureds' by 15 percent, and Asians' by 19 percent. By contrast, whites' average per-capita income dropped slightly. The removal of overt pay discrimination and the convergence of levels of educational attainment both help explain this shift.

A final example is relevant here. In 1985, Regional Services Councils (RSCs) were formed in order to finance and build urban infrastructure not readily constructed by the old local authorities. The RSCs were assigned two sources of revenue: a tax on total production and a payroll tax on businesses within their jurisdiction. Total revenue raised was not enormous—about R1 billion per year in the early 1990s. It was not long before RSCs took on an unintended function: financing capital expenditure within black local-authority jurisdictions, since such local

TABLE—MARGINAL TAX RATES, BY ANNUAL INCOME, 1995–1996

ANNUAL INCOME (R)	MARGINAL TAX RATE
Below 15,000	—
15,000–20,000	20%
20,000–30,000	21%
30,000–40,000	31%
40,000–50,000	42%
50,000–70,000	43%
Above 70,000	45%

authorities were incapable of raising the funds. Some RSCs were more energetic than others, but the best of them took care to consult widely and to prioritize projects within a five- or ten-year time frame. This work prefigures what is now being attempted: a more rapid, but otherwise similar, upgrading of urban infrastructure.

Examined from this perspective, the RDP appears as one initiative in a long chain of developmental efforts, rather than as a radically new approach. Indeed, some of the program's themes can be traced all the way back to the work of the Social and Economic Planning Council established during the Second World War by the second government of Jan Smuts—the closest thing to a liberal administration during the entire period of white rule.

Taxes, Spending, and Poverty

Another perspective on the situation is provided by public-choice theory, according to which the preferences of the median voter govern decisions about taxes and spending. Prior to 1983, the median voter was a member of the white lower-middle class (though it was not until 1975 that the majority of employed whites attained middle-class status). Between 1983 and 1994, the median voter is difficult to characterize, partly because many Coloured and Asian people refused to vote under the segregated, tricameral parliamentary system and partly because the tricameral arrangement was not a straightforward majoritarian system. Since 1994, the median voter has been a member of the urban working class, with an income not far above the poverty line. What we are seeing is a reorientation of the pattern of taxation and spending to reflect the new situation. The pattern of personal-income taxation for 1995–96 illustrates this clearly (see Table). Up to R30,000, income taxation is relatively light; thereafter it becomes much heavier very rapidly. Among blacks, mean household annual income in the cities was about R25,000 in 1995.

Or consider the problem from the expenditure point of view. Local-government spending patterns are illustrative. White taxpayers paid

relatively little in property taxes under apartheid; many local public
goods were paid for not from the public-revenue account, but from
surpluses in the electricity-trading account—a form of populist
redistribution from industrial users of electricity to white suburban
households. White local taxpayers also benefited from the progressive
removal of responsibility for black areas of cities and towns, first to
special boards and finally to separate "city councils" in 1983. By then,
of course, segregated city councils were an idea whose time had passed.
Black areas, left to sink or swim fiscally, promptly sank, and
considerable sums of money had to be pumped in by Regional Services
Councils and provincial authorities to keep essential services going in
conditions where cost recovery had become impossible. Naturally
enough, the ANC goal has been to unravel the privileges of white
households, and to create metropolitan and urban jurisdictions so large
that downward pressure on redistribution through competing
jurisdictions is impossible. The contest over redistribution has already
started, and will continue in new forms after the local-government
elections.

On this view, the RDP is an important strand in the adjustment from
one politically driven public-goods equilibrium to another. It is oriented
to the supply of required new investments, on the assumption that the
recurrent costs of maintaining them will be met out of ordinary
government budgets. At the local-authority level, it is now universally
assumed that the task of supplying infrastructure to hitherto neglected
areas will simply have to be worked at until it is completed. The questions
now concern priorities, financing, and the rate of expenditure.

The RDP might also be seen as a key part of South Africa's war on
poverty. Poverty remains a mass phenomenon among black South
Africans. Using the least generous poverty line regularly calculated in
South Africa (the Bureau of Market Research's Minimum Living Level
[MLL], set at R1,017 per month in 1995), 29 percent of black households
in metropolitan areas, 56 percent of black households in large towns
and immediately adjacent rural areas, and 74 percent of black
households in small towns and remote rural areas live in poverty. The
aggregate poverty gap (the sum of the amounts needed to bring each
poor household up to the MLL) is about R25 billion per year—7.4
percent of aggregate personal income, and half of the revenue to be
received by the state from personal-income taxes in the 1995–96 fiscal
year. There is no way that South Africa can afford an income-support
system to wipe out this poverty, particularly given that no poverty-
alleviation program can achieve perfect targeting. It will take a
generation to reduce poverty from a mass condition to a state
experienced by a small group of unfortunates, and even this is subject
to the proviso that there be sustained economic growth well in excess
of the rate of population increase. For the time being, all that can be

done is to invest in projects that will eventually lead to increased incomes for the poor.

It is therefore no accident that most of the first round of RDP projects in the rural areas are pilot programs, rather than attempts to deliver on a truly large scale. They include efforts at land reform and the development of the skills of small-scale farmers, as well as the provision of water. These projects may pave the way for larger investments down the line, but even the impact of those more extensive efforts will be limited. The RDP reflects no clear view on the considerations that should guide the allocation of public investment between urban and rural areas. The relevant data collection and analysis have not been done. Of course, the political need to please a constituency should not be forgotten; the ANC is strongest in the country's two poorest and most rural regions—the Eastern Cape and the Northern Province—and it cannot afford to be inactive in rural areas.

But the real hope for the poor—rural and urban alike—must lie in formal-sector investment, with the attendant creation of jobs. One way of raising labor-output ratios is to find labor-intensive methods of building urban infrastructure; proposals in this sphere are likely to be put to the test fairly soon.

Moving Toward Cooperation

Adam Przeworski has analyzed the conditions for class conflict and class cooperation in a capitalist society.[10] Cooperation arises when workers see investment as being to their advantage inasmuch as it yields higher wages in the future. This requires that capitalists not devote all their profits to consumption. Both groups agree to defer some of their immediate desires for the sake of larger gains in the future. If time horizons become short and trust is lost, however, conditions of conflict arise, with workers becoming militant and capitalists disinvesting. South Africa was uncomfortably close to being in this latter situation in the 1980s and early 1990s. Rates of savings and investment fell to post-1945 lows in the period of negotiation preceding the 1994 elections. One of the causes was the high level of government dissavings, a factor not taken into account in Przeworski's simple model, but one that also can be taken as a manifestation of pressures for consumption now.

South Africa's economic future depends on moving toward the conditions for cooperation. Without them, Zimbabwean-style stagnation is inevitable. It is inconceivable that savings rates can be boosted to East Asian levels, or that East Asian rates of economic growth can be attained. Yet it may be possible to raise savings rates sufficiently to produce an average growth rate of 3 to 4 percent. The black fertility transition is currently under way, and the rate of total population growth will eventually fall from its present annual rate of 2.1 percent. One might then look for a doubling of per-capita income in 40 years, by which time South Africa would certainly be close to the level of development usually adequate to sustain democratic rule. Whether the delicate political balancing act required to get to that point can be sustained long enough remains an open question.

NOTES

1. African National Congress, *The Reconstruction and Development Programme* (Johannesburg: Umanyano Publications, 1994), 1.

2. *RDP Monitor,* August 1995, 1.

3. *RDP Monitor,* July 1995, 1.

4. Nicoli Nattrass, *Weekly Mail* (Johannesburg), 15 September 1995.

5. *RDP Monitor,* August 1995, 2.

6. See above, Wilmot G. James and Daria Caliguire, "The New South Africa: Renewing Civil Society," on pages 83–93 above.

7. Simon Schama, *Citizens: A Chronicle of the French Revolution* (New York: Alfred A. Knopf, 1989).

8. Heribert Adam, *Modernizing Racial Domination* (Berkeley: University of California Press, 1971).

9. John Kane-Berman, *South Africa's Silent Revolution* (Johannesburg: South African Institute of Race Relations, 1991).

10. Adam Przeworski, *Capitalism and Social Democracy* (Cambridge: Cambridge University Press, 1985).

9

CONSOLIDATION AND PUBLIC OPINION IN SOUTH AFRICA

Robert Mattes & Hermann Thiel

Robert Mattes is manager of the Public Opinion Service at the Institute for Democracy in South Africa (Idasa) in Cape Town. He is currently codirecting a joint project of Idasa, the South African Broadcasting Corporation, the Electoral Institute of South Africa, and Markinor, called Opinion '99. He is also the author of The Election Book: Judgement and Choice in South Africa's 1994 Election *(1994).* **Hermann Thiel** *is a reaearch fellow at the Centre for International and Comparative Politics at the University of Stellenbosch and has recently completed a study of relations between labor and the state in South Africa. He is now doing research on political economy and democratization.*

As recently as January 1990, almost all observers would have agreed that the odds were stacked heavily against a successful transition to democracy in South Africa. In light of the "miracle election" of April 1994, however, the odds might appear, at first glance, to favor a successful consolidation of South African democracy. For the over-whelming majority of South Africa's citizens, long deprived of self-government and common citizenship on the basis of race, a return to the old regime of apartheid obviously is not an option. Democracy, rather than vengeance or group power, has long been a cherished goal for black South Africans and was the mantra of the African National Congress (ANC) and the bulk of those involved in the grassroots struggle against apartheid. Moreover, while white South Africans were the beneficiaries of apartheid, they also have had long experience both with competitive elections and with Westminster-style parliamentary politics, albeit based upon exclusionary and racially defined citizenship.

Yet there are several structural, institutional, and attitudinal factors that point to a much more sober view of the future of democracy in South Africa. In contrast to what might be expected, surveys demonstrate that citizens do not yet feel a widespread attitudinal commitment to democracy.[1] Nor do prospects for creating such a commitment appear bright, given the continuing consequences of the country's history, economy, and present institutional arrangements.

At its core, consolidation has to do with the probability of sustaining democratic processes (defined minimally as free, fair, and regular elections plus all the freedoms—of opposition, association, speech, and the media—that necessarily go with such elections). This conception of consolidation is basically the same as the notion of "democratic endurance" that Adam Przeworski and his three coauthors used in their seminal cross-national and longitudinal study, which appeared in the January 1996 issue of the *Journal of Democracy*.[2] We regard a *consolidated* democracy as one with a *very high probability of endurance*.

Any analysis of democratic prospects in South Africa needs to take into account the key structural correlates of democratic endurance identified by Przeworski and his coauthors: national wealth, economic growth, economic equality, parliamentary government, and favorable international and regional contexts. As we will discuss below, South Africa's prospects appear somewhat dim on a number of these fronts. At the same time, a purely structural analysis of consolidation in South Africa or any other new democracy would have several limitations. In the first place, the relationships between structural factors and democratic outcomes are matters of probability, not certainty, and they are complex. *Some* states that are poor, that fail to grow, that fail to reduce inequality, that have presidential regimes, or that have undergone violent transitions to democracy nonetheless do sustain democracies. Second, as Juan Linz and Alfred Stepan argue, structural factors in and of themselves do not bring about consolidation. Rather, leaders and citizens must act purposefully to preserve or destroy a democratic regime.[3] Thus structural conditions need to be linked to democratic consolidation through purposeful actions and the attitudes that inform such actions.

We argue that democratic commitment is the key factor that links structural background conditions and democratic consolidation. The level of elite and citizen commitment to democratic processes is the single direct determinant of the probability of democratic endurance or consolidation. A very high level of commitment is what Juan Linz and Alfred Stepan refer to as "legitimation."[4] As Larry Diamond argues, when democracy "becomes so broadly and profoundly legitimate among its citizens, it is very unlikely to break down for internal reasons."[5]

While legitimation is not a necessary condition for a democratic transition, it is necessary for democratic consolidation. Democracy can be destroyed only by purposeful actors, motivated at least in part by a belief that democracy is not "the only game in town," that it is not the best form of government available, or that it is no better than all the alternatives. While uncommitted elites may play the electoral game as long as it suits them, or as long as international norms dictate, they are likely to challenge a democratic regime when it no longer suits them. Uncommitted elites will be able to mount such a challenge only where there is an uncommitted, acquiescent citizenry, or a mobilized citizenry that itself becomes an active agent in the breakdown of democracy. In contrast, a society of committed democrats is much less likely to disobey the law, to resort to violence, to tolerate shoddy electoral procedures, to produce undemocratic elites from its ranks, to elect undemocratic elites to office, or to acquiesce in the face of elite challenges to democracy.[6] Ultimately, consensual democratic commitments on the part of citizens and leaders are indispensable to the maintenance of democracy.

While commitments to democracy link structural conditions with consolidation, they are not a simple reflection of these conditions. We need to examine *how, when,* and *why* these factors combine to shape leaders' and citizens' views about democracy. For example, have civil society and the state been able to teach people to value democracy independently of its economic performance? Under what conditions do people connect evaluations of economic performance to views about democracy? And whom do they blame for economic failures—the previous authoritarian regime, international monetary institutions, the present incumbents, or the system of democratic government itself?

This model guides our discussion of the prospects for democratic consolidation in South Africa. We first discuss a range of indicators of mass democratic commitment. Then we discuss various factors shaping this commitment, and in the process, link structural factors to the consolidation of democracy.

Types of Legitimacy

Perhaps the irreducible prerequisite of democratic consolidation is what we call "national legitimacy," meaning a near-consensual agreement on the identity of the state or "people" that is to govern itself democratically.[7] This has been seen as the key challenge posed to democratization and consolidation in "deeply divided societies" like South Africa. The common view is that in such divided societies, people identify primarily with this or that component part—often their own ethnic group or nation—rather than with the multiethnic or multinational state.

In nationally representative surveys conducted by Idasa, only 13 percent of South African citizens in 1994 (and 22 percent in 1995) spontaneously identified themselves as "South African." Most people chose instead a wide range of racial, linguistic, and religious labels. At the same time, however, there is a very strong and very high level of identification with the political community known as South Africa. In

1995, an astounding 92 percent said that they were either "proud" or "very proud" to be called South African. In 1997, overwhelming majorities agreed that they were proud to be called South African (94 percent), that being South African was a very important part of how they saw themselves (91 percent), that "people should realize that we are South Africans and stop of thinking of themselves [in ethnic terms]" (82 percent), and that it would be desirable to create one united nation out of all the groups living in South Africa (83 percent).

None of this is to deny the existence of significant degrees of outgroup rejection and intergroup intolerance, high levels of perceived relative deprivation, or significant group differences in regime norms or support for the government. But the key prerequisite for the legitimacy of the political community has been met: There is widespread agreement on the appropriateness of the South African political community, and a widespread pride in one's place in it.

How can we make sense of this apparently surprising set of findings? One explanation might be that in other divided societies people reject a political identity previously *imposed on* them by authoritarian means, while in South Africa millions claim an identity that was previously *denied to* them by authoritarian means. As Frederik Van Zyl Slabbert, Heribert Adam, and Kogila Moodley put it, "In South Africa, the very real ethnoracial differences in a so-called divided society have facilitated the emergence of a common state."[8]

Legitimation means that a large proportion of the people see democracy as the appropriate way to govern the country, and the democratic, constitutional regime as the correct one. This has a minimalist variant, wherein democracy need only be seen in Churchillian terms as the least-bad option (Larry Diamond calls this "negative legitimation").[9] A second variant, so-called positive legitimation, is the converse: People believe that democracy is legitimate because they believe in its intrinsic worth and inherent superiority to all other forms of government.

One way to assess positive commitment is by looking at citizens' evaluations of how democracy actually works. If we examine the responses of South Africans to negative statements about democracy in the 1995 World Values Survey (WVS), we find that fewer than half disagreed with the statements that under democracy "the economic system runs badly" (48 percent); that democracies "aren't good at maintaining order" (47 percent); and that they are "indecisive and have too much squabbling" (40 percent). In response to another question tapping belief in the intrinsic value of democracy, 76 percent said that having a democratic political system would be a good way of governing the country (though only 44 percent answered that it would be "very good").

Another dimension of democratic legitimacy comes from agreement on the appropriateness of key regime norms. In 1995, Idasa asked people whether a series of procedural elements widely regarded as the *sine qua non* of democracy were, in fact, essential in order for a country to be democratic. The results raise important questions about South Africans' understanding of democracy. Only small minorities rated as "essential" such key procedural elements of democracy as majority rule (30 percent), regular elections (27 percent), complete freedom to criticize the government (25 percent), competition between at least two strong parties (24 percent), and protection of minority rights (21 percent). In contrast, 48 percent said that equal access to houses, jobs, and a decent income was "essential" to democracy, and 23 percent said that having a small gap between rich and poor was essential.

Comparing Political Systems

A key source of negative legitimation in places such as Eastern Europe or the former Soviet Union is citizens' comparisons of the old and new regimes.[10] On first glance, it would seem hard to believe that anyone among the majority of South Africa's citizens who were oppressed by apartheid would favor its return. White minority rule and officially enforced segregation have been thoroughly discredited. Yet a surprising number of formerly oppressed South Africans feel their lives today are actually *worse* than they were under apartheid. In a separate 1996 national survey, 26 percent of black respondents felt that life was better under apartheid, as did 35 percent both of coloured and of Indian respondents. Less surprisingly, 45 percent of whites felt that their lives were better under apartheid.[11] By the time of the 1997 Idasa survey, however, the proportions of those saying that their lives had been better under apartheid had dropped to 13 percent of blacks and 26 percent of coloureds, but had risen to 56 percent of Indians and 67 percent of whites.

A more direct measure of the old and new political systems can be found in the South African version of the 1995 WVS. All racial groups except whites rated the new democratic system as significantly better than the apartheid-era political system. The responses that whites gave probably had less to do with disappointment at the end of apartheid than with their perception that the new nonracial democratic system was not being run nearly as well as "their" old whites-only democratic system had been. Yet all groups, even whites, were significantly more optimistic about the future of the new political system (though whites' evaluations of the future remained lower than their evaluations of the past).

It might seem more likely, however, that South Africans would have positive feelings about some other nondemocratic alternative. One of the reasons that communism and authoritarianism are discredited in

TABLE—COMMITMENT TO DEMOCRACY
WHEN IT "DOES NOT WORK"

	BLACKS (%)		WHITES (%)		COLOUREDS (%)		INDIANS (%)		TOTAL (%)	
	1995	1997	1995	1997	1995	1997	1995	1997	1995	1997
Need Strong Leader	42.9	27.5	44.7	41.7	37.8	26.4	39.1	58.0	42.7	30.2
Democracy Always Best	47.3	61.0	45.3	38.5	46.4	52.7	54.7	27.2	47.0	56.3

Question: "Sometimes democracy does not work. When that happens, some people say we need a strong leader that does not have to bother with elections. Others say that even when things don't work, democracy is always best. What do you think?"

Eastern Europe is that people have experienced them. While South Africans have experienced apartheid, they have no real experience with other pseudodemocratic or authoritarian forms of government, such as the "one-party democracy" that is found in some other southern African nations. In fact, the 1995 WVS revealed that significant proportions of the South African public offered positive evaluations of authoritarian forms of government. A fifth said that military rule would be a "good way to govern the country," 32 percent said that a strong elected leader who did not have to worry about parliament and elections would be "good," and 45 percent gave a favorable evaluation to rule by unelected experts.

In terms of negative commitment to democracy, the WVS found that 72 percent agreed with the Churchill-style dictum that "democracy may have its problems, but it is better than any other form of government" (though only 34 percent strongly agreed). We believe, however, that agreement with this statement represents a fairly abstract and easy form of commitment. The 1995 Idasa survey tested what we call "steadfast" commitment to democracy under duress. It began by stating that "sometimes democracy does not work," and then asked respondents whether under such conditions they would prefer "a strong leader who does not have to bother with elections," or whether "even when things don't work, democracy is always best."

In 1995, only 47 percent said that "democracy is always best," while 43 percent preferred a strong leader if democracy was seen not to be working. While our question places increased pressure on respondents' commitment, this ranks as one of the lowest levels of commitment of all new democracies for which data are available.[12] Yet the 1997 survey showed a significant increase in steadfast commitment (up 9 points to 56 percent) and a decrease in the preference for a strong leader (down 13 points to 30 percent). Thus while steadfast commitment is relatively low, it has been moving in an encouraging direction (see Table).

Thus despite surprisingly widespread consensus on the shape and identity of the political community (national legitimation), South Africa appears to face a difficult path to democratic legitimation, and hence democratic consolidation. Not only are the levels of unconditional democratic commitment generally low, but they have come to differ sharply along racial lines between 1995 and 1997. In 1995, as the Table shows, 55 percent of Indian South Africans were unconditionally committed to democracy, as were 47 percent of the blacks, 46 percent of the coloureds, and 45 percent of the whites. Two years later, those figures had shifted to 61 percent for blacks, 53 percent for coloureds, 39 percent for whites, and 27 percent for Indians.

These differing levels of unconditional commitment to democracy are not based on differences in communal values, socialization experiences, or educational levels. Rather, multivariate statistical analysis reveals that commitment to democracy is based on a series of performance-based evaluations, evaluations that themselves differ sharply along racial lines. These differences did not develop in a vacuum, but grew out of a larger set of structural factors, including the country's history, its present economic circumstances, and its new political institutions.

Broadly speaking, these evaluations can be divided into a global question measuring people's satisfaction with the way democracy works, and a range of more specific questions that reveal how people rate the economic and political performance of the new South Africa. The economic evaluations include assessments of the economy over the past year and expectations for the next year, as well as perceptions of relative deprivation and relative distributions of government resources. The political evaluations include assessments of institutional performance, institutional responsiveness, relative government responsiveness to various groups, the extent of corruption, and the quality of elected leaders.[13]

Apartheid's Legacy

The policy of apartheid created a racially segmented and ranked society with different levels of democratic influence, different rights, and different levels of repression. Among the consequences of this policy are the vastly different experiences with democracy across different racial groups. Whites have participated in competitive elections and a parliamentary system since 1910, and never had to endure a successful coup or subversion of democracy. On the other hand, the value of this experience is limited, if only because the entire system was based on the denial of basic human rights to the majority of their countrymen. Even within the racially exclusive political system, white South Africans (especially dissidents) were exposed to significant curtailments of key democratic rights through apartheid legislation, as well as the security legislation and successive states of emergency of the 1980s that concentrated power in the national security establishment and emasculated parliament.

Black South Africans had little experience with formal, institutionalized democratic practices. They were denied participation in the central government of the land of their birth, and the nominally democratic "Black Local Authorities" or self-governing "bantustans" imposed by Pretoria, lacking resources and legitimacy, became breeding grounds for massive corruption, political assassinations, and successive coups leading to dictatorships and *juntas*.

Another legacy of apartheid was a consequence of the very way in which the struggle against it was carried out. While "one man, one vote" was always the goal, the key liberation organizations subscribed to and spread to their poverty-stricken followers an economic, as opposed to a procedural view of democracy. And while there was a significant amount of pluralism and debate among the various organizations of the mass democratic movement, many of them were based on centralized, disciplined—even Leninist—styles of organization.

But perhaps the most important consequence of apartheid is the way in which it shaped people's perceptions of their access to political power and their stake in the distribution and redistribution of resources. While the dismantling of apartheid ostensibly brought about individual equality, the introduction of the universal franchise may have simply reversed many—though certainly not all—of the key power dynamics of the past, if only perceptually. While there has been significant interest differentiation—including the development of cross-cutting interests among racial groups—apartheid's rigid racial structuring of interests makes it likely that objective differences within groups will remain subordinate to enduring perceptions of homogeneous group interests. Because group membership determined access to power in the past, it is likely that South Africans will continue to perceive access to the state and the distribution and redistribution of resources in this light.

Thus whites, who make up 14 percent of the population, have lost control of the key levers of political power that created and protected their past economic advantages, and now fear the rapid erosion of their interests in favor of black South Africans, who constitute 74 percent of the population. While coloured and Indian South Africans (who make up 8 and 3 percent of the population, respectively) were also oppressed, they have lost some of the apartheid-era statutory advantages (such as the Western Cape Province's Coloured Labour Preference Policy) that they once enjoyed relative to blacks. The relative advantages and small size of the coloured and Indian communities may lead them to feel as threatened as whites do by the black majority.

As mentioned earlier, the findings of Przeworski and his collaborators regarding the structural determinants of democratic endurance do not bode well for South Africa. As a whole, South Africa is not a rich country; as of 1993, annual per-capita income was just $3,127—by Przeworski's calculations, enough to give South African democracy a probable life expectancy of 33 years.[14] Moreover, the country has one of the highest levels of inequality in the world, reflecting the reality of two South Africas. One has First World–style income levels and living standards; the other, and much larger, South Africa belongs squarely to the Third World.

While South Africa's current inflation rate of between 8 and 10 percent is in the optimum range identified by Przeworski and company, economic growth has been sluggish of late and seems unlikely to reach the 5 percent level that has been found to increase the life expectancy of poor democracies.[15] Inequality, moreover, is worsening. Yearly surveys indicate that the income gap which separates the richest from the poorest fifth of black households is now wider than the income gap between whites and blacks as a whole.[16] The new democratic system thus faces considerable pressure to adopt redistributionist policies.

The first place where we can observe the consequences of South Africa's history and its economic disparities is in massive racial differences in agreement with regime norms. Whites are much more likely than blacks to agree that regular elections, party competition, free speech, and minority rights are essential to democracy. This is probably less an indication that whites are better educated about democracy than a reflection of their minority status, which leads them to value potential mechanisms of minority protection. In contrast, whites attach much less importance than do blacks to another key element of democracy—majority rule.

South African blacks, for their part, attach as much or more importance to narrowing the gap between rich and poor as to having regular elections, party competition, free speech, and minority rights. Interestingly, blacks and whites are closer in their responses to a question on the necessity of "equal access to houses, jobs and a decent income." Yet here too, a difference is evident: Blacks seem to focus more on the "equality of result" dimension of the question, while whites stress the "equality of opportunity" dimension. This is borne out by a statistical analysis demonstrating that whites' agreement with this item is related much more strongly to their agreement with other elements of procedural minority protection than to their agreement on a small gap between rich and poor. For blacks, on the other hand, agreement with this item is strongly related to agreement about the need for a smaller wealth gap, and agreement with these two items is also related strongly to agreement on majority rule.

The consequences of South Africa's history and economic circumstances are also apparent in evaluations of the economy. In general, the 1997 Idasa survey found majorities or pluralities dissatisfied with the present state of the country (46 percent), the economy (54 percent), their own group (47 percent), and themselves (42 percent). Tellingly, 66 percent of those polled felt that their own group was not getting what it deserved by comparison with others in terms of educational opportunities; 58 percent felt this about health care; 65 percent felt it about police services; and 72 percent felt it about housing. Such figures manifest the pressures for redistribution that now bear on the government.

Yet while economic satisfaction is low, it seems to be increasing. From 1995 to 1997, the proportion of those saying that national conditions had improved over the previous year went from 29 to 41 percent. Likewise, the share saying that their own group's conditions had improved went from 25 to 33 percent over the same period. Those who felt that the economy had improved went down slightly, however, from 30 percent in 1995 to 26 percent two years later.

Moreover, economic expectations remain optimistic. Pluralities ranging from 43 to 49 percent expect that overall conditions, the national economy, their own group's situation, and their own circumstances will improve over the next year. South Africans also tend to feel that they are better off than most of their fellow citizens. Only 13 percent complain that they are worse off than others, and only 16 percent think that their group is worse off than other groups. These two factors seem to soften the impact of the dissatisfaction indicated above.

Clear racial differences are evident in the answers to all these questions. Blacks tend to be more satisfied and to retain greater optimism about the future. Whites, coloureds, and Indians are more disgruntled and more pessimistic. Contrary to what one would expect given the extensive racial inequalities, the majority of whites feel that they are worse off than other South Africans, while blacks tend to think themselves better off.

Institutions and Leaders

The new South African Constitution's matrix of political institutions and the way in which they were created also have important consequences for democratic legitimacy. The results of six years of constitutional negotiations have been widely interpreted as a broadly inclusive compromise, based largely on crucial "pacts" agreed to during the transition to democracy. Yet popular mobilization and violence also played a role in forcing key constitutional agreements.[17] Neither the Interim Constitution emanating from the all-party talks nor the final Constitution approved by the elected Constitutional Assembly of 1995–96 was totally inclusive in the true sense of a pact. Right-wing parties representing significant proportions of the white electorate remained outside the agreement on the Interim Constitution, and the Inkatha Freedom Party (IFP), representing 10 percent of the total electorate, remained outside the agreements on both the interim and final constitutions. Precisely because the ANC was able to use mass mobilization (in 1993) and its sheer voting muscle in the Constitutional Assembly to force favorable agreements, the new South African constitutional dispensation has a much more majoritarian flavor than its champions would like to admit.[18] It is true that the legislature was elected on the basis of proportional representation (PR), and that the interim executive was comprised of a proportional cabinet. Yet parliament is not run according to proportional principles, and the proportional cabinet—which made decisions by majority rule—was subsequently jettisoned by the ANC in the Constitutional Assembly.

It is true that the constitutional choice of a parliamentary form of government (Mandela's title of "President" is basically a misnomer) is highly favorable for democratic endurance.[19] Yet the particular way in which South Africa's parliamentarism is mixed with four other features may have a pernicious effect on democracy. First of all, South Africa chose a PR-based electoral system with large districts and closed lists chosen by central party structures. (Half the parliamentarians are chosen from national lists and half from provincial lists; in addition, provincial parliamentarians are all elected from provincial lists.) Second, as a result of their respective Leninist or Westminster traditions, all South African political parties harbor traditions of strong internal discipline. Third, the Constitution entrenches even greater discipline by requiring that all legislators who "cease to be members" of their political parties must vacate their seats. And fourth, the governing ANC enjoys such a huge advantage in electoral support that many analysts openly worry about the prospect of one-party hegemony.

The confluence of these factors produces exceptionally strong and highly centralized majority-party control. It also gives the central bosses in each party extraordinary control over the party's MPs, limiting the degree to which MPs can represent their constituencies when constituent opinion runs counter to the party line—if, that is, MPs even knew who their constituents were. In fact, South Africa's electoral system has removed any direct links between legislators and constituents. Some parties have assigned geographical constituencies to their MPs, but there are still no real electoral incentives, and the experiment has come to be widely seen as a failure. For these very reasons, Joel D. Barkan has warned that PR threatens democratic consolidation in Africa, especially in agrarian societies, and runs the risk of creating what Göran Hyden has called the "suspended state," meaning a government disconnected from the electorate and progressively losing legitimacy and authority.[20]

Forced to choose among entire slates of four hundred candidates each, voters find it inordinately difficult to get rid of offensive or corrupt elected officials. This would be a serious problem in any democracy, but is particularly so in a young democracy like South Africa, which is engaged in privatization and other forms of economic restructuring that offer vast opportunities for official peculation. When there is little chance that the governing party will lose power any time soon, the problem is exacerbated. "Good government" is incredibly important for countries like South Africa, where the prospects for improving most people's living standards are limited. An officialdom widely esteemed for probity can help to mitigate the problems that may arise as economic performance inevitably begins to trail surging expectations.

Approval of the government's performance dropped between 1995 and 1997. Even Nelson Mandela's approval rating went down, from 76 to 65 percent. The national government's fell from 57 to 47 percent, parliament's went from 53 to 46 percent, and overall approval of all the provincial governments declined from 42 to 36 percent. In 1997, the approval rating for the new local governments introduced at the beginning of 1996 stood at a meager 30 percent.

The same patterns are evident with regard to evaluations of the quality of representation; perceived responsiveness decreases as voters get closer to the institution. In 1997, 62 percent of all respondents said that they felt that President Mandela was interested in their opinion. Forty-eight percent said the same of the national government, 46 percent said it of Parliament, 40 percent said it of provincial government, and 36 percent said it of local government.

Again, sharp racial differences are evident in the answers. Black approval ratings for the various institutions consistently top 50 percent, while the same ratings among whites ranged in the low teens (the exception is Mandela's 31 percent approval rating among whites). Large percentages of whites and coloureds (43 and 39 percent, respectively) feel that the government treats them unfairly. Two-thirds of whites, coloureds, and Indians indicate that the government is more interested in groups other than their own, while only a fifth of blacks feel that way.

As early as 1995, 25 percent of all respondents believed that the new government was just as corrupt as the old one, and another 41 percent believed that the new one was *more* corrupt. More than half (56 percent) agreed that those in government were "mostly concerned with helping only themselves." By 1997, half of the respondents felt that all or most public officials were guilty of corruption. In contrast with our findings on the other structural factors, there are no significant differences among racial groups when it comes to views about official corruption. It is particularly significant that blacks, even though they have a much more favorable view of the government than other South

Africans, have similarly negative views about the quality of officials. The impact of these perceptions of corruption on popular commitment to democracy shows that citizens are focusing not just on democracy's distributional outputs, but on its quality as well.

Race, Partisanship, and Power

We have argued so far that the link between race and people's evaluations of the economy and government stems primarily from the differing "power positions" originally created by apartheid and now altered by the democratic franchise. Yet the picture is more complicated than that. While race may determine or shape perceptions of access to power in South Africa, race also interacts with partisan loyalties.[21] Not all whites support parties out of power, and not all blacks support parties in power. Further complicating this picture are the nuanced power dynamics introduced by the changing composition of South Africa's interim Government of National Unity (GNU) and by the country's nascent federal structure.

For example, in 1995 white supporters of the National Party (NP) were substantially more sympathetic to the government than were white supporters of the conservative Freedom Front. By 1997, however, one year after the NP left the GNU, this gap had shrunk considerably as NP supporters became more negative in their evaluations of the president, the government, and parliament, and expressed less satisfaction with democracy.

We tend to think in terms of black ANC supporters who favor the new regime and of white, coloured, and Indian opposition-party supporters who are more negative toward it. Yet in the two provinces that the ANC does not control (Western Cape and KwaZulu-Natal), ANC supporters become significantly more negative about the performance of provincial government as well as the legitimacy of that government. Moreover, not all blacks support the ANC, and those who do not have less positive evaluations than those who do. In 1995, black IFP supporters had especially negative evaluations. The IFP, however, remained in the GNU as the ANC's only partner after the NP's departure. In 1997, IFP supporters offered much more optimistic performance evaluations and expressed more satisfaction than they had two years earlier.

The interaction between race and partisan loyalties also helps explain why coloured South Africans have some of the highest levels of commitment to democracy—something that may seem surprising, given their minority status. Yet significant proportions of coloured people identify with the national governing party, the ANC. An even larger share supports the NP. As pointed out earlier, the NP was in the GNU until mid-1995. Perhaps more importantly, the NP still governs the Western Cape, which is home to the vast majority of South Africa's coloured citizens. Significantly, avowed commitment to democracy is ten points higher among coloured voters who live in the Western Cape than among those who live outside that province (58 to 48 percent).

Those who support parties that are out of power not only have especially negative views of government performance, but also take a negative view of the representativeness of government, accord it less legitimacy, and are less satisfied with the way in which democracy works.[22] This indicates that South Africans have not learned to distinguish their feelings about their political institutions and the larger democratic system from their partisan preferences. Yet there has been little opportunity to learn this under the new regime. For both blacks and whites, the new political dispensation is heavily identified with the efforts of Nelson Mandela and the ANC. For blacks, this generally translates into a positive view of the system. For whites (especially Afrikaners), who until very recently were regularly told through their state-supported schools and news media and their state-aligned churches that the ANC was a communist, terrorist organization bent on black power and single-party rule, it translates into a generally negative regime evaluation. All this is only compounded by the widespread expectation that the ANC, given its huge advantage over its nearest rivals in terms of partisan identification, will easily win the parliamentary elections in 1999, and probably in 2004 as well.

What Lies Ahead?

Public commitment to democracy is low but rising. Yet it appears that in the minds of many South Africans, such commitment is premised on the expectation that democracy will improve their daily lives in concrete ways. Many people conceive of democracy as having more to do with performance than with procedures. Those who are committed to democracy tend to tie that commitment to satisfaction with how the government and the economy are "doing."

Ideally, citizens should make a distinction between what they think about the government of the day and what they think about the larger democratic system. Commitment to democracy and the legitimacy of its institutions should not depend on how a particular administration is performing; rather, it should be a function of broad norms and values concerning authority and democracy learned in the family and in school. Thus one might urge South Africa's educational system, civil society, and political parties to shift their emphasis from voter education to the less glamorous task of teaching people to value democratic institutions and processes more for their own sake than for what they may deliver in terms of immediate and tangible benefits.

Yet in a poor and grossly unequal society, it is difficult to preach about the value of democracy for realizing individual dignity and freedom. People struggling to meet basic needs have little time or energy to spend worrying about the survival of democracy. They may see little value in the formal political equality delivered by democracy if their lives continue to be dominated by extreme economic inequality or grinding poverty.

It is difficult to teach the distinction between the incumbents and the system if people have a difficult time influencing or contacting their representatives, or if the party in office, through its electoral dominance, becomes identified in the popular mind with the state. It may simply be impossible to *teach* this distinction: Perhaps it can only be *learned* through the actual experience of voting both for winning and losing parties and candidates, and of living both under governments one supports and governments one opposes. This could explain why some scholars place so much stress upon alternation in government as an indicator of consolidation. South African democracy and its political institutions may first have to legitimate themselves through performance; then, one may hope, they can eventually build a base of support that will turn into a source of legitimacy no longer dependent upon evaluations of this or that set of incumbents.

The new government has made a sharp right turn away from its initial redistributionist Reconstruction and Development Program toward the liberal, growth-oriented Growth, Employment, and Redistribution (GEAR) program. Yet while South Africa's economy is expected to grow, few economists believe that GEAR will lead to the growth rates identified by Przeworski as highly conducive to democratic survival.

Moreover, such growth as does occur will be accompanied by rising social pain caused by the stretching of social services. In fact, most analysts believe that inequality will increase, at least in the short run. Such circumstances will invite the appearance of populists, demagogues, and political entrepreneurs skilled at exploiting ethnic tensions. It will take able managers and courageous leaders just to maintain the optimistic expectations, support for democratic institutions, and level of commitment to democracy that now exist, let alone raise them to the level necessary for legitimation. South African democrats may need to start working on a second miracle.

NOTES

1. The Idasa surveys cited in this essay were supported by grants from the U.S. Agency for International Development, the U.S. Institute of Peace, and the Canadian International Development Agency.

2. Adam Przeworski, Michael Alvarez, José Antonio Cheibub, and Fernando

Limongi, "What Makes Democracies Endure?" *Journal of Democracy* 7 (January 1996): 39–55.

3. Juan J. Linz and Alfred Stepan, "Toward Consolidated Democracies," *Journal of Democracy* 7 (April 1996): 31n. 3.

4. Linz and Stepan, "Toward Consolidated Democracies," 16.

5. Larry Diamond, "Consolidation Challenges of New Democracies" (paper presented to the Centre for Policy Studies, Johannesburg, South Africa, 9 February 1994), 2.

6. For evidence of the effect of democratic values on acquiescence or non-acquiescence to an attempted overthrow of a democratic (or at least protodemocratic) system, see James Gibson, "Mass Opposition to the Soviet Putsch of August 1991: Collective Action, Rational Choice and Democratic Values in the Former Soviet Union," *American Political Science Review* 91 (September 1997): 671–84.

7. Linz and Stepan, "Toward Consolidated Democracies," 24.

8. Heribert Adam, Frederik Van Zyl Slabbert, and Kogila Moodley, *Comrades in Business: Post-Liberation Politics in South Africa* (Cape Town: Tafelberg, 1997), 124.

9. Larry Diamond, "Lecture Delivered to the Idasa Seminar on the New Constitution and Democratic Culture" (Pretoria, 10 March 1997). Speaking to the British House of Commons not long after the Second World War, Churchill called democracy "the worst form of government," then added, "except for all those other forms that have been tried from time to time." *Hansard's* (11 November 1947), col. 206.

10. Richard Rose, "Public Opinion in New Democracies: Where Are Postcommunist Countries Going?" *Journal of Democracy* 8 (July 1997): 92–108.

11. James Gibson and Amanda Gouws, "Support for the Rule of Law in the Emerging South African Democracy," *International Social Science Journal* 152 (June 1997): 187.

12. See Table 3 in Marta Lagos, "Public Opinion in New Democracies: Latin America's Smiling Mask," *Journal of Democracy* 8 (July 1997): 133.

13. These variables explained 19 percent of the variance in commitment to democracy. Satisfaction with democracy had the strongest impact (beta=.23), followed by institutional performance (.15), economic expectations (.15), retrospective economic evaluations (.10), relative group shares of resources (.10), comparisons of the new system with apartheid (.08), corruption (.08), and citizen competence (.08). All are significant at at least the .95 level.

14. See Michael Biggs, *Getting into GEAR: Government and the Economy* (Cape Town: University of Cape Town Press, 1997), 15; and Przeworski et al., "What Makes Democracies Endure?" 41.

15. Biggs, *Getting into GEAR,* 48; and Przeworski et al., "What Makes Democracies Endure?" 42.

16. From 1975 to 1991, the income of the poorest fifth of each racial group in South Africa decreased dramatically, while the income of the richest fifth of each group stayed constant or increased. From 1984 to 1994, the wealthiest fifth of black South African households saw a 40 percent increase in income, while the poorest two-fifths witnessed a 40 percent decline. See Biggs, *Getting into GEAR,* 20.

17. Willem Van Vuuren, "Transition Politics and the Prospects of Democratic

Consolidation in South Africa," *Politikon: The South African Journal of Political Studies* 22 (June 1995): 5–23.

18. For the most consociational reading of the Interim Constitution, see Arend Lijphart, "Prospects for Power-Sharing in the New South Africa," in A. Reynolds, ed., *Election '94 South Africa: The Campaigns, Results and Future Prospects* (New York: St. Martin's, 1994), 221–31.

19. Przeworski et al., "What Makes Democracies Endure?" 49.

20. Joel D. Barkan, "Elections in Agrarian Societies," *Journal of Democracy* 6 (October 1995): 107–8; Göran Hyden, *No Shortcuts to Progress: African Development Management in Perspective* (Berkeley: University of California Press, 1981), 7.

21. Marlene Roefs, "Notes on Perceptions of National and Provincial Government in the Western and Eastern Cape, kwaZulu/Natal, and Gauteng" (paper presented at a workshop on "Democracy and Social Capital in Segmented Societies," Pretoria, 9–12 October 1997).

22. Helen Taylor and Robert Mattes, "Political Parties, Supporters, and Democratic Citizenship" (paper presented at a workshop on "Democracy and Social Capital in Segmented Societies," Pretoria, 9–12 October 1997).

10

SOUTH AFRICA'S EMERGING DOMINANT-PARTY REGIME

Hermann Giliomee

Hermann Giliomee was previously professor of political studies at the University of Cape Town, and is a former president of the South African Institute of Race Relations. He is presently a political consultant and a columnist for several newspapers in South Africa.

South Africa's transition from racial authoritarianism toward inclusive democracy during the first half of the 1990s was managed by two dominant parties. These were the National Party (NP), which had first won power in 1948 and had become the dominant party under apartheid in the mid-1960s, and the African National Congress (ANC), the main movement in the black struggle for freedom. The first nonracial elections, held in April 1994, gave the ANC 62 percent of the vote and set the stage for a Government of National Unity (GNU) that was to rule for five years under an interim constitution. In 1996, however, the NP left the GNU and went into a stance of normal parliamentary opposition, leaving the ANC atop a dominant-party regime that figures to endure through the elections scheduled for 1999, 2004, and beyond.

The dominant-party system has long figured in classifications of party systems and forms of democratic rule. A recent study focusing on industrialized countries suggested three criteria for identifying a dominant-party system: electoral dominance for a prolonged and uninterrupted period, dominance in the formation of governments, and dominance in determining the public agenda.[1] In countries such as Japan, Italy, Israel, and Sweden, a long period of dominant-party rule proved compatible with free electoral competition and the protection of civil liberties. Among developing countries, however, only India has so far succeeded in combining a long period of dominant party rule with liberal democracy.

In the developing world over the past 25 years, three dominant parties besides the ANC have attracted particular attention as they attempted either to intensify their hold on society or to introduce greater democratization. These are the Institutional Revolutionary Party (PRI) in

Mexico, the United Malays' National Organization (UMNO) in Malaysia, and the Kuomintang (KMT) in Taiwan. Most often, a dominant party's embrace of democracy can be described as awkward at best. While not massively repressive or wholly unaccountable, such a party usually displays less willingness to disperse power, more readiness to question the very legitimacy of opposition, and a stronger tendency to abuse state patronage than does a ruling party in a system where the reins of government change hands periodically. It is the fear of losing elections, more than institutional or legal safeguards like the separation of powers or bills of rights, that keeps officials honest and causes them to act in some rough way as agents of the electorate.

Dominant-party regimes in developing countries usually fall short on several key measures of liberal democracy. Such regimes often feature relatively unconstrained executives, minorities that find it hard to advocate their own interests effectively, opposition groups that the government brands as less than fully loyal, less effective protection of rights, more corruption, and—by definition—little or no prospect of any election-induced turnover in government.[2]

In the industrializing world as in the industrialized world, dominant parties are rare. The ANC and its counterparts in Malaysia, Mexico, and Taiwan all sprang from a background of revolution (or mass migration in the case of Taiwan), decolonization, and liberation. All of them quickly ran up against the constraints of the prevailing capitalist system and class structure. In a move that helped them survive, they all staked a strong claim to represent the new nation (or its dominant racial or ethnic group) before the founding election was held. From this strategic position, each could claim that it was the sole credible agent of the nation.

From such a point, there are two possible roads to liberal democracy and a competitive party system. The first has been taken by Taiwan, which experienced the rise of a middle class as the by-product of broad-based social and economic development occurring in the absence of any strong corporatist structures. The other is represented by Mexico, where the dominant-party system was born out of bargaining between business and organized labor under an economy based on import substitution. In recent years, the global economy has put enormous strain on the corporatist consensus that underlies the PRI's power, and the party may well lose its position of dominance in the next national election.

In Malaysia and South Africa, the forces of globalization have caused major tensions within the dominant party, but none severe enough to overcome the force of the ethnic or racial "cement" that holds it together. In neither country does the middle class that has arisen or is arising as a result of ruling-party patronage play any significant role in promoting democracy. On the contrary, there is some reason to fear that middle classes dependent on a dominant party may act to stifle rather than to spread democratic change.

How the ANC Became Dominant

In the late 1980s, on the eve of transition, prospects for establishing a stable nonracial democracy in South Africa looked bleak. The black middle class was tiny, and the ANC's commitment to nationalizing a substantial part of the economy and its rejection of any political movement basing itself on racial, ethnic, or regional identity threatened the interests and values of South Africa's five million whites. Once they gave up power, whites believed, they would never get it back.

South Africa's shift to an inclusive democracy occurred in response to two great pressures. The first was demographic: The white share of the population shrank from 20 percent in 1960 to 15 percent in the mid-1980s, with further shrinkage to 11 percent forecast for 2005. The second was the crisis of domestic capitalism, greatly exacerbated by international sanctions and popular resistance. Plummeting investor confidence drove gross fixed investment from 26 percent of GDP in 1983 to 16 percent eight years later. At this rate, it was impossible for South Africa to grow, for simply replacing worn-out capital stock required an investment level equal to 14 percent of GDP.[3]

Business interests began pushing for a new political order, less because they wanted a competitive liberal democratic system than because they believed that a black counterpart to the NP was needed if political stability and economic profitability were to be restored. By the late 1980s, the ANC had attracted sufficient domestic and international backing to present itself as the only group capable of filling this role.

The transition required the leaders of both the NP and the ANC to be fully in control of their respective followings and (in the NP's case) safe from defeat in an election, referendum, or party caucus vote. Despite difficulties posed by white right-wing opposition in Parliament and a partially free press, President Frederik W. de Klerk and a handful of advisors made all the strategic decisions while the party's MPs and congresses dutifully ratified everything. The endorsement of white voters was acquired through the use of an innocuous-sounding (and, in retrospect, misleading) referendum question. There was no extra-parliamentary revolt, for over the years white business, labor, and civil servants' groups had become so dependent on the NP that they had lost the capacity to organize and act independently of it.

It is also unlikely that a stable democracy would have been established had black politics been fractured. Officially banned in 1960, the ANC languished for decades. It made a comeback during the 1980s, capitalizing on its 80-year history of championing black rights, its standing in world opinion, the immense prestige of Nelson Mandela and other imprisoned leaders, its selective use of violence, and its alliance with the independent trade-union movement. By the end of the decade, the ANC claimed the loyalty of virtually the entire black electorate, excepting only rural Zulu-speakers and a small Zulu professional elite.

The ANC's control of a unified vote and its launching of "rolling mass action" during the negotiations enabled it to secure its core demand of simple majority rule, or what Nelson Mandela has called "ordinary democracy." What might have happened had the ANC faced stiff black competition across the country can be gauged by looking at the bloody conflict with Chief Mangosuthu Buthelezi's Inkatha movement in KwaZulu-Natal, where at least twelve thousand people have died in civil strife since the early 1980s.

There was no real uncertainty about the outcome of the 1994 election. Polls predicted consistently that the ANC would win by 40 percentage points, while the interim constitution adopted in late 1993 virtually assured that the NP would receive cabinet seats and one of the two deputy presidencies. Indeed, this lack of democratic uncertainty helped to guarantee success. Interference by the security forces stopped a few months before the balloting, by which time the handwriting on the wall was unmistakable. The NP condoned the semichaotic way in which the election was conducted in some areas because it was perceived as making only a marginal difference. It is unlikely that the result would have been accepted if it had been a close contest.[4]

Is there enough common ground between whites and blacks to make democracy work? Accounts that see South Africa as a unified rather than a deeply divided society—and hence not in need of special measures to accommodate racial and ethnic cleavages—reflect wishful thinking more than hard-nosed analysis. Opinion polls taken over the past five years point to a dearth of that common feeling of "we-ness" which is crucial to Westminster-style, majoritarian democracy.[5]

Is strong majority rule—Mandela's "ordinary democracy"—the best choice under such circumstances, especially when a single party enjoys predominance? Would power-sharing by a multiparty coalition of races and ethnic groups be better?[6] With the ANC enjoying an outright majority, South Africa is effectively being run according to the West-minster model; consociationalism has disappeared from public dis-cussion. Early hopes for a strong and independent parliament have been dashed, as ANC leaders have shown themselves to be intolerant of criticism of any ANC minister by the party's legislators, no matter how grave or substantiated the charges. The potential alternation of government, the real (and only) safety valve of the Westminster model, is unavailable. There is an eerie echo of the past here, for a highly centralized, sternly disciplined, and executive-dominated form of cabinet government was precisely the instrument that the NP used to implement its radical policy of apartheid beginning in 1948.

It can also be argued, however, that South Africa *needs* a dominant party to preserve stability, consolidate democracy, spur socioeconomic development, narrow class cleavages, and contain populist pressures. Elsewhere, dominant parties have performed some or most of these functions at crucial times, and there is no denying that the NP and the ANC played a vital stabilizing role in the inauguration of democracy. Given what was at stake in 1994, a fragmented party system might have led to competition so fierce as to derail democratization altogether.

A look at dominant-party regimes in nearby countries, however, is not encouraging. With the honorable exception of Botswana's Democratic Party, which has ruled that country since independence in 1962, the dominant parties of southern Africa encroach on civil liberties and barely tolerate opposition formations. It cannot be assumed that dominant parties brought to power through elections will be benign "bridge builders" facilitating the development of a competitive liberal democratic regime. In poor countries, the trend instead is for dominant parties to create bridgeheads for authoritarianism.[7]

Deep ethnic or racial divisions compound the dangers, since questions of "belonging" affect not only the distribution of material goods, but also the amount of prestige and identification with the state that various groups enjoy. Zambia had a successful democratic election in 1991, but its upshot was to repeat the pattern that followed the first post-independence balloting 25 years earlier: A broad multiethnic coalition organized as a dominant party took over, but began to fray as rival ethnic-group leaders within it jockeyed for power. Anxious to stop the bleeding, President Frederick Chiluba is keeping power in the hands of a minority, just as his predecessor Kenneth Kaunda did in the 1970s and 1980s.[8]

South Africa's 1994 interim constitution made only a weak compromise between the power-sharing and majoritarian positions, assuring any party drawing more than 5 percent of the vote at least one cabinet seat in the GNU. The final constitution, adopted in 1996, is in many ways a classic majoritarian document, providing a weak form of federalism, virtually no substantial minority or cultural rights, and no special provision for the inclusion of minority parties in the national cabinet. The Constitutional Court's power to overturn laws on constitutional grounds could become a check on the dominant party, but there are at the moment no judges on the bench whose known views or sympathies on issues like federalism and cultural rights accord with those of minority parties.

Electoral Systems and Party Dominance

Dominant parties in advanced industrial societies almost never secure an outright electoral majority, and must rule instead through a coalition. Many semi-industrialized countries, by contrast, have dominant parties that repeatedly poll more than 50 percent, regardless of the electoral system used. In Malaysia, alliance politics makes it possible for the ruling UMNO to win an absolute majority in a plurality system of single-member districts. In South Africa, the proportional representation (PR) system did prove effective in securing parliamentary representation for minorities, but failed to stop the ANC from gaining over 60 percent of the seats (something not generally supposed to happen under PR).

The use of PR probably reduced the prospect of secession. Under a plurality system, the ANC would have secured virtually every seat in eastern South Africa outside of the rural parts of KwaZulu, while the NP would have taken more than three-quarters of the seats in the Afrikaner and Coloured heartland of the Western Cape.[9] The pressures for a secessionist movement in that province would have been formidable.

The 1994 results showed that only about 3 to 4 percent of both black and white voters crossed over to cast a ballot for a party that had historically represented the other race. There was little evidence that this pattern would change soon. If a liberal democracy is about capturing an "undecided middle," party alternation, and minorities with a real hope of becoming part of a new majority, then the prospects of such a system evolving in South Africa are distinctly unpromising.

The informal ANC-NP coalition of the early 1990s was a marriage of convenience ended by the NP's withdrawal from the GNU in 1996. There had been no pre-election pact and certainly no "coalition of commitment" between the two, which fought each other bitterly during the election campaign. The GNU's collapse has polarized politics. By its nature, PR (especially the closed-list type used in South Africa) provides only limited inducements to racial moderation. Each party's major incentive is to solidify its base, usually by attacking its opponents as mistaken or even sinister. Only once the base is rallied is attention paid to broader appeals, which often take the form of multiethnic candidate lists and a publicly articulated belief in inclusiveness.

Such multiethnic lists, however, only tend to obfuscate discussions of racial and ethnic issues. Precious few of the ANC's white, Coloured, or Indian candidates (most of whom have roots in the South African Communist Party) could win a plurality election among their own coethnics. (The same is true for African NP candidates.) If the leadership of a racially based dominant party dismisses all criticism as racially inspired, representatives of that party who come from the minority communities are unlikely to challenge this interpretation.

South Africa's closed-list PR system allows party leaders to determine the racial mix of the ticket and the order in which candidates appear. It enabled the ANC to build a coalition of commitment that mobilized blacks behind an adroitly balanced array of leading figures from the ten or so different black ethnic groups *before* the first election. This method suited the ANC's purposes superbly in a country where blacks, despite their shared history of subjugation and immiseration, have long been riven by ethnic cleavages that greatly assisted white rule. The ANC has also forestalled charges of bias by drawing up its list in such a way that 30 percent of those elected to Parliament are nonblack, even though nonblacks account for only 6 percent of the ANC vote.

Has race become sufficiently subdued as an issue to allow class interests to supplant identity politics? During the 1994 campaign, both the NP and the ANC displayed indications to the contrary, ranging from the complexion of their respective leaderships to the different ways in which they referred to "the people" and the flavor of their rallies. In the black townships, apartheid's brutality is keenly remembered and bitterly resented. Historically white parties dare not try to campaign there. The Independent Electoral Commission reported in 1994 that as many as 13 million voters (approximately two-thirds of the total) "live in areas where the right to campaign is abridged." As a respected analyst of black politics wrote: "Ideological loyalties are absolute and concepts of political choice and tolerance are at best weakly sanctioned by local leaders. . . . Party adherence is mainly determined by territorial occupation."[10] A recent study found that nearly half of those surveyed felt that it would be difficult to live in their neighborhoods if their political views differed from those around them. While there is no evidence that the ANC's national leaders are encouraging any of this, it cannot be denied that muscular mobilization tactics and rituals of black solidarity serve to boost their power and their party's support.

The ANC captured only two to three percent of the white vote, but the transition did break up the white power bloc. The NP's hopes of playing strategic gatekeeper to the white-dominated civilian bureaucracies, security agencies, and business community were dashed once all these groups made their own deals with the new regime. The NP's presence in the cabinet attracted no further foreign fixed investment, while the integration of ANC personnel into the army's officer corps removed any danger of a military coup. Marginalized, the NP walked out.[11]

Now the only possibility of a competitive party system is through a split in the ANC, perhaps led by MPs close to the trade unions. Yet the 1996 Constitution permits party leaders to expel from Parliament any member who defies party discipline or crosses the floor. This clause, plus the closed list, gives the ANC's leaders a degree of control over party legislators almost unmatched in any other democracy.

The Economic Problem

While dominant parties in industrial democracies invariably rely on a majority coalition of socioeconomic blocs, party dominance in the developing world usually rests on a national-liberation or revolutionary movement whose political ethos and traditions go hand-in-hand with the demand for extensive state intervention in economic life. In racially

or ethnically divided societies, there is added to this a demand for the
redistribution of collective recognition, which is sought along with greater
material prosperity. A particularly receptive audience for this two-pronged
appeal is often found among the emerging middle-class elements in the
dominant group, with their high and rising expectations.

As public-opinion surveys make clear, the black citizens of South
Africa agree that the state and its dominant party should help them realize
their hopes for a better life, but are by no means unified about *how* this
should be done. The wealthiest layers of black society accept capitalism
while insisting on affirmative action and black-empowerment programs
to help their rise. The leadership of the labor movement, meanwhile,
looks to socialism.[12]

Although the ANC came to power promising to ameliorate the plight
of the black poor, the groups that have come to figure most prominently
in government policy are unionized workers and the black middle class,
whether privately employed or civil servants (Indian and Coloured civil
servants also tend to support the ANC). The government is committed
to a program of transformation that seeks as a first step to entrench a
black labor and managerial aristocracy. South African working hours
are now among the shortest in the industrializing world, and wages for
unskilled as well as skilled labor are above the average for midlevel
industrializing countries. Not surprisingly, unemployment is spiraling:
Now at 24 percent, it is expected to reach 40 percent in ten years if
current trends hold. The prospect of an enclave economy, with islands
of prosperity in a vast and widening sea of joblessness, promotes neither
stability nor confidence.[13]

In its attempt to produce an economic transformation that mirrors the
black assumption of political power, the ANC has been inspired in part
by the example of the UMNO, which achieved spectacular success in
advancing a Malay managerial class, boosting Malay equity holdings,
and narrowing Chinese-Malay economic inequalities. Yet major questions surround the ANC's quest to emulate the UMNO by bringing about
both growth and redistribution while holding unemployment down to
single digits. Before the onset of the economic crisis in late 1997,
Malaysia enjoyed tremendous economic growth, averaging about 7 percent a year, during the relevant period. Improvements in the lot of the
poor came from improvements in the labor market rather than from class-
specific redistributionist programs or union bargaining.[14] Then too,
inequalities in Malaysia have remained great, though they are not on
the order of those in South Africa.

Four years into ANC rule, South Africa has a population growth rate
of just under 2 percent and an economic growth rate of just over 2 percent.
Since the early 1980s, moreover, unions have been the key to wage
increases, which come at the price of making it harder for the poor to
enter the formal labor market. The labor market is expected to become

even more rigid after passage of a pending bill that compels businesses to submit plans to the government showing how they intend to bring their labor force profile into line with the composition of the population.

Corporatism and Opposition Politics

In dominant-party regimes, both corporatism and opposition politics take on a special form. Like the PRI in Mexico and the KMT in Taiwan, the ANC tries to use corporatism to blunt opposition. The National Economic Development and Labour Advisory Council (NEDLAC) serves as a top-level industrial-relations forum where big business and organized labor can slug it out. South Africa's unionized workers (one out of every three in the formal sector) aspire to rights comparable to those enjoyed by their counterparts in the Scandinavian social democracies. The Congress of South African Trade Unions (COSATU) has lately turned to strikes and demonstrations in order to press for a more rigid and state-regulated labor market.

Corporatism in South Africa has some other peculiar features. Its model of social partnership is postwar West Germany, a country that enjoyed near-full employment. South Africa currently has no social accord or even informal agreement about a strategy for achieving growth and redistribution. Despite the lag in new fixed foreign investment that is at least partly traceable to the highly constricted South African labor market, COSATU pledged in September 1997 to keep working for socialism and workers' power. NEDLAC, the main corporatist forum, has so far not directly addressed unemployment, the country's greatest crisis, and does not include any representatives of the small and medium-sized enterprises that are the best hope for job creation.

The black-white cleavage aside, the major dividing line now separates employed blacks from their unemployed or informally employed fellows. While the former have enjoyed income increases of up to a third since 1994, the latter have seen their real wages fall since the mid-1970s. In its strivings to reconcile contradictory aims, the ANC increasingly resembles the PRI in Mexico. The support of organized labor must be retained even as the party seeks "national consensus" and a "social balance" between the unions and big business. Meanwhile, union jobs and wages must be protected and business kept happy even as the party pursues its promises to give the unemployed poor access to such badly needed basics as clean running water, electricity, telephones, and minimally decent housing.

Agreements among these contending interests will almost certainly come at the expense of those who lack organization and a strong voice in the debate. The costs could be a worsening of structural unemployment, economic stagnation, a growing fiscal crisis, and even higher levels of crime and disorder.

The ANC's leaders deflect attention away from intrablack cleavages, even though there are now more blacks than whites in the highest-earning fifth of all households. (The average white household has an annual income about 5.5 times greater than that of the average black household, but blacks in the highest income quintile take home, on average, ten times more than their counterparts in the poorest two-fifths of the population.) The ANC's leaders talk as if *all* blacks belonged to the poor majority, and then call for radical transformation to narrow white-black inequalities. It is distinctly possible that this could take the form of a redistribution of wealth from the white to the black middle class, with poor rural blacks left out. Nevertheless, in a pattern manifested by almost all dominant parties, the ANC questions the very legitimacy of opposition, dismissing all criticism as attempts to obstruct nation-building and majority rule.

The opposition parties, although overshadowed by the ANC, could yet perform a valuable service by acting as the "bellwethers or warning devices" that Samuel P. Huntington described 30 years ago.[15] An increase in opposition support, like tensions within the ruling group, can give the dominant party's leaders information about how to maneuver so as to retain dominance. Thus both factionalism within the dominant party and the idea of at least a latent threat from the opposition (however feeble-seeming and vilified) must be considered necessary to dominant-party rule. The ANC continues to attack the NP, which it regularly accuses of pining for apartheid, but has changed its tack with the Zulu-based Inkatha Freedom Party (IFP) and is now trying to coopt its leaders.

The ANC leadership tends to react to any white opposition to its policies in racial terms. President Mandela is known to feel that the white opposition parties, by pandering to their "non-African" constituencies, have not assisted in consolidating the new democracy. In discussing with Mandela an ANC offer of cabinet seats, the Democratic Party (DP) learned that he had in mind the model of Robert Mugabe's Zimbabwe, where members of the ruling coalition cannot discuss contested issues in public. This was hardly the sort of "coalition arrangement" that would appeal to any opposition party, and particularly not the DP, a liberal group that believes in speaking its mind.[16]

The ANC's displeasure with the white opposition and a press that it considers insufficiently sympathetic came to a head in Mandela's December 1997 farewell address as ANC president.[17] In this speech, which was seen as representing the collective view of the ANC leadership, he called the media and white opposition parties "counter-revolutionary forces" that had "essentially decided against the national agenda" and wanted to "propagate a reactionary, dangerous and opportunist position." This dangerous position, according to Mandela, was to declare that a stable and normal democracy has been achieved, and that the opposition parties "have a democratic obligation merely to discredit the ruling party so that they may gain power after the next elections." Mandela's address in effect amounted to a rejection of some of the basic tenets of liberal democracy regarding the role of the opposition.

Other statements by Mandela have made it clear that press criticism also rankles. Any government effort to curb the press will probably come under the guise of the need for "racial diversification" in a white-run institution. A recent official Green Paper calls for a Media Development Agency with statutory powers to investigate the ownership of the media and "promote issues regarded as being of South African interest." Deputy President Thabo Mbeki, widely touted as Mandela's successor, has frequently pleaded for a more "patriotic" press, leading the liberal Institute of Race Relations to ask whether the media will be forced to diversify until it is sufficiently patriotic.[18]

With blacks forming more than three-quarters of the population, ANC rule seems assured as long as any criticism of the government can be tarred with the brush of racism. Oppositionists nourish the hope that a black middle class will emerge to break the racial mold of politics and usher in a truly competitive party system. Malaysia's experience challenges this scenario. The middle class there doubled from 1970 to 1995, growing from 12 to 25 percent of the population, yet Malaysia has regressed politically and is today no more than a semidemocracy.[19] The main reason is that the state's capacity to offer patronage and incorporate a wide range of groups behind the dominant party produces a statist system. The bourgeoisie will not easily challenge or abandon the party that sponsors and underwrites its jobs and interests, especially not in an ethnically mobilized society where belonging to a favored group can boost one's career.

The middle classes in a statist system may waver during hard times or when the ethnic elite is split, but quickly return to the fold once this elite reconsolidates its power.[20] The Malaysian case gives reason to doubt the notion that in ethnically divided societies broad-based economic development goes hand-in-hand with the rise of a middle class committed to competitive politics.

A recent survey has probed the prospects of a power balance emerging in South Africa through strengthened black opposition to government. While about one-quarter of blacks have a strong commitment to the principle of opposition and the notion of limits on majority rule, at least half gave "hegemonically oriented" responses. Significantly, high-school graduates were found to be less tolerant of opposition influence than less educated voters.[21] The emergence of a new black middle class fed by such graduates will not strengthen the middle-class parties. More likely is the strengthening of populist forces imbued with a spirit that will sit uneasily with that of liberal democracy. Alternatively, the ANC may see its one-time supporters fade away into apathy if it fails to deliver on its promises of jobs and houses.

Limits to Dominance

With their firm belief in the primacy of the individual and the ability of class interests to take precedence over ethnic or racial commitments, liberals tend to ignore the possibility that a liberal constitution such as South Africa's may produce only a democratic facade. The ANC enjoys an absolute parliamentary majority, and majoritarian principles are coming increasingly to overshadow any traces of consociationalism. While whites still occupy half the middle and higher positions in the civil service, they are steadily being replaced by ANC supporters. The autonomy of key institutions is eroding, and the lines between state and ruling party are blurring. Provincial attorneys general, for instance, no longer enjoy autonomy, but instead must answer to a politically appointed "super" attorney general empowered to make policy and ensure compliance.

The ANC has concentrated power at the center, particularly with respect to policing, education, health, and sport, and has been taking aggressive steps to increase black representation in numerous settings, from rugby and cricket teams to medical schools and the ranks of government contractors. While the need for black economic empowerment is both pressing and legitimate, there is a danger, as in the Malaysian case, that the dominant party will encroach on the due autonomy of economic and cultural institutions and create opportunities to cut deals, apportion benefits, and mete out punishments.

If it keeps overconcentrating power, the ANC may end up with more and more control over less and less. For example, a continuing refusal to devolve policing functions to the provinces and an overly hasty application of affirmative-action standards to the already under-performing criminal-justice system could have the net effect of putting more real power into the hands of mob bosses, drug lords, and corrupt businessmen in what is already one of the world's most crime-ridden societies.[22]

There has been a growing privatization of security and other traditionally public services. As standards in state schools plummet, private schools grow rapidly. Wary of giving significant power to the provinces, the new government has tried to go around them, building up local authorities as points of decentralized delivery and accountability. But the capacity of these bodies is suspect. The central government itself recently estimated that of the approximately seven hundred local governments, about a third can manage, another third are "salvageable," and the remaining third are collapsing to one degree or another. Bankrupt local authorities may be forced to privatize many services.

Deep in the countryside, the problems are even worse. Closed-list PR means that no legislator is linked to any geographic constituency, producing a phenomenon that is especially pronounced in rural parts of developing countries, and which has acquired the name of "the suspended state." Driven now by power and patronage, the contemporary ANC can offer little to the destitute, who must wrench a hard living out of the land or wait for remittances from relatives working in the cities. Traditional elites, particularly rural chiefs and headmen, feel threatened by the ANC's modernist policies. Rural citizens have little or no access to South Africa's modern infrastructure (by far the continent's finest), and their villages are notoriously underpoliced, leaving the honest majority at the mercy of thugs. Polls reveal severe disillusionment among these impoverished country people. While they pose no immediate threat, a series of rural uprisings in the more distant future is not a far-fetched scenario, with possibly severe consequences for the system.

There are three areas in which the ANC has striking weaknesses that check its dominance of society. First, its party organization has made no strides since 1994, is propped up by foreign funding, and may even be decaying. For the present, the ANC can count on a congeries of black civic groups, student organizations, and trade unions to get out the vote. But its ministerial-parliamentary wing overshadows the party's own structures, which suffer from declining numbers of dues-paying members, dwindling numbers of branches, and severe financial problems necessitating major layoffs of full-time staffers. The ANC has nowhere near the political heft and penetration that India's Congress party had during its early years in power. If major unions make good on their threats to break away over economic liberalization, the ANC will suffer a considerable drop of support at a much earlier stage than other dominant parties did.

Second, the ANC lacks the kind of control over the media that most of its developing-country counterparts enjoy. Although it is tightening its control over the state television network, there is no newspaper that can be considered a party mouthpiece. Meanwhile, the independent media go on exposing high-level corruption in the central and provincial admin-istrations, reporting on the government "gravy train," and publicizing official blunders and inefficiencies.

Finally, whites will continue to dominate the private sector of the economy for some time to come. By refusing to make fixed investments that will create desperately needed new jobs, business manifests the lack of confidence that it feels when contemplating high crime rates, rampant corruption, and constricted labor markets. Gross domestic fixed investment as a proportion of GDP has barely inched up since 1994.

There is some truth in the observation that dominant parties are not what they used to be. The KMT ruled Taiwan for thirty years through martial law and a cohesive security apparatus; in addition to the weaknesses outlined above, the ANC must rely on a weak and divided police and military establishment that is open to wide-ranging press scrutiny and human rights oversight. Moreover, the ANC's grip on its labor wing appears to be much weaker than that of its Mexican counterpart.

On the other hand, the ANC's electoral dominance and control of the policy agenda are as extensive as those of any dominant party anywhere. Its project of transforming society is as ambitious as that of any other dominant party. According to some spokesmen, traditionally white schools, universities, and sports teams must be transformed soon to reflect the composition of the overall population. Pending legislation aims at achieving the same goal within the ranks of management.

Within the bounds imposed by the need not to alienate big business, the ANC is growing ever more majoritarian in its approach to governance. There is little in the Constitution to restrain it, and its dominance has brought considerable benefits to the black bourgeoisie and unionized workers. Ultimately, however, its power depends on the votes of the still impoverished half of the black population. They are still the ANC's shield, but may ultimately prove its Achilles' heel.

NOTES

1. T.J. Pempel, ed., *Uncommon Democracies: The One-Party Dominant Regimes* (Ithaca, N.Y.: Cornell University Press, 1990), 1.

2. For a discussion of the elements of liberal democracy, see Larry Diamond, "Is the Third Wave Over?" *Journal of Democracy* 7 (July 1996): 23–24.

3. I discuss more fully the prospects for democratic consolidation in *Liberal and Populist Democracy in South Africa: Challenges, New Threats to Liberalism* (Johannesburg: South African Institute of Race Relations, 1996), 4–5; and in the conclusion to a book that I coedited with Lawrence Schlemmer, entitled *The Bold Experiment: South Africa's New Democracy* (Johannesburg: Southern Books, 1994), 168–202.

4. The definitive study is R.W. Johnson and Lawrence Schlemmer, eds., *Launching Democracy in South Africa: The First Open Election, April 1994* (New Haven: Yale University Press, 1996).

5. See the survey results published in the *Helen Suzman Foundation Focus,* May 1997, 4–5.

6. See Vernon Bogdanor, "Forms of Autonomy and the Protection of Minorities," *Daedalus* 126 (Spring 1997): 66.

7. Pierre du Toit, "Bridge or Bridgehead?" in Hermann Giliomee and Charles Simkins, eds., *The Awkward Embrace: Democracy and Dominant-Party Rule in Semi-Developed Countries* (London: Harwood Academic Publishers, 1998), ch. 11.

8. Donald Horowitz, "Democracy in Divided Societies," *Journal of Democracy* 4 (October 1993): 25–27.

9. Andrew Reynolds, "Re-Running the 1994 South African and Malawian Parliamentary Elections Under Alternative Electoral Formulae" (unpublished manuscript, 1995).

10. Tom Lodge, "Election of a Special Kind," *Southern African Review of Books* (March–April 1994): 4.

11. There has been criticism of the NP's "myopia" in holding out for power-sharing instead of demanding electoral rules and mechanisms that offered a chance of breaking up the ANC as a liberation movement. See Ian Shapiro, *Democracy's Place* (Ithaca, N.Y.: Cornell University Press, 1996), 210–19. This ignores the fact that when the NP leaders were negotiating the interim constitution, they needed closed-list PR in order to assure their caucus that all members interested in prolonging their careers would be almost certain of retaining their seats. Without that, De Klerk would almost certainly have faced a caucus revolt that would have stopped the transition in its tracks. When the final constitution was negotiated in 1995–96, the ANC had enough power to insist on the perpetuation of closed-list PR.

12. Lawrence Schlemmer and Ian Hirschfeld, *Founding Democracy and the New South African Voter* (Pretoria: Human Sciences Research Council, 1994), 48–50.

13. Lawrence Schlemmer and Charisse Levitz, *Unemployment in South Africa* (Johannesburg: South African Institute of Race Relations, 1998), 1–6.

14. James V. Jesudason, *Ethnicity and the Economy: The State, Chinese Business and Multinationals in Malaysia* (Singapore: Oxford University Press, 1989), 173.

15. Samuel P. Huntington, *Political Order in Changing Societies* (New Haven: Yale University Press, 1968), 147.

16. Anthony Johnson, "Mandela Lets Parties off the Hook," *Cape Times* (Cape Town), 5 March 1997, 9.

17. The quotations in this paragraph from Mandela's address are taken from the *Sunday Times* (Johannesburg), 21 December 1997, 4.

18. South African Institute of Race Relations, press release of 3 December 1997.

19. For an extended discussion, see Jesudason, *Ethnicity and the Economy,* 76–123.

20. James Jesudason, "Statist Democracy and the Limits to Civil Society in Malaysia," *Journal of Commonwealth and Comparative Politics* 33 (1995): 334–36.

21. Lawrence Schlemmer, "Democracy or Democratic Hegemony?" in Hermann Giliomee and Charles Simkins, eds., *The Awkward Embrace,* ch. 13.

22. Over the past two decades, the (reported) crime rate has risen by a third while the conviction rate has fallen by nearly as much. The odds that the perpetrator of a serious crime will be convicted are estimated currently at about 20 to 1. The absolute number of criminal convictions is at a forty-year low despite dramatic increases in both the population and crime rates. A collapse of morale (partly caused by affirmative action) is evident among law-enforcement officials: About one out of every three state prosecutors has resigned over the past two years, and private security firms now employ twice as many people as the police. See Colin Douglas, "Dit lyk of die staat heeltemal in duie stort" ("It looks as if the state is collapsing completely"), *Die Burger* (Cape Town), 25 June 1997, 8.

III

African Ambiguities

11

GHANA'S ELECTIONS: A MAJOR STEP FORWARD

Terrence Lyons

Terrence Lyons, a senior researcher at the International Peace Research Institute in Oslo, Norway, served as a delegate on the National Democratic Institute's December 1996 mission to observe the Ghanaian elections. He is the author of Voting for Peace: Postconflict Elections in Liberia *(1999).*

On 7 December 1996, President Jerry Rawlings won his second multiparty election in Ghana, completing another important step in the building of sustainable political and economic institutions in that West African state. Previous elections, in 1992, ended in charges of fraud and an opposition boycott of the 200-seat, unicameral National Assembly. This time, however, important reforms in the electoral system and a spirited campaign by an opposition coalition gave Ghanaians a meaningful choice on election day. The opposition won a third of the seats in the Assembly, and can use this base both to scrutinize the Rawlings government and to build more effective political parties for subsequent elections.

While the election received less attention than it deserved in the international media, Ghana offers a series of hopeful lessons for African states struggling with the challenges of macroeconomic structural adjustment programs (SAPs) and the transition from authoritarianism to democracy. The case of Ghana also highlights the tendency in a number of African countries for soldiers who seized power through coups to reinvent themselves as democratic leaders. In such West African states as Niger, Togo, Burkina Faso, Guinea, and the Gambia, military leaders have remained in power in part by manipulating elections or by forcing the opposition to withdraw. President Rawlings of Ghana, a former air force officer, has cultivated a rural base of support that has allowed him to go from coup leader to winner of two multiparty elections—all while steering the country through a difficult period of economic reform.

Courtesy of the U.S. State Department

Ghana has served as *the* preeminent test case of structural adjustment
in Africa. Following the virtual collapse of the formal economy in the
early 1980s, the Rawlings government reversed its populist policies and
adopted an SAP with the strong encouragement of the World Bank, the
International Monetary Fund (IMF), and bilateral donors. The results
were dramatic. The country's GDP grew at rates of 6 to 7 percent annually from 1984 to 1988—the highest in sub-Saharan Africa at that time.
These considerable economic accomplishments, however, began to stall
in the early 1990s. The disputed 1992 elections and the subsequent
opposition boycott of parliament raised questions about stability and
made private investors wary.

The stakes in the 1996 election, therefore, were high. As the *Financial Times* put it: "If Ghana falters in its trailblazing role, not only will international confidence in the continent's capacity to recover be jolted, the credibility of the donors' development strategy for Africa will also be eroded."[1] Ghana could not afford to stand pat, and still less to repeat the contentious 1992 elections.

The Rule of Rawlings

To evaluate the transition in Ghana, it is necessary to understand the degree to which both economic and political institutions had deteriorated by the time of Rawlings's 31 December 1981 coup. Ghana had achieved independence in 1957 with a per-capita income roughly equal to South Korea's. Over the next 25 years, however, disastrous import-substitution strategies, sagging export revenues, rampant corruption, and statism laid waste to the economy. Between 1974 and 1981, for example, GDP dropped 15 percent and cocoa exports, the leading source of foreign exchange, shrank by more than 40 percent.

The independence movement in Ghana was led by Kwame Nkrumah and his Convention People's Party (CPP). In 1966, after a decade of increasingly authoritarian rule, a coup toppled him. Following an election three years later, the military returned power to civilians. The winners of this election, Prime Minister Kofi A. Busia and his Progress Party, ruled for just over two years. Senior military officers retook power in early 1972. In June 1979, then–Flight Lieutenant Rawlings led the Armed Forces Revolution Council in a junior-officers' putsch. Later that year, Rawlings handed power over to President Hilla Limann and his People's National Party (PNP), the winners of national elections. It was Limann whom Rawlings overthrew on the last day of 1981.[2]

This thumbnail sketch shows that elections and established political parties are as much a legacy of recent Ghanaian history as military coups. In 1969, 1979, and 1992, elections followed a period of military rule and served to select and legitimate civilian leaders. "Few African countries have experienced either the frequency, the heterogeneity, or the tenacious commitment that is associated with the electoral process in Ghana," notes Naomi Chazan.[3] Until 1996, however, no elected government had completed its term in office.

When Rawlings's Provisional National Defence Council (PNDC) took power as 1982 began, "Ghana was in the midst of a multifaceted crisis of political enfeeblement, social fragmentation, and economic decline."[4] During his first 18 months in office, the government tried to manage the economy through administrative controls and mass mobilization. Rawlings's radical populist rhetoric and ties to domestic leftist groups evoked the image of a radical military government along the lines of Daniel Ortega's Nicaragua or Thomas Sankara's Burkina Faso.[5]

By the close of 1983, however, Ghana was becoming the steadiest economic reformer in Africa, and the continent's showcase example of structural adjustment. Rawlings pursued an Economic Recovery Program (ERP) that accepted World Bank and IMF conditionalities largely because he had no choice: The economy was dead in the water and sinking fast. A dramatic currency devaluation, the removal of price controls and social-service subsidies, the privatization of some state-owned enterprises, and strict limits on government spending led to generous assistance from multilateral and bilateral donors. Bilateral donors provided $800 million in both 1987 and 1988 and $900 million in 1989, an extremely high level of assistance for an African country.[6] As a result of the reforms and aid, Ghana achieved significant growth rates. The early stabilization programs have since been followed by a broader adjustment agenda. These economic reforms have favored farmers, enabling them to command higher prices for their crops. Urban workers, more reliant on subsidized services and government jobs, have suffered.

Structural adjustment created severe hardships for many Ghanaians, but before reform, much of the economy's formal sector was dormant. While households have had to pay more for schooling and other social services, such services were nearly nonexistent prior to reform. The very weakness of formal institutions at a time when most Ghanaians were either emigrating or eking out a hand-to-mouth living in the informal sector meant that there was little organized opposition to the ERP. A small group of technocrats around Finance Minister Kwesi Botchwey, shielded from popular pressures, implemented their program with a free hand.[7]

In addition, Rawlings's economic policies remained insulated by his authoritarian style and wide powers of coercion. Decision making was strongly centralized, with the president's populist rhetoric serving in place of governmental institutions. The security apparatus, originally designed to mobilize the population in defense of the revolution, quashed dissent. Summary executions and the rough tactics of the local militants who staffed the Committees for the Defence of the Revolution (CDRs) imposed acquiescence and a "culture of silence." According to Albert Adu Boahen, one of Ghana's leading scholars, "We have not protested or staged riots not because we *trust* the PNDC but because we *fear* the PNDC!"[8]

The Transition

Authoritarian control and populist rhetoric sufficed to carry out stabilization in the short run, but greater popular support and regime legitimacy were needed for longer-term economic and political reforms. The dearth of political institutions meant a lack of channels to carry information from the countryside to decision makers in the capital, and also worried private investors. The rigors of adjustment sapped some of the regime's original support among radical students and urban groups.

The SAP's main beneficiaries were farmers, but their support was diffuse and difficult to organize effectively. Ghana's significant economic progress had reached the stage where it needed popular legitimacy and political institutions to support it.

The political reform process—Rawlings called it "political structural adjustment"—began under strict control from above.[9] Rawlings organized "no-party" district-assembly elections in 1988–89 in order to mobilize rural support. Turnout was good, demonstrating the PNDC's strength in the countryside.[10] The district assemblies, however, had serious drawbacks. One-third of their members, as well as the powerful district chief executives, were government appointees. The new assemblies lacked links to the center, and did nothing to diminish growing national-level demands for a return to multipartism. In the end, these assemblies were a stopgap that gave the regime breathing room but left the government without institutionalized social roots.

The next step in the political reform process was a series of carefully managed deliberations on a new constitution. At first, Rawlings seemed intent on institutionalizing the no-party political system used in the district assemblies, but Ghanaian human rights groups such as the Movement for Freedom and Justice objected fiercely. After debate, the government-appointed National Commission for Democracy issued a report concluding that the "generality of Ghanaians were not against party politics."[11] Rather than resist, Rawlings co-opted the opposition's agenda and presented a multiparty Constitution to a referendum in April 1992. Despite controversy over a last-minute provision granting full immunity to all PNDC members, the Constitution passed with an overwhelming 93 percent.[12]

Following the referendum, the government lifted the ban on party activity and began preparations to hold a vote for president in November 1992 and for parliament a month later. Opposition leaders objected to the government's lack of neutrality in the electoral process, and to continued restrictions on political freedoms. The strongest opposition party was the New Patriotic Party (NPP), led by Adu Boahen and linked to the political tradition associated with Kofi Busia and the anticolonialist leader J.B. Danquah. Former president Limann led the People's National Convention (PNC); it and a variety of other parties competed to represent the heritage of Nkrumah. Rawlings ran at the head of a new party, the National Democratic Congress (NDC).

As many observers recognized, the playing field was far from level. The presidential election was marred by a hastily compiled and clearly bloated voters' register, an electoral commission appointed by Rawlings that the opposition regarded as partisan, and an electoral process open to manipulation. The opposition complained when Rawlings began campaigning before the official unbanning of political parties. The president freely used his powers as incumbent, initiating public-works projects (electrification in the Brong Ahafo and Northern regions, water projects in many regions) and giving public employees a 60 percent pay raise during the run-up to the voting.[13] Finance Minister Botchwey later claimed that certain expenditures had been politically imperative: "We were more or less obliged to award a substantial wage increase to buy the peace and enable the democratic transformation to go ahead."[14]

In the end, the Electoral Commission declared that Rawlings had won 58 percent of the vote to Boahen's 30 percent, with the remainder split among smaller parties. Turnout was 50 percent. Rawlings is from Volta Region, a long, narrow strip of land between the winding eastern shore of manmade Lake Volta and the border with Togo, Ghana's neighbor to the east. He gained more than half the votes in every region except Ashanti in south-central Ghana, and carried his home region by an almost incredible 93 percent. He ran particularly well in rural districts. Boahen, who is from Ashanti, won his home region and generally got more of his votes from the cities.[15]

The reports of international observers recognized the irregularities in the poll but concluded that the results probably reflected the voters' wishes. The Carter Center, for example, acknowledged "irregularities and inconsistencies," but saw no "systematic pattern that would suggest fraudulent conduct or the rigging of the elections."[16] In a controversial report released before balloting had been completed, the Commonwealth Observer Group declared the vote "free and fair."

The four opposition parties issued a joint statement calling on the Electoral Commission to withhold results until investigations of irregularities were completed. Demonstrations occurred in several cities. Rioting in Kumasi, the capital of Ashanti Region, led to a dusk-to-dawn curfew for several days. Citing a long list of irregularities, the opposition decided to boycott the December parliamentary balloting. Facing only token independent candidates, the NDC swept those races. Turnout, however, was a paltry 29 percent.

Rather than pursue their complaints through established legal channels that they considered biased, opposition parties made their allegations publicly and tried to undermine the new government's legitimacy. The NPP published *The Stolen Verdict,* a detailed list of its charges. Most of the problems, however, were known to the opposition prior to the presidential election in which they participated. Two scholars who reviewed the opposition's charges concluded that "it remains difficult to believe that there was any centrally directed plan to rig the presidential election."[17] Rawlings's skills as a politician, his avid use of the advantages of incumbency, and splits within the opposition better explain the outcome than do theories about fraud. The old political elites, however, regarded themselves as the legitimate guardians of Ghanaian civic virtue and simply could not accept that Rawlings could be so popular among so many of their compatriots.

On 7 January 1993, Ghana returned to constitutional rule, officially launching its Fourth Republic. The de facto one-party parliament, however, lacked legitimacy and exerted only limited powers of oversight regarding Rawlings. The opposition, lacking seats in parliament and hampered by a continuing preoccupation with the irregularities of the 1992 poll, had a difficult time playing a constructive role.

This unfortunate outcome led some observers to conclude that Ghana had experienced a "transition without change." What was needed above all was an electoral system reliable enough to banish controversies about vote fraud, thereby allowing energy to be rechanneled toward the building of effective parties, the selection of articulate leaders, and the development of popular programs.

The 1996 Elections

Despite the disappointing outcome in 1992, Ghana continued to build on its initial tentative steps toward consolidating democratic rule. Between 1992 and 1996, the Supreme Court demonstrated increasing independence from the ruling party. Independent newspapers began publication. Opposition parties continued to operate outside of parliament, holding rallies and press conferences. The next round of elections in 1996 provided another opportunity to assess the political reform process. For the first time in Ghana's history a government that emerged from a competitive election had served its full four-year term and stood for reelection.

By 1996, the Ghanaian economy was beginning to weaken as inflation quickened while job creation and poverty alleviation lagged. Still, cocoa prices remained good, the mining sector was booming, and the timber industry was developing. In contrast to the mid-1980s, when weak organization prevented effective opposition to structural adjustment, mass demonstrations in 1995 forced Rawlings to withdraw a proposed value-added tax.[18]

In 1996, a number of important changes had been made in the electoral process, demonstrating that the Electoral Commission and the parties had learned important lessons from 1992.[19] The opposition had initially questioned the neutrality of the Electoral Commission, whose members were government appointees. Mutual distrust among political parties had been eased in part through the Inter-Party Advisory Committee (IPAC), an innovative mechanism that brought the parties together to discuss election preparations with the Electoral Commission. IPAC began holding regular monthly meetings in March 1994—more than two years before the election date—and met more frequently as the pace of preparations increased in late 1996. Kwadwo Afari-Gyan, the chairman of the Electoral Commission, skillfully calmed the fears of political parties and activists regarding electoral procedures. Even though some of the charges contained in *The Stolen Verdict* lacked credibility, the Electoral Commission treated them all seriously and put in place multiple measures to reassure the opposition that any attempts at fraud on election day would be detected.

International donors also recognized that controversy over procedures in 1992 limited the ability of elections in Ghana to serve as a mechanism for public choice and acceptance of the results by all parties. The U.S. Agency for International Development provided assistance for a Supporting the Electoral Process (STEP) program in Ghana, with technical assistance from the U.S.-based International Foundation for Election Systems. U.S. officials also encouraged all parties to participate in the IPAC meetings. Other donors supported other components of the electoral process.

Electoral Commission officials paid particular attention to the question of registration, designing an exemplary process that involved all political parties. The register was compiled afresh, with almost 9.2 million voters registering at nearly 19,000 polling stations. Voters generally registered at the place where they would vote, an important improvement over 1992, when many voters had not known where they were to cast their ballots. Party agents monitored each step and reviewed the lists. Each polling station exhibited the list in order to allow voters to confirm their names. An astonishing 73 percent did, permitting the Commission to make additional corrections. By election day, the opposition had by and large accepted the accuracy of the voter rolls, removing a major controversy that had undermined the legitimacy of the 1992 elections. A decision to hold presidential and parliamentary elections on the same day and the use of see-through ballot boxes with numbered seals further increased the confidence of voters and opposition parties.

These steps created a commendable, transparent process which assured Ghanaians that the results would accurately reflect their choices on election day. The Electoral Commission, political parties, and donors demonstrated that years of serious work prior to an election are critical to its success. While an effective system for administering elections does not by itself result in a meaningful contest, in Ghana such procedures addressed most of the opposition's concerns from the 1992 election and gave political leaders the opportunity to devote their time and attention to campaigning and building up their organizations.

In addition to the party agents, who monitored every stage of the election at every polling place, the election was monitored by large groups of international and local observers. The U.S.-based National Democratic Institute (NDI) sponsored a 33-member delegation. This group deployed 16 teams on election day and observed the voting in approximately three hundred polling sites in each of Ghana's ten regions. Other international groups included the Commonwealth Observer Group (23 members who visited nearly three hundred polling centers), the European Union, and the Organization of African Unity. As in 1992, the Commonwealth again issued an early, interim statement. This time, however, it waited until the polls had closed, and generated no controversy.

Ghanaian nongovernmental organizations created a nonpartisan Network of Domestic Election Observers (NEDEO), which won the support of a broad range of civic groups, including trade unions, religious groups, and student organizations. With support from NDI, NEDEO trained approximately 4,100 local poll-watchers. Some NDC activists initially objected to NEDEO, claiming that some of its constituent groups were partisan opponents of the government. On election day, however, the NDC made no move to interfere with NEDEO's operations. Still, tardiness in getting the appropriate accreditation for all its observers combined with logistical difficulties to hamper NEDEO's deployment. Some regions were more effectively covered than others.

While both the international observer groups and NEDEO played important roles, the more important contribution was played by the more than 60,000 candidate agents who were present at nearly every polling site. These agents not only monitored the voting process throughout the day in a given polling place but signed the relevant reporting forms and reported the results ballot box by ballot box to their respective party leaders. This parallel vote-tabulation system meant that each party had an independent report from each polling site to compare with the official results from the Electoral Commission.[20]

The Campaign and the Results

The 1996 election ended up being a contest between Rawlings's NDC and the Great Alliance formed by the opposition. The Great Alliance brought together the two main opposition parties and political traditions, the New Patriotic Party (NPP), representing the heritage of Busia, and the People's Convention Party (PCP), standing in the tradition of Nkrumah and his similarly named CPP. The Great Alliance's main purpose was to make a common stand behind a single presidential candidate. In practice, however, this meant months of bitter wrangling that inflicted deep wounds and delayed the start of the opposition's presidential campaign.[21] The Great Alliance's candidate, John A. Kufuor, was a 58-year-old lawyer, former MP, and onetime minister under Rawlings (in 1982). A compromise choice, he may not have been the most forceful figure to lead the race against the formidable Rawlings and his NDC.

The Great Alliance attempted to back a single candidate in each of the two hundred parliamentary races, but in a number of constituencies both the NPP and PCP were on the ballot, threatening to split the opposition vote. A melding of two competing political traditions, the Great Alliance was held together mainly by a shared desire to defeat Rawlings; it had difficulty articulating a clear positive message of its own. Another party, former president Limann's PNC, backed Edward Mahama for the presidency.

Many oppositionists believed that "Rawlings fatigue" had made the 15-year incumbent beatable. They emphasized the recent downturn in Ghana's economy and asked voters to consider their living conditions and vote accordingly. The opposition, however, lacked a clear message on how it would change economic policy. The current reality in much of Africa is that economic policy is determined largely by international financial institutions, with local leaders able to make changes only at the margins.

Competing against a sitting head of state is always a challenge. Rawlings made development—"always for the people, always for development"—his main message. He campaigned vigorously, traveling the country to dedicate new buildings, open new roads, and stump for his own reelection. Refusing to distance himself from structural adjustment, he promised to continue the reform process if reelected. Rawlings is a formidable campaigner and public speaker, with a knack for addressing many Ghanaians, particularly farmers, in a manner that exudes a powerful impression of concern for their problems. In the end, no major policy differences dividing Kufuor and Rawlings were articulated. The campaign turned on personalities.

The distrust between the ruling NDC and the Great Alliance often made for a contentious campaign. Oppositionists complained about the incumbents' unfair use of state resources, particularly the state-owned media. The youth wings of the parties sometimes clashed, and many Ghanaians expressed concerns about unofficial security forces. Intimidation and violence in several areas, including more riots in Kumasi, created a tense atmosphere in the days prior to the voting.

Despite these concerns, the December 7 voting was peaceful. Turnout was an impressive 78 percent. The two main parties had agents in almost all polling places. Some relatively minor problems occurred, such as inadequate parliamentary ballots in one constituency (Mfantsiman West), underage voters (particularly in the north), and a shortage of indelible ink. The new election-watching and vote-counting safeguards went a long way toward creating a transparent electoral system in which all parties could place their confidence.

According to the Electoral Commission, Rawlings won 57 percent of the vote to Kufuor's 40 percent. In the Assembly, the NDC took 133 seats to the opposition's 67. The parliamentary opposition is dominated by the NPP, which took 61 seats while the PCP garnered only 5 (the PNC won a single seat). A number of leading NDC figures, including several ministers and regional executives, went down to defeat. While beating Rawlings was always a long shot, the opposition might have done better in the parliamentary races if they had presented a clearer, more unified message.

Evaluations by international observers were encouraging. NDI stated that the manner in which the elections were conducted "represents a positive step forward in the strengthening of Ghana's democracy and its electoral process" and singled out the Electoral Commission for praise. The Commonwealth Observer Group similarly concluded that conditions existed "for a free expression of will by the electors."[22]

One remarkable characteristic of the 1996 voting was how closely it compared to the 1992 results—the ones that the opposition had decried as fraudulent. In both elections, the opposition carried Ashanti Region and a few constituencies in the Eastern and Greater Accra regions while Rawlings won overwhelmingly in Volta (the home of his own Ewe ethnic group) and did well in every other region. While the opposition complained that Rawlings's victory in 1996 was due to "ethnic voting" by the Ewe of Volta, its own vote was heavily dominated by Akan-speaking people from the south. The Great Alliance received fewer votes than expected in the Northern, Upper East, Upper West, and Brong Ahafo regions. Brong Ahafo, for example, had been Busia's stronghold in the 1969 election and had been widely expected to turn out for the NPP in 1996. In general, the opposition again did better in the cities while the NDC received more support in the rural constituencies.

Postelection Developments

The opposition accepted the results of the 1996 election and played its role as the opposition in parliament. The presence of a 67-member opposition bloc encouraged more open debate and served in part as a check on the ruling party. Ghana's political leaders engaged in extensive debate over government appointments, tax policy, corruption, and a severe energy crisis, indicating that the assembly could serve as the focus of democratic deliberation. The NPP, led by ex-Finance Minister J.H. Mensah, is now among the strongest legal opposition parties in Africa.

The 1992 Constitution limits presidents to two terms; Rawlings cannot run again. After a flurry of rumors that he would find a way to remain in power, Rawlings threw his support behind Vice President John Evans Atta-Mills to succeed him in 2000. Splits within the NDC erupted as political factions maneuvered to control the party in the post-Rawlings era. The opposition NPP went through its own internal struggles for leadership and remained poorly institutionalized in the countryside. No party has effectively mobilized the original Nkrumahist political base, and it remains to be seen if a new party alignment will develop before the elections in 2000. The political salience of ethnicity, seen in the pattern of voting in Ewe and Ashanti areas, may increase as parties scramble for votes in a post-Rawlings era.

The 1996 Ghanaian elections demonstrate that a well-led and scrupulously independent electoral commission with sufficient time and resources can play a critical role in shifting the focus of politics away from election-day voting and toward issues of party leadership and program. The irregularities of 1992 diverted the opposition from efforts to broaden its appeal and expand its base beyond the Ashanti region. The success of the electoral process in 1996 not only led all parties to accept the results, but also has made them think about what they must do to succeed in future elections. In the days immediately after the election, NPP leaders began developing strategies to use their parliamentary base to build a more effective party and to put forward more popular leaders and a more persuasive message in the next elections. This represents an important step forward.

The success of political reforms to date should reinforce earlier economic reforms. By building new institutions with legitimacy and popular support through competitive elections, Ghana has made it possible to sustain the reform process. The further development of a stronger economy and political system will remain difficult; success is by no means assured. Poverty alleviation remains a major challenge. Balancing the need to maintain fiscal discipline with voter demands for higher spending is never easy, in Ghana or anywhere else. Rawlings campaigned on his economic program, and his victory will be seen as an endorsement for continuing reform.

Despite these future challenges, the December 7 elections represent an encouraging step forward in the democratization process. The ability of the people to make an effective choice, not alternation in government, is the criterion for meaningful elections. The large opposition bloc in the next parliament will increase accountability and may serve as the base for a stronger opposition in future elections. The civic organizations that NEDEO galvanized may play an important role in monitoring political developments in the postelection period. Improvements in the electoral process, coupled with a commitment by all parties to accept the outcome, resulted in an election that served to lay the basis for further development of democracy in Ghana.

NOTES

1. Michael Holman and Michela Wrong, "Ghana 1996: African Trailblazer Begins to Falter," *Financial Times* (London), 9 July 1996.

2. For a recent political history, see Albert Adu Boahen, "Ghana: Conflict Reoriented," in I. William Zartman, ed., *Governance as Conflict Management: Politics and Violence in West Africa* (Washington, D.C.: Brookings Institution, 1996).

3. Naomi Chazan, "The Anomalies of Continuity: Perspectives on Ghanaian Elections Since Independence," in Fred M. Hayward, ed., *Elections in Independent Africa* (Boulder, Colo.: Westview, 1987), 61.

4. Naomi Chazan, "The Political Transformation of Ghana Under the PNDC," in Donald Rothchild, ed., *Ghana: The Political Economy of Recovery* (Boulder, Colo.: Lynne Rienner, 1991), 22. For more on the collapse of Ghana prior to 1981, see Donald Rothchild, "Rawlings and the Engineering of Legitimacy in Ghana," in I. William Zartman, ed., *Collapsed States: The Disintegration and Restoration of Legitimate Authority* (Boulder, Colo.: Lynne Rienner, 1995).

5. Donald Rothchild and E. Gyimah-Boadi, "Populism in Ghana and Burkina Faso," *Current History* 28 (May 1988): 538.

6. Matthew Martin, "Negotiating Adjustment and External Finance: Ghana and the International Community, 1982–1989," in Rothchild, ed., *Ghana,* 251.

7. Jeffrey Herbst, *The Politics of Reform in Ghana, 1982–1991* (Berkeley: University of California Press, 1993); Richard Jeffries, "Leadership Commitment and Political Opposition to Structural Adjustment in Ghana," in Rothchild, ed., *Ghana,* 157–71.

8. Albert Adu Boahen, *The Ghanaian Sphinx: Reflections on the Contemporary History of Ghana, 1972–1987* (Accra: Academy of Arts and Sciences Press, 1989), 51–52.

9. Jerry Rawlings as quoted in Colleen Lowe Morna, "A Grassroots Democracy," *Africa Report* 34 (July–August 1989): 20.

10. See Kwame A. Ninsin, "Strategies of Mobilisation Under the PNDC Government," in E. Gyimah-Boadi, ed., *Ghana Under PNDC Rule* (Dakar, Senegal: CODESRIA, 1993).

11. Quoted in Kwasi Afriyie Badu and John Larvie, *Elections in Ghana 1996,* Part 1 (Accra: Electoral Commission of Ghana and the Friedrich Ebert Foundation, 1996), 72.

12. Richard Jeffries and Clare Thomas, "The Ghanaian Elections of 1992," *African Affairs* 92 (July 1993): 335–37.

13. E. Gyimah-Boadi, "Ghana's Uncertain Political Opening," *Journal of Democracy* 5 (April 1994): 82; and "Ghana: Elections and the Rawlings Factor," *Africa Confidential,* 20 November 1992, 5–6.

14. Collen Lowe Morna, "Interview: Kwesi Botchwey, Ghana's Finance Minister," *Africa Report* 40 (March–April 1995): 38. See also Todd J. Moss and David G. Williams, "Can Ghana's Economic Reform Survive the 1996 Elections?" *CSIS Africa Notes,* No. 175, August 1995.

15. Jeffries and Thomas, "The Ghanaian Elections of 1992," 356.

16. Carter Center, "Ghana Election Mission—Executive Summary," 6 November 1992.

17. Jeffries and Thomas, "The Ghanaian Elections of 1992," 354.

18. "Ghana: Last Chance Alliance," *Africa Confidential,* 29 March 1996, 6–7; Michela Wrong, "Ghana 1996: Rawlings Faces Tougher Test," *Financial Times,* 9 July 1996.

19. Richard Soudriette, "Ghana's Democracy Is a Good Model for Africa," *Washington Times,* 26 December 1996, A15.

20. See Larry Garber and Glenn Cowan, "The Virtues of Parallel Vote Tabulations," *Journal of Democracy* 4 (April 1993): 95–107.

21. On the fight for the nomination, see "Ghana: Last Chance Alliance," *Africa Confidential,* 29 March 1996, 6–7; and "Ghana: Together Against Jerry," *Africa Confidential,* 21 June 1996, 4–5.

22. National Democratic Institute, "Preliminary Statement by the NDI International Observer Delegation to the December 7 Elections in Ghana," 10 December 1996. Commonwealth Observer Group, "Interim Statement by the Chairperson, Sir Paul Reeves," 8 December 1996.

12

GHANA'S ELECTIONS: THE CHALLENGES AHEAD

E. Gyimah-Boadi

E. Gyimah-Boadi teaches political science at the University of Ghana, Legon, and is executive director of the Center for Democracy and Development, a think tank for democratic development based in Accra, Ghana. He was a fellow at both the Woodrow Wilson Center and the International Forum for Democratic Studies in Washington, D.C.

The Ghanaian elections of December 1996 raised two sorts of questions. The first were narrow but urgent: Would the electoral process be free, fair, and transparent? Would the outcome be broadly accepted rather than strongly disputed, as it had been in 1992? Happily, the predominant answer to this line of inquiry is yes. The presidential and parliamentary polling of December 7 went ahead peacefully; violence, though widely expected, never materialized. Moreover, the 1996 elections were freer and more transparent than those of 1992.

The second sort of questions are broader and harder to answer concisely; they will preoccupy us here. These questions ask whether the elections will advance, delay, or even reverse democratic progress; whether they will weaken or strengthen governmental accountability; whether the entrenched, neopatrimonial "party-state" will flourish or wither; whether the prospects for economic reform and renewal will wax or wane; whether civilian control over the military will grow or shrink; and whether the development of civil society and its participation in the political process will be fostered or not. Our responses to such queries can be at best tentative; they will also require a look at the four years following the return to constitutional rule in 1992.

The elections of 1992, though disputed, ushered in a period of modest but significant gains in democratic governance. These included political liberalization, allowing Ghanaians to enjoy a much wider range of rights and liberties and giving vibrant, privately owned media scope to emerge. The period also saw a modest improvement in governmental transparency and accountability—thanks to the new media as well as to the resumed publication of the Auditor General's Reports, the institution of parliamentary debate, and the increasing activism of constitutionally established watchdogs like the Media Commission and the presidentially appointed Commission on Human Rights and Administrative Justice (CHRAJ).

Renewed efforts to foster an environment conducive to economic growth and private-sector development also bore fruit. Constitutional provisions protecting private property were generally respected. With one exception, the state refrained from confiscations of private property, and the official commitment to economic renewal remained strong, despite increased popular pressure to reverse some reform measures.

Constitutional rule also opened a larger political space for civil society in Ghana. Civic associations and nongovernmental organizations (NGOs) proliferated. Many were devoted to the protection of human rights and the promotion of democratic governance. These included the Institute of Economic Affairs (IEA), the Ghana Legal Literacy and Resource Foundation, and the Ghana Committee on Human and People's Rights. Indeed, the years since 1992 have seen many initiatives by Ghanaian society to promote democratic development. Civic groups and public-interest organizations sought to improve the quality of analysis and deliberation in the National Assembly through memoranda and expert testimony, and some even attempted to mediate a dispute between President Jerry Rawlings and his vice-president. These society-based initiatives were not always welcomed by the ruling National Democratic Congress (NDC), but they bespoke a new level of independent societal involvement in politics.

Such achievements notwithstanding, the hope that 7 January 1993 would mark a fresh start in democratic governance was frustrated in many respects. In fact, Ghana's latest attempt at democratic governance began on a decidedly inauspicious note and faced a number of critical challenges. In the parliament that emerged from the elections, Rawlings's NDC and two allied parties held 198 out of 200 seats. Presidential nominees to key posts came under only the most casual legislative scrutiny, and the new government sought to pass illiberal laws.

Relations between the government and the extraparliamentary opposition turned highly acrimonious. Political society became polarized, with the NDC and its supporters at one end, and the older postcolonial elites at the other. The latter elites included figures from both of the two main pre-Rawlings political traditions—the conservative Kofi Busia–J.B. Danquah camp and the left-leaning Nkrumahist tendency—as well as former Rawlings supporters who had left the president's camp.

Relations between the government and key elements of civil society also reflected mistrust. Consensus remained elusive regarding such key questions as how best to promote direct investment and fund basic and tertiary education.

Ghana's economy began to falter. Economic growth decelerated. Macroeconomic imbalances reemerged, at least in part because of election-inspired public spending.[1] The enviable record of fiscal prudence compiled since the 1980s appeared to be in jeopardy. Paralyzing strikes and violent protests compelled the government to slow the pace of reform measures such as public-sector job retrenchments and caps on the growth of salaries and allowances. The newly enacted value-added tax was dropped. The Ghanaian economy, many analysts concluded, was headed "back to the intensive-care unit."[2]

The Fourth Republic's experiment in democratic governance seemed about to break down as violent ethnic and communal clashes erupted in many parts of the country, especially the northern regions, during 1994 and 1995. In the middle of the latter year, antigovernment demonstrations rocked the larger cities, killing at least five people and wounding several others. Meanwhile, a bitter falling-out between Rawlings and Vice-President Kow Nkensen Arkaah threatened to provoke a constitutional crisis.

It was against this background of unmet aspirations for enhanced democracy and renewed economic growth that Ghanaians began to prepare themselves for the next multiparty elections, slated for December 1996. These became the object of great expectations, especially as regards the revival and consolidation of political reform.

Positive Signs

The December 7 elections marked the first time in Ghanaian history that two multiparty elections had occurred under the same constitutional system. On the surface, Rawlings and opposition candidate John Kufuor appeared equally confident of winning. For a short while, there even appeared to be a slight but real chance that Rawlings might lose.

The rather hard-fought campaign produced an instant "democracy dividend." Accountability and transparency got a boost as Rawlings found himself compelled to campaign seriously, to defend his record, and to address some of the issues that his opponents raised. For instance, he conceded the truth of the widely heard criticism that, at a time of public-sector contraction and general austerity, his cabinet was bloated. He promised, if reelected, to employ fewer ministers. To refute widespread allegations of self-dealing and opacity in the process of state-enterprise divestiture, the government published a list of enterprises divested from 1 January 1995 to 31 July 1996, their new owners, the purchase prices charged, and the balances outstanding.[3] Indeed, President Rawlings made history of a sort when, in midcampaign, he broke his 15 years of silence toward the domestic media and granted a personal interview (including a public phone-in session) to a privately owned radio station.

Most significantly, the official outcome of the elections appears to have been broadly accepted. Opposition parties are looking toward the next elections, scheduled for the year 2000. This betokens both a belief that elections offer at least the possibility of winning office and a broad (albeit provisional) consensus that the ballot box is, in any case, the sole legitimate instrument for seeking power. Many of the candidates who had complaints about the 1996 results are seeking redress through the Electoral Commission and the judiciary instead of resorting to colorful but dubious tactics such as marching naked through the streets (as some female New Patriotic Party [NPP] supporters reportedly did in 1992).

The great improvements made in the electoral system since the last election and the presence of 60,000 party agents at polling stations on election day were crucial to the success of the 1996 elections. A share of the credit must go to civil society. Having played only a limited role in 1992, it emerged as a major player in the latest election. Determined to avoid the mistakes of 1992 and the bitter disputes that they engendered, and desiring to assert a stake in the electoral process, key elements of civil society mounted programs to support the election. Prominent national organizations such as the Christian Council, the Conference of Catholic Bishops, the Ghana Legal Literacy and Resource Foundation, and others undertook campaigns of voter education.

The epitome of societal involvement was the emergence—despite strong opposition from the ruling party—of two society-based domestic poll-watching bodies: Ghana Alert, led by veteran journalist Ben Ephson, and the Network of Domestic Election Observers (NEDEO), led by Joseph Kingsley-Nyinah, a retired Appeals Court judge and former Electoral Commission chairman. NEDEO comprised prominent national organizations such as the Christian Council, the Catholic Secretariat, the Federation of Muslim Councils, the Ahmadiyya Muslim Mission, the Ghana National Association of Teachers (GNAT), and the National Union of Ghana Students. The groups helped to mobilize most of the available domestic resources for nongovernmental election monitoring. In addition to selecting suitable personnel from their organizations for training and deployment as monitors, the member groups of NEDEO placed communications and transport equipment at the network's disposal.

The domestic poll-watching groups began preparing to monitor the elections as early as July, five months before the election. They were better placed than most international observers to monitor developments before, during, and after the voting. The IEA initiated a program that trained and deployed personnel to 35 key constituencies to observe and report on the preelection environment up to three months before polling day. It also commissioned a team based at the School of Communications of the University of Ghana to monitor the coverage of the election in the local media, both state-owned and private. But the domestic poll-watching groups' most ambitious efforts involved the training of election monitors at the national, regional, and district levels and their deployment to polling stations across the country on election day. In the end, more than 4,200 domestic monitors were deployed to polling stations.

All this presented a sharp contrast to 1992, when only about two hundred domestic monitors took part. At that time, the government and its agencies dominated the field, with external observers (including the African-American Institute, the Carter Center, the Commonwealth Secretariat, and so on) playing only a limited role. In 1996, local NGOs and civic organizations were heavily involved. Before the voting, they provided their own independent analyses of the situation to international observers. In 1996, moreover, a sizeable share of outside contributions for the support of democracy flowed to local NGOs and civic groups, whereas four years earlier the government had received almost all such funds. This funding shift was the second major factor in the growing sense of local ownership of the electoral-cum-democratization process and the leveling of the institutional playing field.

The full cooperation that the Electoral Commission gave to domestic election-observation groups, including complete access to Commission officials and facilities, did much to enhance both the election's transparency and the Commission's credibility. The Commission accredited domestic poll-watching groups and ensured their unhindered access to polling places. Such cooperative actions, combined with the ability of NEDEO to set up independent mechanisms for a crude parallel vote count, assisted efforts to check claims of fraud, deterred chicanery, and boosted public confidence in the voting and its outcome.

In 1992, the capital city of Accra had but a single FM radio station, which was government-owned. By the last quarter of 1996, Accra had a half-dozen privately owned FM stations. The independent print media, too, had become stronger. The active presence of these media, as well as court orders mandating equal opportunity for political-party broadcasts, helped to generate a high degree of public interest in the election and contributed greatly to the unprecedented 78 percent turnout. By providing channels of discourse outside the state's control—and by leading cheers for the opposition—these media were largely responsible for keeping the election somewhat competitive and saving opposition candidates from total despair about their chances against the incumbents, who had ample resources and the vocal support of the state-run media.

The campaign confirmed the presence of a modest consensus regarding at least the broad outlines of economic policy. The NDC ran largely on its economic record, openly embracing neoliberal economic reforms and the search for global markets and investments.[4] The opposition offered few if any clear alternatives, contenting itself with jabs at aspects of the Rawlings-NDC reforms such as "cash-and-carry" health care and cost-sharing in education. The platform of the NPP, the largest opposition party, hewed fairly closely to the NDC's neoliberal line, though it promised to strengthen the welfare content of reforms, offer more support to domestic investment, and restore fiscal discipline. In the heat of the campaign, opposition presidential candidate John Kufuor pledged that his government would retain Rawlings's *Vision 2020* economic-policy document.

The opposition vote in the presidential race was a solid 43 percent (Kufuor took almost 40 percent, and the remainder was split among minor candidates). Non-NDC representation in the National Assembly went from zero to 66 out of 200 seats. The government has close to a controlling (two-thirds) majority, but faces a bloc studded with opposition stalwarts. At a minimum, they should enliven parliamentary debate and bring future presidential appointments and proposed bills under more than casual scrutiny. Their presence on committees should help to improve policy making. Governmental accountability and transparency, never strong in the previous Assembly, should also get a boost.

Danger Signs

Nonetheless, a close look at the December 7 elections and the four years leading up to them reveals the persistence of formidable obstacles to democratic consolidation. Despite all the money that was spent and the extensive preparations that were made, the 1996 elections were marred by serious lapses.[5] The voter-registration figures alone are disturbing: How could 9.2 million voters be enrolled in a country with only about 17 million people, very many of whom are under age 15? Add to this the episodes that domestic monitors witnessed of voting by children, especially in remote areas, and the integrity of voter registration comes gravely into question. The relatively high incidence of rejected ballot papers, meanwhile, suggests inadequate voter education, while the evidence of polling stations that were badly lit or left vulnerable to the elements betrays poor preparation.

The elections of the 1990s have revealed a troubling pattern of bloc voting by region and ethnicity. The four main ethnolinguistic groups are the Akans (a designation that includes the important Ashanti subgroup), who all told make up 44 percent of the population; the Mole-Dagbani (16 percent); the Ewe (13 percent); and the Ga-Adangbe (8 percent). The Ewe predominate in Volta Region, the Mole-Dagbani are found mainly in the northern half of the country, and the Akans are concentrated most heavily in the south, center, and west. During the 1990s, bloc voting by Ewes has risen to levels not seen since 1969, when the National Alliance of Liberals, under the leadership of Ewe politician

Komla Gbedema, captured 14 of the 16 parliamentary seats available in Volta Region. Rawlings, whose father was a Scotsman, is an Ewe on his mother's side. His roots are in Volta. In 1992, he captured 93.2 percent of the vote in that region, his best showing. His opponent that year, the NPP's Albert Adu Boahen, won 60.5 percent of the vote in the NPP bastion of Ashanti Region. This pattern repeated itself in 1996, with Rawlings getting 94.5 percent of the vote in Volta and Kufuor making his strongest showing (65.8 percent) in his own home region, Ashanti.

It is likely that there is more than just ordinary communal solidarity at work here. The pattern of ethnoregional voting is at least in part a reflection of the parties' decision to play the "ethnic card." They have done so in different but disturbing ways. Only a handful of the leading figures in the 1996 opposition coalition, known as the Great Alliance, could claim Ewe origins. Its presidential ticket—Kufuor and his running mate, disaffected former Rawlings vice-president K.N. Arkaah—were both Akans. With the Great Alliance barely campaigning in Volta, the public use of ethnic taunts and slurs by some young NPP supporters reinforced the impression that the formation was a vehicle for Akan-Ashanti chauvinism.

While the NDC's campaign covered all ten of Ghana's regions, the most avid mining for votes was done in "stranger quarters"—those neighborhoods in many villages and towns where migrants from other regions of the country come to settle. In those cities where Akans are concentrated, the NDC courted non-Akans; in the countryside, migrant farmers were the targets of its appeals. NDC candidates and their operatives engaged in scare-mongering among migrant communities, suggesting that an NPP-dominated government would expel them, just as the Busia regime had expelled undocumented aliens several decades before. Ewes were told that only a vote for Rawlings could avert a return of Volta to its preindependence status as part of Togo. Rawlings may have been joking, but he hit a raw Akan nerve when he declared at a rally in Ho, Volta's capital, that the region was his "World Bank" of votes. Whatever the intention behind the president's remark, the lopsided nature of the pro-Rawlings vote in that region is bound to reinforce the widespread perception, especially among Akans, that the Rawlings regime harbors a strong pro-Ewe bias.[6]

Ghanaians of non-Ewe descent, Akans in particular, have been complaining bitterly (though usually behind closed doors and among their ethnic compatriots) about the lopsided voting in Volta. Some Ewes have been voicing embarrassment over the phenomenon, but again mainly in private. The present prevailing atmosphere, where stony public denial masks seething private resentment, can only be described as unhealthy. At best, it is delaying true national reconciliation. At worst, it is creating an environment in which the next election will assume even more fully the character of a sharp contest among rival ethnic groups. Pride in region and ethnicity is not about to disappear from the Ghanaian scene; how to combine it with competitive multiparty elections will remain a challenge.

Advantages and Drawbacks of Continuity

A second Rawlings-NDC victory could be said to help the cause of democratic transition in at least two ways. First, it may facilitate a smoother, if rather protracted, transition away from the quasi-militarized authoritarianism that Rawlings first rode to power. The continuity entailed by a second consecutive electoral triumph for the president and his party creates the opportunity for the gradual (and therefore, perhaps, more politically tenable) negotiation of the trickier passages in this transition. Members of Rawlings's Provisional National Defense Council (PNDC) and its affiliated paramilitary groups may be offered concrete guarantees of unlimited indemnity and "sunset" arrangements to ease their reintegration into "civilian" life.

The second advantage comes from the assurance of continuity in economic reform. The Rawlings administration can continue its infrastructure building and rehabilitation projects, and follow up on promising contacts with prospective foreign investors. There remains, however, the problem of promoting domestic private investment in the face of poor relations between the Rawlings regime and key elements of the local capitalist class. The president's preferred solution, it seems, has been to sponsor the creation of a new domestic capitalist class beholden to the regime, but this approach faces doubtful prospects.

Unfortunately, the continuities between an elected Rawlings administration and its military-authoritarian predecessor offer no advantages from the standpoint of democratic consolidation. The election of 1996 was only a second transitional election. As such, it did not satisfy the maximalist criterion for democratic consolidation, which requires that democracy become "so broadly and profoundly legitimate, and so habitually practiced and observed, that it is very unlikely to break down."[7] Perhaps more importantly, the election of 1996, like that of four years earlier, involved no change of government. At best, it was a case of an incumbent regime renewing its mandate to govern through the ballot box. The crucial test—a peaceful and orderly transfer of power to a new government that bests the incumbents in multiparty elections—remains to be passed.

The first democratically elected NDC administration was composed principally of holdovers from the PNDC era; new faces were few. As many as 13 out of the 34 substantive ministerial posts (including all the most influential portfolios) in the first post-PNDC government went to persons affiliated with the PNDC. In fact, many retained the same ministries that they had supervised under the PNDC regime, while others filled positions as top presidential advisors and staffers or as NDC party bosses.

Moreover, the exploitation of incumbency and the commandeering of state resources were key factors in the Rawlings-NDC victories in both 1992 and 1996. The playing field was not level in a contest in which the ruling party had cornered state resources, including the state print and electronic media,[8] and the opposition parties had only the very weak private sector to rely on for resources. The NDC's campaign was a lavish affair. Its billboards were splashed around the country; its fleet of 250 campaign vehicles outnumbered the opposition's five to one. It sustained a months-long blitz of slick advertising, and reportedly threw plenty of money around (where the money came from is largely a mystery).

With no mechanisms in place to enforce postelection accountability, the NDC has no reason to abandon questionable methods of mobilizing its war chest in future elections. It appears that Rawlings and his followers have simply traded mastery at coup-making for mastery at election-winning; the NDC could become a frozen-in-place majority party, driving the opposition to despair of the ballot box as a route to power.

Another concern is the further entrenchment of an undemocratic political culture left over from the PNDC's heyday. It is far from reassuring to note that the newly elected NDC government seems bent on continuing to celebrate the anniversaries of the "uprising" of 4 June 1979 and the coup of 31 December 1981 as national holidays. All this can only heighten the alienation of political opponents and retard the process of national reconciliation. When the Supreme Court recently upheld an opposition lawsuit seeking to bar the celebration of December 31 as a national holiday, the president responded with an intimidating outburst, claiming that the courts were staging a coup against the other branches of government.

At bottom, the NDC retains attitudes derived from the early years of the authoritarian PNDC era. That was a time when subversives seemed to lurk in every corner, and several countercoups had to be defeated. The party operates like a former national-liberation movement, akin to Robert Mugabe's Zimbabwe African National Union. There is little intraparty democracy. In about 70 cases in 1996, the results of parliamentary primaries were overturned by NDC higher-ups. Rawlings remains the "supreme leader"; in most cases, it seems, his word is final. Loyalty to the leader and the party are esteemed above all. Principled dissent is severely frowned upon.

The political liberalization of the last four years did not encompass the separation of the state from the ruling party. Departments in some ministries, including the Education Ministry and the state media (especially the *Ghanaian Times*), are practically colonies of the NDC. Some of these bureaucracies were established during PNDC days: Their chiefs are holdovers from that period, and nearly every official in them of middling to higher rank has ties to the PNDC "revolution." There are reported cases of resources allocated to such departments for their regular functions being diverted to NDC political tasks. Editors of the *Ghanaian Times* and other state-owned newspapers have continued to propagandize in favor of the NDC government while spewing venom at its perceived opponents.

There is also a high degree of fusion between the NDC regime and key parastatals such as the ubiquitous Ghana National Petroleum Corporation (GNPC), the Ghana National Procurement Agency, the National Mobilisation Programme, the Social Security and National Insurance Trust (SSNIT), and several state-owned banks run by PNDC-era appointees. The officials who manage these bodies know that their tenure depends on the NDC; they line up alongside the ruling party with varying degrees of openness, and some have served as top political advisors to the regime. By accident or design, some of these government-aligned parastatals, notably GNPC and SSNIT, are also some of the most active institutional investors in the state companies now undergoing privatization. The strong relationship between the heads of such parastatals and the NDC creates possibilities for self-dealing, and gives the NDC huge advantages in building an electoral war chest.

The 110 rural district assemblies and the 110 presidentially appointed district chief executives supposedly have nothing to do with partisan politics, yet are fused with NDC political structures. Many "bush governors" hold appointments dating back to the late 1980s and have close ties to the minister of local government (a key NDC political operative) and the old authoritarian instruments of mobilization such as the 31st of December Women's Movement, the Association of Committees for the Defense of the Revolution, and other groups. Along with the party hierarchy and many traditional rulers, this array of people and organizations constitutes the political machine that makes Rawlings and the NDC so strong in the countryside. This strength, in other words, comes not simply from the regime's record of rural development, but flows in at least equal measure from the resilient clientelist network that the PNDC developed in the late 1980s and nurtured into the 1990s.[9]

The continued fusion of party and state suggests that political liberalization has failed to bring such democratic essentials as separation of powers or checks and balances to Ghanaian political life. That there has been no alternation in power is all the more significant in view of the military antecedents of the incumbent regime. The PNDC may have been unconventional as military regimes go, but it was undergirded by an extensive paramilitary security and police apparatus controlled politically, along with the regular army, through mostly informal and personalized channels. Rawlings and his chief national-security advisor, Kojo Tsikata (like the president, a former military officer), have been at the helm. These agencies, once subjected to no public oversight, now receive only slight oversight.

The return to constitutional rule has so far done little or nothing to bring Ghana's military and security establishment into conformity with democratic standards. The question of the military's proper role under democracy has been broached, but only indirectly and with great circumspection, at IEA seminars featuring visiting U.S. military officers and academic experts on civil-military relations. With Rawlings as commander-in-chief, Tsikata (a member of the Council of State) as his unofficial security advisor, and Defense Minister Alhaji M. Iddrisu in office ten years now and counting, the military command structure remains largely unchanged.

Parliamentary oversight of military and security agencies has been extremely superficial. The chairman of the Committee on Defense and Interior, a retired army colonel, has been highly accommodating to the Ministry of Defense.[10] In general, the Committee has agreed with the defense minister's insistence that his budget is a national-security document that should be mostly shielded from public scrutiny or debate.

Military and security arrangements dating from the period before competitive elections have largely persisted since 1992. In theory, the old PNDC-sponsored paramilitary units have been disbanded or integrated into the regular military. In practice, this has been only partly accomplished; the paramilitaries have mostly gone underground, resurfacing occasionally to act against opponents of the government.[11]

The 1996 campaign period saw a number of ominous reminders of the stick that lurks behind the facade of democracy in contemporary Ghana, and the distance that must be traversed before civilian supremacy is achieved. Two months before the elections, the veteran head of the Bureau of National Investigations, one of the dreaded security organs of the PNDC era, was appointed to head the national police. In the military high command, the positions of Ewe officers appeared to have been strengthened at the expense of Akan officers.[12] A pro-Rawlings group published misleading newspaper advertisements calling attention to what it claimed were antimilitary statements by opposition stalwarts.

Civil Society and Consolidation

While civil society has developed substantially since 1992, it continues to suffer severe handicaps. Civic groups in Ghana are enthusiastic, but beset by organizational and financial shortcomings. They depend heavily on external agencies for funding, and sometimes for moral or political support. Domestic election-observation groups, for instance, depended almost completely on foreign donors. NEDEO had a strong human-resource base, but little money of its own, slender material resources, and no experience in something as massive and complex as monitoring an election. NEDEO could not have trained and deployed its monitors, or collated reports on the election, without the generous funding it received from the U.S. Agency for International Development and the National Democratic Institute.

Yet such dependence was not an unmixed blessing. The prospect (or hope) of individual organizations' receiving their own donor money and being able to report directly to their external backers seems to have provoked factionalism, turf battles, and one-upmanship among civic groups. Credibility, efficiency, and democracy-building all suffered. At the same time, NEDEO also survived in part because donors preferred to give to a coalition of observers rather than to individual groups.

Negative official attitudes have also inhibited the growth of civil society. The NDC government is openly hostile to organizations not under its control, especially if they are not apolitical. The government was happy to invite international election observers, but objected vehemently to the presence of domestic observers. Its agents attempted to compromise the domestic observer groups, especially NEDEO. They opposed the Electoral Commission's decision to grant accreditation to domestic observer groups, and made outrageous demands that NEDEO change its name and drop key members (such as the Christian Council, the Catholic Secretariat, and GNAT) deemed to oppose the government. The entire domestic observation process was threatened when the government publicly contemplated forming an alternative network of domestic election observers out of NDC-aligned groups unless NEDEO agreed to bring such groups under its umbrella.

Some of NEDEO's member groups (including the Christian Council, the Catholic Secretariat, GNAT, and the Ghana Union Traders' Association) had a long history of struggles with the state—a circumstance that reinforced the NDC's erroneous perception that NEDEO was partisan. The problem derives largely from Ghana's prevailing political culture, in which dissent is often viewed as treason and government officials are not used to the presence of countervailing domestic forces. NEDEO broadened itself to include Muslim and other organizations not normally seen as anti-NDC, and carefully selected and trained its monitors, but this availed little in the government's eyes. In the event, with domestic-observer reports favorable to the incumbent, the regime decided to tolerate NEDEO, and did not arrest or detain any domestic observers (as President Frederick Chiluba had done after the 1996 elections in Zambia).

Tasks Remaining

Despite its unpromising beginnings, Ghana's experiment in democratic governance has survived into its fifth year—a record for Ghana as well as for many other African countries. The first four years brought marked political liberalization and advances in democratic governance, suggesting that even a flawed transition can set the stage for democratic progress. The widely acclaimed success of the 1996 elections shows that an electoral system (and an Electoral Commission) with suspect origins can become credible enough to produce an outcome that meets with broad public acceptance. Finally, the continued, if somewhat diluted, official commitment to economic renewal and accelerated investment promotion indicates that democratic reform is not necessarily inimical to economic renewal.

Ghana's experience, however, also shows that keeping democratic transitions on track is costly. It takes a considerable amount of donor support to construct a credible electoral system and help build an efficacious civil society. Most of all, the Ghanaian experiment underscores the intractable problems of democratic consolidation and deepening that lie beyond successful multiparty elections and mere democratic survival. The modes and orders of authoritarianism may linger despite political liberalization; replacing them with the norms and institutions of democracy is a slow and arduous affair.

Consolidating existing gains in democratic governance over the course of the next Rawlings administration will be extremely difficult, in spite of a stronger opposition presence in parliament, a resurgent civil society, and a vibrant independent press. The opposition parties, like other key institutions of democratic politics, remain weak. Civil society does not yet present a strong countervailing force to the state. The independent media continue to struggle with an unfriendly legal system, slender resources, and government machinations designed to circumvent constitutional guarantees of free speech. The courts have expanded the scope of the country's already strict criminal-libel laws, and have shown themselves eager to punish journalists who run afoul of the powers that be. Official attitudes toward watchdog agencies such as CHRAJ and the Media Commission have ranged from lukewarm to plainly hostile.

Clearly, Rawlings and his NDC government are not inclined to enhance transparency and accountability. There is little in civil society or the Constitution capable of compelling a significant degree of governmental openness. And against the background of continuity in the executive branch and the government's controlling majority in parliament, the party-state and all its neopatrimonial habits and trappings are likely to persist.

The conclusion is clear: For its democratic progress to continue, Ghana needs stronger opposition parties, a more securely independent press, and a more vibrant civil society, as well as constitutional bodies (the courts, the CHRAJ, and the Media Commission, for instance) that can restrain undemocratic governmental impulses.

NOTES

1. Nii Sowa, *Adjustment in Africa: Lessons from Ghana* (Overseas Development Institute Briefing Paper No. 3, London, England, July 1996).

2. Michael Holman and Michela Wrong, "Ghana 1996: An African Trailblazer Begins to Falter," *Financial Times* (London), 9 July 1996; see also Todd J. Moss and David G. Williams, "Can Ghana's Economic Reform Survive the 1996 Elections?" *CSIS Africa Notes,* No. 175, August 1995.

3. See *Daily Graphic* (Accra), 5 September 1996, 10–11.

4. See the NDC's 1996 election manifesto, "Moving Ghana Forward," printed as a supplement in *Daily Graphic,* 1 October 1996; and the presidential report to parliament of 6 January 1995, entitled *Ghana—Vision 2020, The First Step: 1996–2000* (Accra: Government Printer, 1995).

5. It has not been possible for me to get the full details of funding for the elections and their sources. My own estimates suggest external funding of between $12 and $15 million for Electoral Commission activities. Partial details of external funding for the Commission are provided in Kwasi Afriyie Badu and John Larvie, *Elections in Ghana 1996,* Part 1 (Accra: Electoral Commission of Ghana and Friedrich Ebert Foundation, 1996), 75–76.

6. Albert Adu Boahen, *The Ghanaian Sphinx: Reflections on the Contemporary History of Ghana, 1972–1987* (Accra: Academy of Arts and Sciences Press, 1989).

7. This maximalist definition is from Larry Diamond, Juan J. Linz, and Seymour Martin Lipset's introduction to *Politics in Developing Countries: Comparing Experiences with Democracy* (Boulder, Colo.: Lynne Rienner, 1995), 53.

8. There was a clear pro-NDC bias in news coverage and editorial opinion in the state-controlled print and electronic media—though the opposition parties had equal opportunity in the holding of press conferences and to broadcast on Ghana Television.

9. For a recent analysis of the PNDC-NDC rural political machine, see Paul Nugent, *Big Men, Small Boys and Politics in Ghana* (Accra: Asempa Press, 1995).

10. He apparently believes that there is sufficient accountability and transparency in the internal process involved in the drawing up of budget estimates within the military. See E.K.D. Anku-Tsede, "Defense Budgeting: Accountability and Transparency, the Experience of Ghana in the Fourth Republic, 1993–1996" (paper presented at a conference on "The Military and Civil Society in Africa," sponsored by the Africa Leadership Forum, Lilongwe, Malawi, 23–25 September 1996).

11. The Association of Committees for the Defense of the Revolution had reportedly been used to quell antigovernment riots in Accra in May 1995. "Kume preko—Kill Me Now!" *Africa Confidential,* 26 May 1995, 1–2.

12. *Africa Now,* October 1996, D3.

13

KENYA TRIES AGAIN

Joel D. Barkan & Njuguna Ng'ethe

Joel D. Barkan, professor of political science at the University of Iowa, was a senior fellow at the United States Institute of Peace in 1997–98. In 1992–93, he served as the regional democracy and governance advisor for Eastern and Southern Africa at USAID. Njuguna Ng'ethe is senior research fellow at the Institute for Development Studies at the University of Nairobi. From 1993 to 1996, he served as the first director of the Institute for Policy Analysis and Research (IPAR) in Nairobi.

The lesson that one election does not a democracy make was painfully learned by Kenyans in December 1992 when their country held its first multiparty elections in 26 years, but continued to be ruled by an *ancien régime* that was returned to power with barely one-third of the vote.[1] Compared to the decade preceding the elections, during which Kenyans endured a combination of kleptocratic dictatorship and declining income, the period that followed was marked by substantial political liberalization and modest economic advance—but not democratization or full-scale economic renewal. Indeed, the return to multiparty politics resulted in a protracted five-year stalemate pitting President Daniel arap Moi and his ruling party, the Kenya African National Union (KANU), against an increasingly divided opposition.

That stalemate might now be broken, but it is hard to predict whether it will give way to an increasingly intense struggle between Moi and his opponents—possibly even leading to civil war—or to wide-ranging negotiations that establish the constitutional framework for democracy. On 29–30 December 1997, Kenyans went to the polls again in an exercise that many hope will prove a turning point in their country's torturous transition to democratic rule. Although the outcome was similar to 1992, with Moi and KANU besting a divided opposition, the process of democratization and the groups that drive it were reinvigorated to a degree that would have seemed impossible even six months earlier. This is particularly true of civil society, which now occupies a pivotal position in Kenyan politics.

A perpetual theme of Kenya's democratic transition, like its desultory efforts at macroeconomic reform, is that reform has been the product of domestic and international pressure upon a resistant government. Calls for a return to multiparty politics were first voiced domestically in 1989. Moi stonewalled them until December 1991, relenting only after international donors suspended $350 million in "quick-disbursing" aid.[2] Moi's acceptance of reform was—and is—purely tactical. His strategy then was to amend the Constitution to permit the existence of more than one political party, with the idea of harassing or bribing the leaders of any new parties until splits occurred or key members defected to KANU. Moi would go on ruling much as before, but at the head of an emerging one-party-dominant system with enough democratic trappings to satisfy the donors.

Moi appointed all 11 members of the Electoral Commission, thus compromising its independence. Even more controversial, he forced through a second constitutional amendment that required any presidential candidate to win not only a plurality or majority of the popular vote, but also at least 25 percent in no fewer than five of Kenya's eight provinces. This was meant to wreck the presidential prospects of popular opposition figures, particularly politicians such as Mwai Kibaki, Kenneth Matiba, and Oginga Odinga, who drew the bulk of their support from their ethnic homelands. With their support concentrated in Nairobi, Central Province, some sections of the Rift Valley, and Nyanza, they could not hope to clear this hurdle.

The run-up to the 1992 elections and the outcome went according to Moi's plan. The opposition split into three major and six minor parties. Although the voting itself was administered passably well, and although both domestic and international observers stated that the outcomes reflected the preferences of the electorate, the entire period before the elections was one of continual state harassment of the opposition.

Most sinister was Moi's self-fulfilling prophecy that multipartism would lead to "tribal conflict" because opposition parties would become vehicles for tribal interests. Throughout 1992, there were "ethnic clashes" in which mysterious "raiders" attacked members of those groups (especially though not exclusively the Kikuyu) that formed the core of the opposition's support. These attacks, which occurred mainly in minority ethnic areas of the Rift Valley Province, left more than 1,500 people dead and a quarter of a million homeless. Private death squads, acting on the orders of KANU hard-liners close to the president, were widely held to be responsible.

Within days of Moi's 1992 win came the shutdown of the limited political opening that he had permitted during the campaign. Although the opposition parties had won 88 of the 188 elected seats in the 200-member National Assembly, Moi began his fourth presidential term as if nothing had changed. He refused to engage opposition MPs in the legislative process. KANU as a party followed suit, though it had to tolerate opposition critiques of government policy.

The opposition, in its turn, refused to recognize Moi as the legitimate leader of government, or to engage KANU. Opposition leaders, claiming that "rigging" had cost them victory, cried simply that "Moi must go!" while also refusing to engage one another. Within a few years, two of the principal opposition parties had each split in two, while several leaders of the third had defected to KANU. Moi both abetted and enjoyed the spectacle.

Though splintered, the opposition did not disappear. In marked contrast to what had happened in Kenya and most of the rest of postcolonial Africa during the 1960s, neither defections to the ruling party nor any other government efforts could make the opposition fold.[3] From 1993 through 1996, the regime "persuaded" 24 opposition MPs to defect to KANU,[4] triggering a constitutional provision under which a legislator who switches parties in midterm must face a special by-election. Out of 29 such elections, KANU gained only 12 seats. As 1997 approached, the opposition was thus weaker but still standing with 76 Assembly seats.[5]

1997: Déjà Vu?

With elections on the horizon, Moi began preparing to repeat 1992. In late 1996, he reshuffled his cabinet to strengthen the hard-liners who opposed both further democratization and full implementation of the IMF-approved economic-reform program. The leaders of this group, which came to be known as KANU-B, were Vice-President George Saitoti and Energy and Natural Resources Minister Nicholas Biwott, both widely seen as among the regime's most corrupt figures. Opposition leaders allege that the latter is also the mastermind behind the ethnic clashes. The elevation of the hard-liners also revealed the emerging struggle within KANU over the succession to Moi, who is constitutionally barred from running again in 2002. Those demoted in the reshuffle included so-called moderates and pragmatists such as Simeon Nyachae, who had been minister of agriculture and who is known to covet Moi's job. This faction acquired the label KANU-A.

Continuing the widely disliked practice of entrusting election administration to officials handpicked by himself, Moi reappointed 7 of 11 Electoral Commission members, including the chair. Opposition leaders and representatives of the international donor community had argued since 1992 that Kenya's electoral process would be compromised until the Commission became truly independent and included opposition members. The reappointments signaled that Moi and his hard-liners, deaf to such appeals, were ready to take an "in your face" attitude toward critics and were set to replay the 1992 strategy. Because international donors had been relatively quiescent throughout most of the interelection period and had resumed "quick-disbursing" aid in 1994, Moi felt secure in ignoring their calls for a more level playing field.

One of the new Commission's first acts was to draw up 210 constituencies, an increase of 22 over 1992. While the additional constituencies were distributed across all provinces in a rough approximation of their relative population, Nairobi received none. Even though the capital region had Kenya's highest population growth, KANU had won only one of its eight seats in the previous election. As in 1992, and indeed as in every election since 1961 and 1963 (when the British drew the constituencies), the number of inhabitants varied greatly from one constituency to another.[6] The purpose, now as then, has always been to overrepresent the members of Kenya's smallest and most spatially dispersed ethnic groups by giving them more constituencies than the larger and more concentrated groups receive. The former groups, such as the Kalenjin, Masai, Turkana, Somalis, and Majikenda, reside mainly in the Rift Valley, Northeastern, and Coast provinces. They have been the core of Moi's support and that of his allies for more than 30 years.[7]

Save for complaints about the failure to allocate more seats to Nairobi, opposition leaders virtually ignored malapportionment in both 1992 and 1997. Yet had opposition leaders done their arithmetic, they would have discovered that KANU's *parliamentary* majority of 1992 (as contrasted with Moi's victory) was due as much or more to the systematic overrepresentation of KANU voters than it was to the divided state of the opposition majority. In most of the constituencies where the winner took a large (65 to 90 percent) majority, that majority was highly concentrated geographically. In other words, it did not matter whether one or many opposition candidates ran in most KANU-dominated constituencies, for such constituencies were set up to be "sure things" for the ruling party. This led one observer to predict that continuing this practice in 1997 would let KANU win another parliamentary majority with a minority of the total vote.[8]

Most troubling was a significant increase in state harassment of opposition leaders during the first half of 1997. Opposition MPs were denied rally permits, blocked from entering certain districts, and had their campaign meetings disrupted. In several instances, prominent opposition leaders such as Paul Muite suffered physical assault by the police. The government also targeted civil society organizations, especially those with active civic and voter education programs, which were ominously described as possible threats to "the security of the state." A new opposition party, Safina, was denied registration.

These tactics, plus the increasing opposition fragmentation, demoralized many Kenyans. Some said that they would not register or vote, preferring to wait until the next election cycle in 2002. Some major opposition leaders, most notably Kenneth Matiba, the second-leading vote getter in 1992 and the head of the Forum for the Restoration of Democracy–Asili (FORD-A), promised a boycott. Several knowledgeable observers predicted that KANU might win as many as 135 seats in the National Assembly. With 12 seats to be filled by presidential appointment, KANU would then enjoy (if just barely) a two-thirds majority and the power to amend the Constitution on its own. Notwithstanding these predictions, 9.1 million Kenyans, or 70 percent of the voting-age population, had registered by the end of June, the same percentage as in 1992.

The Quest for Constitutional Reform

Faced with almost certain defeat because of their inability to unite behind a single slate, opposition leaders nevertheless agreed on the need for fundamental constitutional reforms. This became the opposition's rallying cry. By year's end, it would change the political landscape.

The call for constitutional reform was voiced first in 1995, when a group of reformist lawyers published a proposal for a new Kenyan constitution in the *Nairobi Law Monthly*.[9] Their basic thrust was greatly to reduce the president's power vis-à-vis the National Assembly. In addition, the reformists called for a comprehensive bill of rights and a reduction in the powers of the Provincial Administration—the instrument of state harassment, and under Moi's direct command. Opposition-party leaders backed this initial call for a new constitution, but the sustained push for constitutional reform came from civil society.

In classic fashion, Moi publicly alternated between endorsing the idea of constitutional change and contending that it was not needed. He announced that he would appoint a task force to study the matter, but never did. Fearing how Moi and KANU might rewrite the Constitution after a big victory at the polls, both civil society and the opposition demanded that reform occur *before* the 1997 balloting. Led by the Citizens' Coalition for Constitutional Change (popularly known as the "4 Cs") and other nongovernmental organizations (NGOs), and joined by Kenneth Matiba and the leaders of two other opposition parties, a National Convention Executive Council (NCEC) was formed to convene a National Constitutional Assembly (NCA) similar to those held in Francophone Africa during the early 1990s. The plan was straightforward: threaten to boycott the elections, and take the debate to the streets through mass demonstrations and civil disobedience.

Consistent with its longstanding strategy, the KANU government refused any dialogue with the NCEC and tried to repress the reformers.

Moi said that while he accepted in principle the need for constitutional changes, such changes could be negotiated only *after* the elections and only by parliament, home to the "true representatives" of the Kenyan people and a forum that the president expected to control. In the meantime, he warned, his government would deal firmly with anyone who provoked disorder.

Moi's tactics soon led to the confrontation that both sides wanted. Denied a permit to hold a rally at Uhuru Park in downtown Nairobi, the NCEC leaders went ahead anyway on 7 July 1997. They were teargassed, and several, along with their supporters, were beaten senseless by riot police. The scene, soon broadcast to the world by CNN, shocked many Kenyans, angered the donor community, and gained Kenya unwanted notoriety. Between 20 and 25 people died in Nairobi and at other rallies around the country. The battle lines were now clearly drawn, and the government had come out the loser. In the court of public opinion, both domestic and foreign, Moi had been put on the defensive for the first time since he had been forced to legalize the opposition in 1991.

Moi and the hard-liners also stonewalled the IMF on macroeconomic reform, particularly the issue of ending corruption by senior regime figures. At the end of July, the Fund responded by suspending its $220 million Enhanced Structural Adjustment Facility (ESAF) program. The World Bank and certain bilateral donors followed suit, pushing the withheld-aid figure to over $400 million. This was more than the total amount of aid suspended in 1991, and quickly led to a massive flight of short-term private investment and a 25 percent drop in the value of the Kenyan shilling. The government's recalcitrance on corruption, like its resistance to constitutional reform, was a gross miscalculation that played into the hands of the opposition. Although neither the IMF nor the Bank was particularly concerned with the need for political reform, bilateral donors, led by the United States, publicly urged the government to open a dialogue with the opposition.

In a final and tragic replay of 1992, a new round of "ethnic clashes" occurred in late August. The killings, on the coast south of Mombasa, pushed Kenya to the brink. The victims were "foreigners from upcountry," primarily Kikuyu and Luo residents who opposed the ruling party. As in 1992, regime hard-liners were behind the attacks, a fact that was underscored by orders to the army not to intervene. Approximately 65 people were killed, with 10,000 left homeless. Tourism in the coastal region fell by roughly half, depriving Kenya of needed foreign exchange and throwing hundreds out of work. As in 1992, the attacks provoked a broad-based response by the opposition parties and civil society—including the Catholic Church and the (Anglican) Church of the Province of Kenya—as well as the donor community. All demanded reform, fearing that Kenya, like some of its neighbors, might descend into civil war.

The Emergence of the IPPG

With the polity and the economy unraveling and pressure from the international community and the opposition rising, Moi beat a tactical retreat. Realizing that his own legitimation hinged on getting most if not all of the opposition parties to take part in the elections, the president conceded the necessity of constitutional reform before the poll. Listening now to the pragmatists of KANU-A, he turned away from the hard-liners who had undercut his position. For the first time, he agreed to negotiate with the opposition, albeit on a highly circumscribed basis. First, talks would be limited to the crafting of "minimal" reforms, i.e., those demanded by the opposition to create a "level playing field" for the elections and guarantee their participation. Fundamental issues such as the powers of the presidency vis-à-vis the legislature, the devolution of authority to local or regional government, and the redesign of the electoral system would all have to wait until after the elections, although Moi did agree to legislation creating a constitutional-review commission. Second, negotiations would take place within parliament, not the NCA sought by civil society. Third, there would be no talk about getting rid of the "25-percent-in-five-provinces" requirement for winning the presidency.

Moi's strategy split the reformers, but still produced a package that went farther than he or his advisors intended. Led by maverick opposition MP George Anyona, a former detainee who had not joined any of the three main opposition parties in 1992, a group of 30 to 40 opposition legislators joined with 70 to 80 moderate KANU back-benchers to form the Inter-Parties Parliamentary Group (IPPG). The size of the group varied daily as negotiations proceeded through September. Its purpose was to defuse the political crisis by staking out the middle ground between the opposition NCEC leaders, whose concepts of reform were extensive and who remained committed to civil disobedience and an election boycott, and the KANU hard-liners who had precipitated the troubles.

Moi delayed on enacting the IPPG package into law, but ultimately did so after coming under pressure from the international community, particularly the United States. The reforms, as passed by the National Assembly in late October and early November, contained the following provisions:

• The addition of ten opposition representatives to the Electoral Commission.

• The repeal or amendment of laws used by the Provincial Administration and the police to prevent candidates from campaigning freely around the country.

• The immediate registration of all unregistered political parties, including Safina.

• The establishment of a separate independent court to hear all petitions and complaints regarding alleged election irregularities.

• Amendment of the Kenya Broadcasting Corporation Act to require balanced coverage of all candidates.

• Repeal or amendment of the sedition laws, the legal basis for government harassment of the press and civil society.

• Repeal of the constitutional provision declaring that only ruling-party MPs may serve as cabinet ministers (this cleared the way for the formation of a coalition government).

• Agreement that the 12 presidentially appointed seats in parliament would be filled proportionally from among all parties in parliament, rather than solely from the ruling party.

• Agreement to establish a constitutional-review commission after the elections.

Although the IPPG package did not fundamentally change Kenya's constitutional framework, it was significant in at least three ways. First, the negotiations themselves marked the first time that KANU and the opposition had engaged each other since the return to multiparty politics in 1991. The participants felt good about the exercise, a healthy sign in a fledgling democracy. Irreconcilables in both KANU and reformist ranks grumbled about the IPPG, but the vital center on which democracies are founded had finally emerged.

Second, the reforms cleared the way for a more equal conduct of the 1997 elections. Although it was too late for them to match KANU's levels of funding and organization, all the opposition parties except Matiba's FORD-A decided to participate. Beating Moi was out of the question, but mounting an effective parliamentary challenge to KANU was not.

Third, the reinvigoration of the opposition and civil society as a result of the struggle for constitutional reform suggested that the sands were starting to shift under the regime. Although civil society failed to force Moi and KANU to accept a constitutional assembly, it did bring them to the bargaining table. In the process, civil society broadened its organizational base. Opposition parties, human rights NGOs, and, most significantly, the Catholic and Protestant churches had worked together as never before to challenge the regime. There was now a real prospect that this coalition might play a more active and decisive role in advancing democratization during, and especially following, the elections.

The Electoral Interlude

The balloting itself produced few surprises. Nineteen political parties nominated 15 candidates for the presidency and 887 candidates for

TABLE—Presidential Elections in Kenya, 1992 and 1997
(Percentage of Vote by Province)

Candidates	Total '92	'97	Nairobi '92	'97	Central '92	'97	Eastern '92	'97	Coast '92	'97	North-Eastern '92	'97	Rift Valley '92	'97	Western '92	'97	Nyanza '92	'97
Moi (KANU)	36	41	17	21	2	6	37	35	62	63	78	73	66	69	40	46	14	24
Matiba (FORD-A)	26	—	44	—	60	—	11	—	11	—	11	—	19	—	38	—	2	—
Kibaki (DP)	19	31	19	44	36	89	50	28	10	13	3	21	8	21	3	1	7	15
Ngilu (SDP)	—	8	—	11	—	3	—	33	—	9	—	1	—	1	—	1	—	2
Odinga (NDP)	17	11	20	16	1	1	2	1	16	6	8	—	6	2	18	2	76	57
Wamalwa (FORD-K)	—	8	—	7	—	0	—	1	—	3	—	5	—	6	—	48	—	2
Turnout as % of registered voters:	68	68	56	50	84	75	62	72	48	51	41	56	76	76	63	67	63	68

Average number of voters in the 107 parliamentary constituencies won by KANU: 36,350
Average number of voters in the 103 parliamentary constituencies won by the opposition: 53,387

the 210 elected National Assembly seats. In addition, more than 8,000 candidates stood for 2,955 local-council seats. The presidential results by province and compared to those for 1992 are summarized in the Table on the previous page.

The 1997 turnout, as in 1992, was 68 percent—higher than expected given the widespread predictions that disillusionment over the opposition's fragmentation would keep many Kenyans away from the polls. Indeed, the only significant declines in turnout occurred in Nairobi and Central Province, places won in 1992 by FORD-A's Kenneth Matiba and where his 1997 boycott calls appear to have found a hearing.

The relatively strong turnout may reflect the success of the IPPG. In contrast to the period before the passage of the IPPG reforms, candidates campaigned freely, while civil society organizations were permitted to conduct voter education and to train more than 28,000 domestic observers. Police and Provincial Administration officials, once instruments of state harassment, now facilitated the campaign process. In what may have been the most comprehensive domestic observation of an African election, observers were posted at nearly all of Kenya's 12,600 polling stations and at each counting station to monitor the tabulation of the votes. This pervasive observer presence may also have helped the turnout.

The relatively strong turnout, marked by long lines of patient voters, is particularly significant given that the election was the worst-run in Kenyan history.[10] Fifty-six percent of polling stations opened two or more hours late, forcing the Electoral Commission to add a second day of voting. Local and international observers did not deem these problems serious enough to affect the final results, however, since foul-ups occurred with equal frequency in both KANU and opposition strongholds. Most serious observers found the Electoral Commission merely incompetent, not corrupt.

Only 5 of the 15 presidential candidates were serious contenders. In addition to Moi, there were former vice-president Mwai Kibaki (Democratic Party), Raila Odinga (National Development Party [NDP]), Kijana Wamalwa (Forum for the Restoration of Democracy–Kenya [FORD-K]), and Charity Ngilu (Social Democratic Party[SDP]). As in 1992, Moi garnered a nationwide plurality by winning large majorities in his traditional bastions of Coast, Northeastern, and Rift Valley provinces, and by making a strong showing in Western Province, where he lost narrowly to Wamalwa. Moi alone cleared the 25 percent threshold in five provinces (his narrow plurality in Eastern Province was key). Most significantly, he raised his vote share by 5 points over 1992's figure of 36 percent, with his greatest, albeit modest, gains coming in such opposition strongholds as Central Province, Nairobi, and Nyanza.

Mwai Kibaki, who had finished third in 1992 with 19.5 percent, was the 1997 runner-up with 31 percent as a result of Matiba's boycott. Like Matiba, Kibaki drew most of his strength from his fellow Kikuyu, who live mainly in Nairobi and Central Province and in pockets of the Rift Valley, and from related groups such as the Embu and Meru in Eastern Province. He nevertheless failed to inherit most of the Matiba vote outside of Central Province, Kibaki's home region. Indeed, his total vote was more than 600,000 votes below the combined total for himself and Matiba in 1992. Kibaki's candidacy was also hurt by Charity Ngilu, the first woman to campaign nationwide for the presidency. An MP from Eastern Province and a former member of Kibaki's Democratic Party, she entered the race to block Moi from passing the 25 percent threshold in her home province. She failed, but her presence in the race reduced Kibaki's percentage from 50 to 28 percent as they divided the anti-Moi vote. Ngilu also appears to have cut into Kibaki's vote in Nairobi and Central Province.

Negotiations over comprehensive constitutional reform could lay the foundation for bringing the democratic transition to a successful conclusion.

The two remaining major candidates, Raila Odinga and Kijana Wamalwa, had both been MPs from the same party, FORD-K, one of the three principal opposition parties that challenged Moi and KANU in 1992. Following the death of Jaramogi Oginga Odinga, Raila's father and the first leader of FORD-K, Raila Odinga and Wamalwa headed rival factions that ultimately split the party in two. They then divided the original FORD-K vote along provincial lines with Odinga winning his home province of Nyanza as the candidate of the NDP, and Wamalwa winning narrowly in his homeland, Western Province, as the candidate of what remained FORD-K. But even in Nyanza, the younger Odinga ran nearly 20 percentage points lower than his father had.

Two important observations can be made about the presidential race. First, despite Matiba's boycott and the further fragmentation of the opposition, 1997 repeated the basic voting pattern of 1992. As depicted by the shaded areas of the Table, all the leading candidates, parties, and successor parties drew the bulk of their support from the same areas as five years before. Second, with the exception of Moi, and to a much lessor extent Kibaki, no candidate ran well outside his or her home province. None of the other presidential candidates passed the 25 percent threshold outside their respective home provinces. Conversely, all five major candidates received 47 to 78 percent of their total votes from their respective home provinces. These patterns indicate a very high geographic concentration of the vote, reflecting Kenyan voters' penchant for defining their political interests in regional and ethnic terms.

The same regional patterns that marked the presidential race were repeated in the parliamentary contests. Here again, each party drew mainly on its regional ethnic base. The picture that emerges, as in 1992, shows a series of one-party or one-party-dominant areas rather than a large number of true multiparty races—with the difference that in 1997 more parties won seats. Indeed, of 198 contested races, only 19 could be called truly "competitive" (meaning that the winner beat the runner-up by no more than 10 percent). The unusually high geographic concentration of the vote is also revealed by comparing the average number of candidates for each parliamentary seat (4.4) with the average vote share garnered by the winners (65 percent).

Notwithstanding these patterns, the most significant result was KANU's failure to achieve its expected massive victory. Although it won 12 of its 107 seats unopposed and increased its share of the parliamentary vote to 38 percent (from 30 percent in 1992), it finished with only a four-seat edge over the combined opposition. Since Moi can now name only half of the 12 appointed MPs, the division in the new National Assembly is 113 to 109. This means that the opposition will, on occasion, be in a position to block government legislation. Most important, the two sides must now bargain if there is to be any further progress on constitutional reform.

Three additional outcomes merit consideration. First, 62 percent of the MPs from the previous parliament were either not renominated (whether by their original party or another party) or were defeated. This includes 12 of the 25 outgoing cabinet ministers. Turnover was especially high in KANU ranks, where 48 percent of the outgoing class was not renominated by the party. This suggests that Moi was cleaning house, but it is hard to say whether his aim was to improve candidate quality or to dump IPPG participants. Some credence must be given to the former possibility, as 75 percent of the renominated KANU MPs won their races.

Second, the fragmentation of the opposition appears to have increased the number of voters who engaged in split-ticket voting. This is particularly true among Kibaki voters, who deserted the DP for the SDP or Safina when voting for parliament.

Third and most striking, had parliamentary districts been drawn to be roughly equal in numbers of registered voters, the opposition would have defeated KANU by approximately 123 to 87! Once the opposition grasps the impact of malapportionment, the redesign of the electoral system is likely to become an issue in any future constitutional talks.[11]

The reinvigoration of civil society is one of the most significant outcomes of the elections. Following the IPPG, civil society divided between elements, like the NCEC that rejected the deal as "too minimal," and those prepared reluctantly to accept it and participate in the elections. The NCEC and its associated NGOs thus did not play a major role in the elections. Instead, the principal vehicle for civil society became an alliance bringing together the Catholic Justice and Peace Commission (CJPC), the National Council of Churches of Kenya (NCCK), and the Institute of Education and Democracy (IED), the successor to a local NGO that had monitored the 1992 elections.

With financial and technical support from the donor community, including trainers from the U.S. National Democratic Institute, these organizations fielded a virtual army of observers who monitored the campaign, watched the polls, and scrutinized the count. The IED started the entire effort months before the election, but the real muscle came from the church organizations, which provided over four-fifths of the more than 28,000 observers. Denmark, the Netherlands, Sweden, the United Kingdom, and the United States picked up the tab, spending about $2 million all told and coordinating their support through the Donors' Democracy Development Group (DDDG). The CJPC, the NCCK, and the IED accepted the election results, though with many caveats.[12]

Supplementing the efforts of Kenyan civil society were approximately 90 teams of international observers drawn from the 22 diplomatic missions of the countries that composed the DDDG. These observers monitored the entire process, from voter registration in May and June through the final count. Like the local observers, the international observers reported the outcome of the election as "in the main . . . credible . . . [except] for 5 percent of the parliamentary contests [where] the irregularities in the poll and count [were] so great as to invalidate the elections in these particular constituencies and consequently the legitimacy of the overall KANU majority in the National Assembly."[13]

The extent and sophistication of both domestic and international observation were far greater than in 1992, when barely 4,500 domestic observers could cover no more than a third of the polling stations, and when the donors relied on short-term international observers who flew in a few days before the voting. In a rare display of donor coordination and collaboration with Kenyan organizations, both donors and civil society built on the lessons of 1992. The result was a poorly administered but closely monitored election acceptable to most voters and candidates (Mwai Kibaki being the notable exception). The involvement of the churches also mobilized civil society across the rural areas for the first time.

The Future of Kenyan Democracy

The elections were carried out in a more mature environment in 1997 than in 1992. Although the IPPG package failed to address most of the basic constitutional issues that divide the government from the opposition, the atmosphere in 1997 was less confrontational and more issue-oriented. The real significance of the IPPG package was that it required Moi formally to recognize the opposition as a bargaining partner. He and his lieutenants can no longer treat Kenya as a one-party state. This in itself has led to a vastly improved electoral atmosphere and can only be good for democracy.

The question now is whether the protagonists can negotiate more far-reaching and fundamental reforms, or whether the post-1992 stalemate will return. The opposition and civil society are more powerful than ever. They will not wait indefinitely for negotiations to resume. If no movement is evident, they are likely to block the government's legislative agenda and take to the streets again. Yet the elections also further entrenched Kenya's ethnic divisions. Such divisions need not prove an insurmountable obstacle to the building of a pluralist democracy of an African variety. Still, it will take a great deal of political good will and imagination from *both* the government and the opposition to turn this natural African pluralism into a non–zero-sum game that many players can join, guided by a tolerant political culture. This is now the basic challenge facing Kenya's political elites.

The elections did not produce new leaders of the kind emerging elsewhere in Africa, which complicates the prospects for bargaining. Moi and Kibaki have been major figures in Kenyan politics since independence. Each depends on a distinct ethnoregional base. Wamalwa and Raila Odinga, though younger, did not articulate a democratic vision, but imitated the older generation by directing their campaigns to their ethnic heartlands. Though she was a new and refreshing face in national politics, Charity Ngilu was unable to generate much support outside her home province.

Prospects for a full transition to democracy will depend heavily on the Moi succession and constitutional reform. The split between KANU-A and KANU-B has greatly weakened the ruling party, which is now held together solely by incumbency. Moi's refusal to groom a successor has not helped matters. His postelection decision to leave the vice-presidency vacant is likely further to shake the delicate KANU coalition. At worst, it could unravel just when the party and its leaders are expected to negotiate constitutional reforms. Continued fragmentation and instability among the opposition will also complicate negotiations. If this happens, Kenya is likely to go through a very unstable period.

Negotiations over comprehensive constitutional reforms could lay the foundation for bringing the democratic transition to a successful conclusion. The talks, however, will demand from all parties precisely the flexibility and readiness to give and take that are so conspicuously missing in Kenya's fractious political culture. There is little trust between the two sides. Some opposition leaders, joined by the NCEC and, most significantly, the churches, have already announced their opposition to the creation of the IPPG-mandated constitutional-review committee on the grounds that Moi will control its composition and agenda.

Moreover, with opposition-aligned urban lawyers dominating the constitutional debate, so much stress has been placed on the protection of individual rights that the crucial issue of *group* rights has been neglected. Most important among these are the rights of ethnic minorities to land and to a fair share of other resources that they regard as rightfully theirs, including state-funded infrastructure and social-welfare services. The institutional guarantee of group rights will likely take the form of a demand by the leaders of Kenya's smallest ethnic groups, the core of the KANU coalition, for some form of decentralization or federalism that will address their dual need for resource guarantees and meaningful political representation vis-à-vis the larger groups.

Because the constitutional debate to date has focused mainly on the protection of individual rights within the context of a more accountable unitary state, discussion of decentralization, and therefore communal rights, has largely been treated as illegitimate. This will need to change. Indeed, failure to address the vital interests of the KANU constituency as well as those of the opposition will undermine the entire process and lead to renewed political paralysis.

The issue of federalism, however, is one of the most emotionally charged in Kenya. KANU has used the cry of "Majimbo," the Swahili term for regional government based on Kenya's eight existing provinces, to justify the creation of KANU zones in which members of ethnic communities that support the opposition are to have limited rights or no rights. The demands for "Majimbo" voiced by KANU hard-liners before the 1992 ethnic violence have forever tainted the idea of a federal solution in the minds of most opposition leaders, particularly those who are Kikuyu. Nor has the renewal of ethnic clashes in 1997 and *after* the elections in 1998 helped matters. One can, however, imagine a federal framework based on geographical units that are smaller than the present provinces, especially Rift Valley Province, yet larger than the current administrative districts, and that could provide secure areas and accountable government for all. (Forty years ago, India redrew its internal boundaries in the same way to protect linguistic groups.) One can also imagine other mechanisms for power sharing and the protection of group rights—for example, a bicameral legislature, perhaps combined with a constitutional provision (like that in the interim South African Constitution) guaranteeing one or more cabinet posts to each party exceeding some fixed percentage of the total vote. Constitutional provisions that protect individual rights and those that protect group rights need not be mutually exclusive. Kenya can have both.

The successful negotiation of basic reforms will turn on the political will and perseverance of Kenya's principal political actors. Moi will be a key player, though many doubt that the elderly president still has the energy or inclination for prolonged discourse. His refusal to appoint a coalition government after the elections is not encouraging. The opposition must also be forthcoming, not only on the "big" issues of constitutional reform, but on giving Moi and individual hard-liners an exit option, perhaps in the form of guarantees against prosecution for acts committed in office.

Kenya may have now entered what Guillermo O'Donnell and Philippe Schmitter would describe as the "pact phase" of its democratic transition.[14] The IPPG is a textbook example of soft-liners gaining the initiative for the purpose of controlling the pace and content of the transition after hard-liners have failed to protect the vital interests of the incumbent authoritarian regime. What is different about Kenya, and other countries where incumbents have used multiparty elections to fend off donor pressure while staying in power, is that the negotiation process has come only *after* elections.

The future of democracy in Kenya, as elsewhere, depends on more than electoral politics, important as elections might be to the transition. The agenda is much wider and deeper. But the protracted electoral process of 1996–97 has served as a welcome catalyst encouraging Kenyans to renew their pursuit of that agenda to its logical conclusion.

NOTES

1. On the 1992 elections, see Joel D. Barkan, "Kenya: Lessons from a Flawed Election," *Journal of Democracy* 4 (July 1993): 85–99; and David Throup and Charles Hornsby, *Multiparty Politics in Kenya: The Kenyatta and Moi State and the Triumph of the System in the 1992 Elections* (London: James Currey, 1998).

2. Quick-disbursing aid refers to cash payments to cover a country's budget and current-accounts deficits to facilitate reforms that reduce these deficits.

3. Kenya became a de facto one-party state in 1964 when the main opposition party, the Kenya African Democratic Union (KADU), of which Moi was chairman, folded after Moi and many KADU legislators defected to KANU.

4. The "persuasion" was a carrot-and-stick affair. "Carrots" included cash bribes to defectors, along with the promise of the KANU nomination and funding for the by-election. "Sticks" included police harassment and the cutting off of government resources to the constituency of the targeted MP.

5. Defections did not trigger every by-election. Four were necessitated by the resignation or death of the incumbent, while one resulted from a court's determination that the initial balloting was invalid because of irregularities.

6. The mean number of registered voters per district is 43,307, but district size varies widely. The smallest district is Ijara in Northeastern Province, with 7,501 voters. The biggest is Embakasi in Nairobi, which, with a registration of 114,354, is more than 15 times larger.

7. Before Moi's 1964 defection to KANU, these groups voted solidly for KADU.

8. Roddy Fox, "Bleak Future for Multi-Party Elections in Kenya," *Journal of Modern African Studies* 34 (December 1996): 597–607.

9. "Proposal for a Model Constitution for Kenya," *Nairobi Law Monthly* 51 (January 1995): 8–32.

10. See the editorial in the *Daily Nation* (Nairobi), 30 December 1997. The major problems included the late delivery or nondelivery of ballot boxes to polling places; the delivery of insufficient numbers of ballot boxes; improperly secured ballot boxes; the delivery of ballots to the wrong polling places; ballots printed with incorrect party symbols, incorrect names, or no names at all; the nondelivery of ink pads, seals, and other crucial supplies; and the relocation of some polling stations. Flooding caused by unusually heavy late-December rains in Northeastern Province further complicated the process.

11. The average number of voters in districts won by KANU is 36,350, while the average for districts won by the opposition is 53,387. We have used these figures to calculate the extent of over- and under-representation by comparing them with a hypothetical district having the mean average number of voters. Our estimate of what seat shares would be without malapportionment is based on these calculations.

12. IED, CJCP, and NCCK, "Final Statement," (Nairobi, 3 January 1998, mimeograph). See also "Observers Accept Election Results," *Sunday Nation* (Nairobi), 4 January 1998.

13. Donors' Democracy Development Group, "The Kenya General Election, 1997: Final Report," January 1998, Executive Summary I.

14. Guillermo O'Donnell and Philippe Schmitter, *Transitions from Authoritarian Rule: Tentative Conclusions About Uncertain Democracies* (Baltimore: Johns Hopkins University Press, 1986), especially chs. 3 and 4.

14

"NO-PARTY DEMOCRACY" IN UGANDA

Nelson Kasfir

Nelson Kasfir, professor of government at Dartmouth College, is the editor and coauthor of Civil Society and Democracy in Africa: Critical Perspectives *(1998). He is currently writing on state creation and state-building in Africa.*

Have Uganda's President Yoweri Museveni and his National Resistance Movement (NRM) invented a form of "no-party democracy" more suitable for Africa than Western-style multiparty competition? Under the NRM government, Uganda has made remarkable strides in recovering from the insecure, lawless, and economically immobilized regimes that came before, even if some sections of the country have not yet reaped the benefits. Since the NRM took over in 1986, it has organized three national elections. Each, according to local and foreign observers, was freer, fairer, and more open than the 1980 election, the only other one held since Uganda gained its independence from Britain in 1962. Moreover, in a development never seen before in Uganda, the NRM has repeatedly held elections in every village. In the no-party presidential election in 1996, Museveni won more than 70 percent of the vote, soundly defeating Paul Ssemogerere, the candidate of a coalition formed by groups with allegiances to the Democratic Party (DP) and the Uganda People's Congress (UPC), the two most important among the old political parties.

To most Ugandans, Museveni's victory seemed to validate no-party democracy, and for two reasons. First, he won by a landslide; few impartial observers felt that he would have lost to Ssemogerere even had parties been allowed to campaign. Second, the bankruptcy of the old multiparty system was made manifest by the willingness of Ssemogerere, the "real" winner of the 1980 elections, to ally himself with the UPC, the party that he had always charged with cheating the DP of its victory by threatening to use the army.

Were Museveni to cite as evidence for the superiority of no-party democracy the Kenyan multiparty elections of 1992 and 1997—which

featured multiple candidate defections from one party to another as
well as ethnic bloc voting in half of all legislative constituencies—few
in either country would dispute him. Indeed, most would probably
agree that Kenya can hardly be said to be more democratic than
Uganda, though the former has 27 parties and the latter has none.

Many foreign donors, who have become entranced by Uganda's
economic and political recovery, have praised its new form of democracy. "What is happening in Uganda is . . . your own type of democracy
that is trying to fit into the Ugandan context," said one. The new British
Labour government has decided that it "will not press for multiparty
reforms in Uganda."[1] This is particularly significant because elsewhere
in Africa, donors have insisted that aid depends on continued progress
toward permitting parties to form and compete freely. What envy Kenyan president Daniel arap Moi must feel when he hears the praise that is
heaped upon Uganda for its staunch refusal to allow parties!

Both the foreign and the domestic audiences are right in one respect
and wrong in another. They are right to think that Uganda has never
been as democratic, either at the village or the national level, as it is today. But they are wrong to imagine that the no-party system has made it
so. The great puzzle is to figure out what no-party democracy stands
for, and whether it has a future. A look at the treatment of no-party
democracy by top NRM officials helps to show why these questions are
hard to answer.

While the NRM's leaders prefer to speak of "movement" democracy, I refer here to "no-party" democracy because its authors actually
discuss it more in terms of what they wish to avoid (parties) than in
terms of what they claim to have created (a movement). In the Ugandan
version, all adults, by virtue of residence, are members of the Movement and of their village Resistance (now called Local) Council (RC).
An interlocking structure of elected RCs reaches up through five
administrative levels that culminate in district government. Parties may
exist, but are barred from political activity. This, says the NRM, is
necessary to prevent appeals that smack of "sectarianism"—a term that
in Ugandan usage refers not only to conflicts based on religion, but also
to those based on ethnicity or regional ties (in Uganda, the three are
often closely linked). In theory, elections at every level are conducted
on the basis of personal merit rather than political affiliation. Officials
make great efforts to ensure that all candidates have an equal
opportunity to present themselves in each locality within their constituencies. The Movement has a small national secretariat, funded by the
state, that supervises a few political schools and engages in modest
mobilizational activities.

No one in the NRM has done much to develop or articulate the
principles behind no-party democracy, other than to insist that parties
may not nominate candidates or campaign for them, and consequently

cannot form a government. Besides the NRM's original manifesto, known as the "Ten-Point Programme," and brief discussions by Museveni in some of his speeches and articles, very little has been written about no-party democracy.[2] Nor has there ever been a concerted campaign to educate the public about it. Oddly, after putting great energy into developing RCs in every village and at higher levels, the NRM quietly handed over the shaping of Ugandan democracy to a state-appointed Constitutional Commission and a subsequent Constituent Assembly.

In lieu of a solid justification for no-party democracy, the regime has put forth a series of rationales marked by internal inconsistencies and occasionally abrupt shifts in reasoning. The only thing that has not changed is the insistence that no-party democracy means no parties may participate. Although establishing motives is difficult, the NRM leadership may support no-party democracy primarily to help itself maintain its rule in the face of the various local conflicts that it has inherited and to which it must respond. It would be wrong to conclude from this, however, that Uganda is merely a dictatorship with an attractive but misleading facade. In fact, the country is much more democratic today than it was before the NRM took power. Nevertheless, one wonders whether any of its new democratic forms can outlast the tenure of their founder, the current president.

Sectarianism and Politics

To understand Ugandan no-party democracy, it is necessary to know something about the nature and origins of political "sectarianism" in Uganda. The NRM's analysis of this problem lies at the root of each of its successive rationales for restricting parties. The NRM's initial premise is that competition among the old parties exacerbated sectarian tendencies, and hence could never produce democracy. This argument is plausible, though it may go farther toward explaining the NRM's use of no-party democracy than toward justifying its acceptance as a system of government.

A look at Uganda's history of political and economic conflict helps to clarify what the NRM government has had to take into account. When Museveni's National Resistance Army (NRA) marched into Kampala in January 1986, it inherited a series of complex relationships that each preceding government had in its turn made considerably worse. From the inception of their collaboration with the British, the leaders of the southern kingdom of Buganda—then as now the largest, richest, most coherent, and most assertive political entity in Uganda—made their relationship to the British Protectorate (1894–1962) and later the independent state an enduring political issue. The more Buganda pressed its own dominance or autonomy, the more other groups tried to combine to hold it in check—or to assert an equivalent political coherence. Ethnic identity became a central factor in Ugandan politics because it became bound up in these conflicts.

So did regional identification, partly because there was somewhat greater cultural similarity within each region, but also because the southern regions, particularly Buganda and the east, achieved greater economic development and thus had more in the way of social services, schools, hospitals, and jobs than did the west or especially the north. Before independence, rank-and-file military recruitment was concentrated in part of the east and in the north. Afterwards, officers also came mostly from the north. Cultural similarities notwithstanding, each region played host to several fractious political conflicts. In addition, rivalries among missionaries left behind a degree of political competition among Catholics, Protestants, and Muslims that is unusual for sub-Saharan Africa.

Consequently, Ugandan politics has always been extraordinarily local, based on complicated and highly unstable political and economic alliances. The DP and the UPC, not surprisingly, took on the coloration of these conflicts. From the late-colonial period on, each party sought to mobilize votes on the basis of ethnicity, region, and religion. Museveni and his colleagues argued, correctly, that the parties' behavior made the country's conflicts worse and diverted attention from economic problems. This attack on sectarianism resonated with Ugandans, who had coped for some time with the consequences of the parties' penchant for using religion, ethnicity, and regionalism to expand their support, and thus lent greater legitimacy to the NRM's early espousal of "popular democracy" as an alternative to multiparty democracy.

In the 1960s, the complex federal arrangements embodied in the independence Constitution and the relationships among politicians from the DP, the UPC, and the Kabaka Yekka (or KY, a party representing Baganda ethnic interests) gave these conflicts room to grow. The UPC government of Milton Obote, the northern, Protestant politician who became independent Uganda's first prime minister, jettisoned its original allies from Buganda and strengthened the central administration. In 1966, Obote made himself president and scrapped federalism, trying to achieve through unitary presidential rule and coercion what had not previously been achievable through bargaining.

In its growing isolation, the Obote government became ripe for a coup. The ax fell in 1971, when power was seized by General Idi Amin, Uganda's highest-ranking military officer and a Muslim from a different part of the north than Obote. Both Amin's religious identity (Muslims make up less than a sixth of the population) and his regional affiliation were disadvantages when it came to creating a political base broad enough to allow the possibility of consensual rule. In 1972, he expelled most residents of Indian descent—traditionally the mainstays of business and mercantile life—pushing the economy into a downward spiral. Shortages and growing corruption soon followed. Arbitrary government and the application of military force to existing local conflicts led to widespread killing.

The Tanzanian army, accompanied by a Ugandan faction under Obote and a rival one under Museveni, overthrew Amin in 1979 after he had foolishly invaded and ravaged northwestern Tanzania. The transitional government that followed included several civilian groups that collectively added another layer of conflicts, immobilizing administrative activity and deepening Uganda's impoverishment. Eventually, Obote gained the preponderance of power in the army and shaped the rules ensuring that the 1980 elections, which returned Uganda to "civilian" rule, would be party-based.

When Obote used his military edge to declare the UPC the winner, Museveni and a few of his followers turned to guerrilla war, in competition with several other small groups. This war probably resulted in the deaths of as many civilians—perhaps 400,000—during Obote's second period of rule as had been killed under Amin. In July 1985, Obote was overthrown by officers from a northern district other than his own. Six months later, the NRA defeated this rump army and the factions, including some of Amin's old troops, that had rallied to it.

At the time it took power, the NRM had only a limited political base. It had done most of its fighting in Buganda, drawing most of its recruits and social support from the south, and taking control of the west only in the ten months preceding victory. Much to the alarm of northerners, it became the first Ugandan government to be run by southerners. About six months after the NRM took over, rebellions broke out in parts of the north and east. The eastern insurgency ended after several years, but the war in the north continues. The NRM's legitimacy has thus remained in question, especially throughout most of the north.

The NRM was caught in a dilemma. Having taken power by force, it nonetheless aspired to a democratic justification for its rule. The NRM proclaimed no-party democracy as a new approach to government that would bar the expression of sectarian loyalties, though all the sectarian conflicts inherent in the old political issues still had to be faced, as well as the new ones produced by the NRM's victory.

The Original Rationale

The NRM has never engaged in extensive analysis of its notion of no-party or movement democracy, offering instead justifications that are frequently ambiguous or mutually contradictory. Moreover, the NRM has made surprising changes in the later rationales it has used to justify no-party democracy, ignoring its most creative political contributions. It has never formally asked whether its original approach—developed by the NRA, not its civilian wing, the NRM—should be changed to fit peacetime conditions. This absence of sustained attention by its founders leaves open several fundamental questions about what can be considered democratic about Uganda's no-party democracy, questions that include some familiar disputes in the literature of democratic theory.

The "Ten-Point Programme" espouses a complex definition of democracy that combines important ideas often thought to be in contradiction with one another. Democracy "must contain three elements: parliamentary democracy, popular democracy, and a decent living for every Ugandan."[3] Each of these notions has received significant attention in discussions of democratic theory. The combination promises an original approach.

It would be best to start by considering how the founders of the NRM regarded each of these ideas, and then to ask how they responded (or failed to respond) to the difficulties of joining them together. The NRM's approach to popular democracy involved its most exciting democratic initiative, even if popular democracy was undercut both in design and later in practice. The village-level RCs are a textbook example of participatory democracy, with all adult residents gathering to decide village issues, electing a council to govern and judge local cases, and recalling any elected officials who have lost their confidence. In Museveni's words, they are involved in "making the decisions which affect their daily lives."[4]

In 1986, the NRM devoted enormous energy to instituting an RC in every village. Greeted at first with widespread popular enthusiasm, the councils represented a local governmental structure wholly new to Ugandans, who had always been ruled by chiefs or male elders before, during, and after colonialism. The village councils may turn out to have been the NRM's most important democratic initiative. So long as they remained the institutional expression of popular participation, they supplied no-party democracy with its most persuasive justification.

Above the village level, however, the case for popular democracy is more difficult to defend. Higher RCs are composed of the Resistance Committees elected from the next lower level, a system that holds all the way up to the fifth, or district, level. In other words, they are ever more indirectly representative of the villagers acting at the bottom level, and are chosen by ever smaller electorates. In addition, indirect representation erodes the right of recall, since only the council that elected a committee has the right to recall one of its members. Thus even if a village RC wanted to remove someone whom it had originally elected, say on grounds of corruption, it could not do so after that official had been elected to a higher level. A 1987 commission of inquiry argued that it would be more democratic to permit voters in the villages to elect officials at all levels, but the NRM government rejected this suggestion, claiming that it would lead to more sectarianism. Employing indirect representation at higher levels is a substantial departure from participatory democracy.

Since participatory democracy means that the people govern themselves directly, it can only remain meaningful if the RCs' function as deliberative bodies is retained as fundamental. Yet it was their administrative utility rather than their deliberative quality that seems to have recommended them most strongly to the NRM's founders. The RCs were first organized to enlist sympathetic civilians in the acquisition of food, recruits, and intelligence for the NRA war effort; "later on," Museveni has written, "we made them elective."[5] Their administrative origin is not surprising, and the NRM deserves much credit for taking the risk of introducing a degree of democracy while it was fighting a war.

The RCs have always been closely supervised in what they can discuss, with most power remaining in the hands of the Central Committee of the National Resistance Council (NRC)—originally the commanders of the NRA, but after the takeover, the parliament. A 1987 law placed the RCs under the direction of the minister of local government, who has broad powers to suspend them. In addition, each district has a presidentially appointed resident commissioner, who may intervene to reverse RC decisions and even remove existing councils.

Early enthusiasm notwithstanding, the years after 1986 saw widespread demoralization among RC officials and a drop in RC participation.[6] This happened in part because ministries heaped unpaid village-RC officials with responsibility for tasks such as tax collection, road building, and security provision. Many rural officials complained that they no longer had time to work their farms. In addition, the leaders of the NRM, governing between 1986 and 1989 without benefit of national elections, had no gauge of their own legitimacy and were worried that the old parties, particularly the DP, had enough grassroots support to capture the RC hierarchy from the bottom up. Indeed, in 1988 the DP held a large majority of the seats in two-thirds of the District Councils and thus in all lower RCs as well.[7]

Thus the real question was not whether the state could create popular democracy from above, but whether the NRM could live with the risk that letting people choose freely might open the door to an embarrassing challenge from the parties. Since the adoption of the 1995 Constitution and the 1997 Local Government Act, local councils at all levels have become more clearly part of the state and less part of the NRM, though the adoption of an entrenched decentralization scheme protects their autonomy to a modest degree. Yet the reduction in their role as genuinely deliberative assemblies greatly diminishes the justification that they can provide for no-party democracy. And if they can no longer be justified on the basis of participatory democracy, why should parties be barred from running candidates to serve on them?

Participatory versus Parliamentary Democracy

The "Ten-Point Programme" neither defines "parliamentary democracy" nor even specifies that parties are to be banned. Indeed, despite the NRM's subsequent refusal to allow party activity, an earlier NRM manifesto had stated that while constituent-assembly candidates would "have to run on a nonparty basis," the enactment of a new constitution would mean that "political party activity shall be permitted to resume."[8] Clearly, the eventual decision to ban parties did not grow out of a longstanding NRM vision of a no-party parliament. On the other hand, as late as 1989 Museveni offered a proposal (quickly withdrawn) that parliament would simply be the culminating RC, comprising the members of all the district-level resistance committees. But in that case, it need not have been singled out as a separate element essential to the definition of Ugandan democracy.

The first test of the electoral meaning of parliamentary democracy occurred in the 1989 elections for the NRC, which also included all the lower RCs. The rules that the NRM leaders designed for this contest betrayed their anxieties about the extent of their popular support.[9] Upon taking power three years before, the leaders had declared that their interim rule would last four years. With that deadline looming and so many problems still unresolved, they knew that they would extend the interim period, and thus felt the need to seek some sort of democratic legitimation for it. Yet aside from the lower-level RC elections and the 1980 races (in which they had done poorly), their electoral appeal was untested. With that in mind, and without the time or money to conduct a conventional election, they designed an electoral scheme that would be quick, cheap, and (last but not least) hard to lose.

The elections began at the village (RC1) level only three weeks after the original announcement. Open-queue voting was used at all levels, doing away with the need for ballot boxes and voter registration. Counties were adopted as NRC constituencies and candidates were elected by convening all the subcounty councils (RC3). These "territorial constituencies," however, accounted for only five-eighths of the seats in the NRC. The 38 previously appointed "historical members," comrades of President Museveni from the guerrilla war, simply retained their seats. Museveni also named 20 new members, while the NRA, under his direct control, named 10 more. Thus almost one quarter of the seats were controlled by the government. The presidency was not contested, nor were parties allowed to participate. Nonetheless, the government carefully followed the rules that it had set. Most neutral observers concluded that, within those limits, the elections had been free and fair and the votes honestly counted.

By connecting the removal of poverty, the third element in the definition, to democracy, the NRM manifesto makes a familiar argument recognizing the importance of substantial economic development for the success of democracy. Many analysts agree that a high level of national income is a necessary precondition for sustaining democracy.[10] But, if by "a decent standard of living for every Ugandan," NRM leaders mean the achievement of economic wealth in any way comparable to that of industrialized nations, then the leaders must have an extremely long time horizon—one that would render suspect their claims that democracy *currently* exists in Uganda. Thus if no-party democracy is to apply to contemporary Uganda, in terms of this definition, it can only take its meaning from its other two elements—parliamentary and popular democracy—despite the difficulties that each of them presents for an NRM rationale.

Putting them together creates an additional challenge, for students of politics have usually seen these two forms of democracy as contradictory. Indeed, the distinction between representative and participatory (or "popular") forms of self-government is a staple of democratic theory. The former is typically thought to center on elites who compete in elections, usually through parties, in order to represent the voters.[11] Its advocates insist that the process of creating the set of policies through which each party tries to make its voter appeal broader than that of its rivals makes the system democratic. Participatory democracy is usually thought to privilege direct participation by ordinary citizens, particularly their deliberations concerning issues that directly concern them.[12] Proponents of this system usually assert that no one can fully represent the views of someone else and, for reasons of difference in culture or wealth, will more likely misrepresent them.

Proponents of participatory democracy frequently reject parties, complaining that in the process of creating a common program out of the preferences of some citizens, parties are likely to distort the views of many others. But in anything other than a very small polity, insist defenders of representative democracy, direct citizen participation in governing is awkward if not impossible, so that representative institutions actually offer greater opportunities for improving the quality of deliberation. Finally, advocates of popular democracy place a high value on the notion of individual equality in actually influencing outcomes, while proponents of representative democracy are typically content with the equal opportunity to participate. Thus parliamentary and popular democracy are rarely found in the same definition, and most of those in either camp would say that they cannot be.

Whether the NRM leaders believed that they could square this circle is difficult to say. They thought about making parliament the top tier in a hierarchy of no-party RCs. Such a parliament, required to consider important policy positions adopted by directly elected autonomous lower councils, could have become the apex institution in a popular democracy. But the NRM never accepted any of these conditions. Alternatively, the leaders could have opted for a straightforward representative democracy by allowing open party activity. Instead, they have permitted a de facto, though unacknowledged, form of party competition to become the basis for the actual practice of Ugandan electoral democracy. In the first years after the NRM came to power, the old parties, especially the DP, had considerable success in running candidates at all RC levels, even though they could not publicly admit what they were doing. Even the UPC—in effect the loser of the guerrilla war— managed to win four parliamentary seats in 1989. The NRM itself, meanwhile, became sufficiently organized to win a majority of seats at every level in the 1989 and subsequent elections, even while denying that any parties were participating.

The interesting question is whether, in spite of the analytic difficulties, the NRM could have combined popular and parliamentary democracy, as its manifesto proclaimed. Indeed, the Constitutional Commission's 1992 report dismisses any possibility of combining a movement and a multiparty system.[13] Yet the "Ten-Point Programme" suggests that parliament and the local RCs could be handled differently. It might have been possible to let parties run in national elections while banning them from RC races. Checks and balances might have helped to maintain a creative tension between partyless popular councils at lower levels and parties at the national level. Using parliamentarism at one level and popular democracy at another might have attracted wider support from both the middle and lower classes, thereby enhancing political stability.[14] Despite the foundational status ascribed to the "Ten-Point Programme," neither the NRM nor the constitution-making bodies paid any serious attention to combining popular and parliamentary democracy once the guerrilla war was over.

The Rationales After Taking Power

Just after the NRM took power, it stressed the importance of building a "broad-based" government in order to bring all political tendencies together. A few years later, it sought to highlight its own singular inclusiveness by denying that there were any basic economic cleavages dividing Ugandans. The notion of inclusiveness—and hence the rationale for no-party politics—had changed, but in both cases their intention was to distinguish the NRM from all previous parties and governments by characterizing them as inherently sectarian and thus incapable of ruling Ugandans democratically. .

"Broad-based government" meant appointing erstwhile opponents to high positions in both the government and the army. The new rationale gave the NRM a brilliant opportunity to avoid appearing as one more narrow government bent on appointing only its own supporters to power. At first, its performance was as unprecedented as its creation of the RCs. The NRM's rivals received many of the most desirable posts. Yet once it installed them, the NRM gave these new officials no basic direction. As Mahmood Mamdani points out, the NRM did not create a program to reconcile groups, but simply expanded its base of support by offering jobs to their leaders.[15]

In Uganda as elsewhere, buying loyalty with patronage is a time-honored practice. But for the NRM, it meant squandering what little ideological coherence it had achieved during the war. The NRM's willingness to include people who had been cabinet ministers or army officers under Amin or Obote meant relinquishing any claim to policy consensus. "Broad-based government" expanded nominal support for no-party democracy, but only by making it even harder to establish its basic tenets. Over time, the rhetoric of "broad-based government" has faded along with the practice of appointing opponents to high office. For example, the proportion of significant cabinet portfolios held by members of parties has declined in each succeeding cabinet.

"In our own model, which we call no-party democracy," Museveni recently insisted, "there is no exclusion at all." This time he made no reference to RCs as the core of participatory democracy. Instead, he justified no-party democracy with an argument premised on the claim that Uganda has no salient economic or class cleavages. Unlike Western societies, where parties represent different classes and interests and thus offer different economic programs, Uganda, according to Museveni, is a rural society composed predominantly of peasants with essentially the same economic interests. Unable to attract votes by advocating distinctive economic policies, Ugandan parties turn instead to ethnic, regional, and religious appeals, breeding strife and diverting people from the important issues that affect their livelihoods. In short, says the president, "Tribalism, religion, or regionalism becomes the basis for intense partisanship. There is no healthy basis for honest competition." Consequently, given Uganda's social structure, it would be foolish to adopt Western-style multiparty democracy. But Museveni insists that his system is different from the former dictatorial "one-party states in Eastern Europe" because in Uganda, all belong to the movement and "everyone who wants to stand for election is free to do so."[16]

With this rationale, Museveni has revived the now-discredited defense that Tanzania's then-President Julius Nyerere made of his country's single-party system 30 years ago. Nyerere also insisted on "the historical difference between parties in Africa and those in Europe or America . . . [which] came into being as the result of existing social

and economic divisions." Since Tanzanians were not "divided over
some fundamental issue," a two-party system would "merely encourage
the growth of factionalism." Given "fundamental agreement, it would
be far more sensible . . . [to] let the electorate choose the best individuals from among them all." Nyerere also distinguished between his
own country and one-party communist states, insisting that "as long as
TANU [Tanganyikan African National Union] membership is open to
every citizen, we can conduct our elections in a way which is genuinely
free and democratic."[17]

Aside from his use of the term "movement" rather than than "party"
(Uganda's 1995 Constitution outlaws a single-party system), Museveni
adds two important points not found in Nyerere's argument. The first is
the assertion that "Ugandans are overwhelmingly of one class, peasants."[18] Taking a familiar if no longer highly regarded view, he sees
peasants as ignorant, undifferentiated, self-sufficient, and not dependent on markets. A peasant, he claims, is "not worried about markets,
because he has little to sell. . . . The hill is the outer limit of his horizon." He "tries to build his own house, collect his water from the well,
cultivate all the food he eats, look after his own cows, and become an
informal teaching instructor for his children."

There are many problems with this argument.[19] First, it is foolish to
say that peasants have nothing to do with markets when they have been
responsible for growing and selling the coffee, the cotton, and a large
part of the tea on which Uganda has long depended for almost all its
foreign earnings. Economic surveys show that Uganda's small farmers
invariably know the current prices for their crops. In addition, all Ugandan peasants, however poor, have to pay taxes and school fees and buy
certain foodstuffs, clothing items, and tools that they consider essential
but can no longer make for themselves.

Second, there are enormous differences in wealth among farmers in
Uganda. Some hire others as laborers. Even if all of them—including
those who serve as models for modernized agriculture—are labeled
peasants, it makes little sense to consider them members of the same
economic class. In truth, there is a considerable degree of class differentiation in rural Uganda. Third, the business of growing and marketing
each of Uganda's food and export crops brings competing economic
interests into play. It stretches the imagination to regard all these interests as belonging to one class. In fact, class interests might well be
expressed by different parties, were full party competition openly permitted.

Certainly Uganda's social structure differs from that of an industrialized country. Museveni may be correct that copying a multiparty system lock, stock, and barrel from a Western country will fail to respond
to local conditions. It is shortsighted and deeply chauvinistic for Western donors to press on other states not merely multipartism, but almost

always a form of multipartism based directly on the historical experiences of the particular Western state from which that donor comes.[20] But the one-class analysis that leads Museveni to the NRM version of no-party democracy is questionable enough to suggest that it has been designed to meet his immediate political goals rather than to support a new political theory.

The second novel point raised by Museveni is his suggestion that once Uganda modernizes, it should adopt a multiparty system:

> What is crucial for Uganda now is for us to have a system that ensures democratic participation *until such time* as we get, through economic development, especially industrialization, the crystallization of socio-economic groups upon which we can then base healthy political parties.[21]

The clear implication is that no-party democracy has become a transitional device pending the day when Uganda can become a "real" multiparty democracy. Museveni has not offered even a rough idea of when this day will arrive. How long will it take for Uganda's peasants to become members of the working or middle class? Is the NRM saying that it must remain the guardian of no-party democracy until that happens? What seems disturbingly clear is that the NRM has abandoned any ground on which it could lay plausible claim to democratic legitimation, and now seeks to justify its rule on the basis of a highly suspect theory of modernization.

Given its claim of inclusiveness, it is paradoxical—under any rationale—that the NRM has resisted internal democratization. Until the 1995 Constitution required Parliament to establish a structure for the Movement, the NRM had never held an election for any of its officers, never convened a body to deliberate or vote on its policies, nor even written a charter for itself. Its response to the constitutional mandate evoked unhappy memories from Africa's recent past by proposing a structure that basically identified the Movement and the state. Its first bill declared the president of Uganda the chairperson of the Movement, thus avoiding election for the top position, and made all members of parliament *ex officio* members of a new body, the NRM "National Conference," regardless of the preferences of any individual MP. Parliament rejected this bill, but a rewritten draft, mandating elections for the chairperson of the NRM while changing few other details, passed in 1997.[22] The NRM leadership's evident lack of interest in its internal democracy further underlines the hollowness of its post-1986 rationales for no-party democracy.

Has the experience of no-party democracy made Uganda more democratic? Uganda today is undoubtedly more democratic than it ever has been before. It is also currently more democratic than any of its neighbors, Tanzania possibly excepted. Though there are significant exceptions, there is an impressively free press, considerable respect for human rights outside the zones of armed conflict, and a relatively independent judiciary. In addition to the 1989 election, Uganda held national elections for a Constituent Assembly in 1994 and, separately, for the presidency and Parliament in 1996. Parties were not permitted to participate in any of these, and there were severe restrictions on campaigning. All candidates were limited to presentations of their personal merits in public meetings with their rivals. There seemed to be little room for anyone to argue about policy. In an odd way, Museveni's idea that Ugandans entertain no fundamental policy differences became true by fiat. Otherwise, the elections were conventional, following the usual norms regarding registration and secret balloting. Most Ugandans consider them to have been fairly conducted on the whole. After a long dry spell, both voters and election officials are becoming adept at handling the mechanics of these exercises.

Museveni's landslide election to the presidency in 1996 and the victory of many of his followers in the parliamentary elections have been a mixed blessing. Museveni in particular and the NRM in general have been democratically legitimated. Most Ugandans, and especially the rural dwellers, clearly believe that Museveni and the NRM have made fundamental contributions to improving life in Uganda and should continue to rule. But what is the NRM now? Without institutions, without an ideology, and, finally, without a rationale that can justify its no-party democracy, it no longer has any existence apart from its leader.

NOTES

1. These quotations are from *The East African* (Nairobi), 3–9 February 1997; and *New Vision* (Kampala), 8 October 1997.

2. See Yoweri Museveni, *Selected Articles on the Uganda Resistance War* (Kampala: NRM Publications, 1985).

3. Museveni, *Selected Articles,* 46.

4. *New Vision,* 30 January 1991, quoted in Ingvild Burkey, "People's Power in Theory and Practice: The Resistance Council System in Uganda" (B.A. thesis, Yale University, 1991), 10.

5. Yoweri Museveni, *Sowing the Mustard Seed: The Struggle for Freedom and Democracy in Uganda* (London: Macmillan, 1997), 134.

6. Burkey, "People's Power in Theory and Practice," 11–13, 32, and 53; and Expedit Ddungu, "Popular Forms and the Question of Democracy: The Case of Resistance Councils in Uganda," in Mahmood Mamdani and Joe Oloka-Onyango, eds., *Uganda: Studies in Living Conditions, Popular Movements, and Constitutionalism* (Vienna: JEP, 1996), 377–78, 391–97, and 401–2.

7. Nelson Kasfir, "The Ugandan Elections of 1989: Power, Populism, and Democratization," in Holger B. Hansen and Michael Twaddle, eds., *Changing Uganda: The Dilemmas of Structural Adjustment and Revolutionary Change* (London: James Currey, 1991), 255.

8. *Towards a Free and Democratic Uganda: The Basic Principles and Policies of the National Resistance Movement* (Kampala: no publisher, no date), 16–17.

9. Kasfir, "The Ugandan Elections of 1989," 257–73. Nevertheless, the NRM did not try to reverse any results. Fourteen ministers and deputy ministers lost their NRC seats, while several DP and even four UPC candidates were victorious.

10. Adam Przeworski, Michael Alvarez, José Antonio Cheibub, and Fernando Limongi, "What Makes Democracies Endure?" in Larry Diamond et al., eds., *Consolidating the Third Wave Democracies: Themes and Perspectives* (Baltimore: Johns Hopkins University Press, 1997), 297.

11. The classic statement is Joseph Schumpeter, *Capitalism, Socialism and Democracy* (New York: Harper and Brothers, 1950), 269–83.

12. See Carole Pateman, *Participation and Democratic Theory* (Cambridge: Cambridge University Press, 1970).

13. *Report of the Constitutional Commission* (Entebbe: Uganda Printing and Publishing Corporation, 1992).

14. Nelson Kasfir, "Popular Sovereignty and Popular Participation: Mixed Constitutional Democracy in the Third World," *Third World Quarterly* 13 (1992): 587–605.

15. "NRA/NRM: Two Years in Power," in Mahmood Mamdani, *And Fire Does Not Always Beget Ash: Critical Reflections on the NRM* (Kampala: Monitor Publications, 1995), 48.

16. The quotations in this paragraph are taken from Yoweri Museveni, "Democracy and Good Governance in Africa: An African Perspective," *Mediterranean Quarterly* 5 (Fall 1994): 7 and 6. In the "Ten-Point Programme," 49–50, the NRM insisted that it would exclude "anybody that impedes the unity of the people of Uganda," a category that seems to embrace proponents of all forms of sectarianism and thus could have excluded most Ugandans.

17. The quotations in this paragraph are taken from Julius Nyerere, "Democracy and the Party System," in idem, *Freedom and Unity: A Selection from Writings and Speeches, 1952–65* (Nairobi: Oxford University Press, 1967), 198, 196, 197, and 200.

18. Museveni, *Sowing the Mustard Seed*, 195. The additional quotations in this paragraph come respectively from "Democracy and Good Governance in Africa," 5; and *Sowing the Mustard Seed*, 197.

19. The points in the paragraph are more fully discussed in Nelson Kasfir, "Are African Peasants Self-Sufficient?" *Development and Change* 17 (April 1986): 335–57.

20. Thomas Carothers, "Democracy Assistance: The Question of Strategy," *Democratization* 4 (Autumn 1997): 121–22.

21. Museveni, *Sowing the Mustard Seed*, 195 (italics added).

22. This bill is known as the Movement Act of 1997.

15

THE GAMBIA: FROM COUP TO ELECTIONS

John A. Wiseman

John A. Wiseman, senior lecturer in politics at the University of Newcastle upon Tyne, is the author of The New Struggle for Democracy in Africa *(1996). He gratefully acknowledges funding for repeated research visits to the Gambia over 20 years from the British Academy, the Nuffield Foundation, and the Research Committee of the University of Newcastle upon Tyne.*

Explaining the readiness of his fellow Nigerians to accept the contrived and limited process through which their country was supposed to return to democracy in 1993, Nobel prizewinning author and dissident Wole Soyinka observed that "Nigerians made up their minds that even a moldy loaf was better than nothing and that the immediate target . . . was to get rid of the military [dictatorship]."[1] In the event, of course, the regime of General Ibrahim Babangida annulled the 1993 presidential election *tout court*. Instead of a moldy loaf, Nigerians ended up with nothing at all.

Although the circumstances surrounding the 1996–97 legislative and presidential elections in the Gambia differed in some ways from those that took place a few years earlier in Nigeria, Soyinka's metaphor vividly captures the character of the political change that did occur in that much smaller West African state, which contains slightly more than a million people in a territory, virtually surrounded by Senegal, running for about two hundred miles along the lower reaches of the Gambia River. The elections, which were supposed to mark a democratic transition from military to civilian rule, were deeply flawed and left the military head of state, Colonel Yahya Jammeh, still in charge as a nominally civilianized president. Yet despite the sharp limits and serious distortions besetting the whole exercise, there was genuine movement in a democratic direction. This was owing largely to the activism of Gambian civil society and the decision of domestic opposition groups to put aside their thoroughly justifiable misgivings in order to take part in the electoral process.

Until the army coup led by then-Lieutenant Jammeh on 22 July 1994, the Gambia had had a multiparty democracy that dated back to independence from Britain in 1965—the longest-surviving such regime in Africa. For nearly three decades after the country's peaceful acquisition of self-rule, it had been governed by President Dawda Kairaba Jawara and his People's Progressive Party (PPP). Free and relatively fair multiparty elections were regularly held. It was ironic that the military takeover came just as most other African states were moving in precisely the opposite direction, reintroducing more democratic and competitive party systems after decades of authoritarian rule.

The coup was the work of a group of young officers calling themselves the Armed Forces Provisional Ruling Council (AFPRC). Jammeh, their leader, promptly promoted himself to colonel and promised "a new era of freedom, progress, democracy, and accountability." Meanwhile, he was banning all existing political parties and ordering the arrest of most political leaders who had not already fled the country, as well as many senior army and police officers. Lawyers' and doctors' groups, trade unionists, the independent press, and most Western nations condemned the takeover, but could not prevent Jammeh and his cohorts from embarking on 30 months of increasingly authoritarian rule.[2]

The AFPRC's media policy, for instance, significantly restricted open discussion of political matters. The newly established national television station and government-controlled newspapers such as the *Gambia Daily* and *Upfront* (the latter's masthead proudly styled it "The Voice of the Armed Forces Provisional Ruling Council") specialized in undiluted praise for Jammeh and unadulterated attacks on anyone who appeared to be a critic. From the start, Jammeh showed extreme hostility toward the independent press. Restrained from banning it outright by fear of international opprobrium, he used a number of strategies to harass and intimidate journalists. That newspapers such as the *Observer*, the *Point*, and *Forayaa* managed to keep publishing and maintain even a cautiously critical stance testifies to the determination, and in many cases the personal courage, of their editors and staffers.

Since 1994, independent journalists have regularly been arrested and beaten or abused in other ways by members of the security forces (one I spoke to on a recent visit had been the victim of a suspicious house fire, set while he was sleeping). Many journalists have been hauled into court on the flimsiest of charges, sometimes under colonial laws dating to the Second World War. In many cases, judges have exercised independence in dealing with politically motivated charges. Yet even if eventually cleared, defendants have had to put up with a great deal of inconvenience and lost time. The AFPRC also deported significant numbers of journalists from other West African states, especially Liberia and Sierra Leone; such reporters have historically played an important role in the independent Gambian press. In a move plainly meant to cause problems for newspapers operating on tight budgets, the AFPRC in 1996 suddenly declared a hundredfold increase in the financial bond required from any independent newspaper.

Although many members of the Gambian judiciary have attempted to act as buffers against military authoritarianism, they have themselves been subjected to considerable pressure and harassment. Some have been sacked or prematurely retired, to be replaced by more pliant judges recruited from Nigeria. Leading members of the Gambia Bar Association, known for its criticism of military rule, have been subjected to the most onerous treatment.

In the summer of 1995, the military regime issued decrees restricting protections for civil liberties and human rights. The death penalty was reestablished and applied to a vaguely defined category of "treasonable offences." A new secret-police organization, the National Intelligence Agency (NIA), was created with virtually unlimited powers of surveillance and arrest. In its brief career, the NIA has created a climate of fear and gained a reputation for intimidation and torture. In November 1995 came a decree, backdated to the time of the coup, that gave the interior minister unlimited power to arrest and detain without charge any person deemed a threat to "security, peace, and stability." To complete this assault on the rule of law, the same *ukase* banned all applications for the writ of *habeas corpus.*

The military regime used its extensive powers in a highly partisan fashion. Particularly vulnerable to arrest and long-term detention without charge were major political figures who might otherwise have been expected to figure prominently in anti-Jammeh activities, whether as candidates, party organizers, or opposition spokespersons. In some but not all cases, these leaders were associated with the banned precoup parties. Most of these potential opposition leaders were released (without explanation or apology) only *after* the elections.

The AFPRC tightened its grip on the rural areas by naming soldiers to replace the civilian commissioners of each of the five administrative divisions into which the up-river areas are divided. Control was also established over the traditional rural network of chiefs and village headmen. Those suspected of less than total support for Jammeh's regime were replaced by more pliant individuals.

Although Jammeh often spoke ambiguously about whether elections would take place and whether he would run, he embarked on what was, essentially, two-and-a-half years of campaigning. With all other political parties and organizations banned until shortly before the elections, Jammeh toured the country at government expense, trying to persuade Gambians of his leadership qualities. He was backed by a large and well-funded civilian support group (really a political party in all but name) called the July 22nd Movement. It was not much of a surprise when, in time for the elections, this movement transformed itself into a pro-Jammeh party, the Alliance for Patriotic Reorientation and Construction (APRC).

The political legacy of the AFPRC period was such that participation by the personnel of the military regime in the electoral process by itself precluded the possibility of anything resembling a level playing field. This would have been so, moreover, even if the organization and conduct of the elections had been impeccable, which they most assuredly were not.

The Constitution and the Electoral Arrangements

Although Jammeh had been uttering promises of a return to democracy ever since his seizure of power, the course of events leading to the 1996–97 elections was anything but smooth or straightforward. At various times, the AFPRC cast doubt on whether there would even be elections and denounced the very idea of political parties. In October 1994, the regime announced that military rule would last for four years. When condemnations rolled in from Gambian civil society groups as well as from outside sources such as Britain and the Commonwealth, the United States, the European Union, and the African Commission for Human and People's Rights, the regime set up a National Consultative Committee (NCC) to sound out public opinion. In February 1995, following the suppression of two attempted coups within the AFPRC, Jammeh publicly accepted the NCC recommendation that the projected period of military rule should be cut from four to two years.

In April 1995, funding from the United States, Britain, Canada, and various foreign nongovernmental organizations supported the establishment of a Constitutional Review Commission (CRC). Chaired by a Ghanaian attorney, this expert body submitted its recommendations for a draft constitution to the AFPRC in December 1995. Nothing was made public until March 1996, by which time Jammeh had given himself a free hand to accept, amend, or reject the CRC's ideas.

Although many Gambians expressed serious objections to various aspects of the CRC draft, it was put to a referendum in August 1996. The referendum split both the pro- and anti-Jammeh camps. Many in the former, especially members of the July 22nd Movement, backed a simple continuation of military rule. Their more astute colleagues, however, realized that Jammeh was sure to win the presidential election, and favored the adoption of the constitution. Jammeh himself was coy about whether he would be a candidate. In April 1996 he even said that elections would be postponed indefinitely, only to announce a few weeks later that they would take place in September and December (the latter subsequently changed to January).

Many AFPRC opponents urged a "no" vote, arguing that the proposed constitution was badly flawed and a device to perpetuate and legitimize Jammeh's hold on power. Others, most notably those associated with the People's Democratic Organisation for Independence and Socialism (PDOIS), a small but influential party from the precoup period, argued for a "yes" vote on pragmatic grounds.[3] To them, even a flawed election and constitution seemed preferable to the continuation of undiluted military rule. This split produced in opposition ranks an animosity that would last through the elections.

Many Gambians unaffiliated with the opposition questioned the meaningfulness and advisability of an up-or-down vote on a complex 174-page legal document that most voters could not read. Yet the referendum went ahead as scheduled on 8 August 1996, and 70 percent of the voters approved the new Constitution (turnout was 87 percent).

Although Jammeh probably would have preferred otherwise, the new Constitution did allow for competing political parties: The Gambia's long tradition of competitive politics, combined with the trend toward multipartism that was sweeping Africa during the 1990s, made this step virtually inevitable. Nonetheless, Jammeh's critics were not mistaken in suspecting that the Constitution and its associated electoral arrangements contained many aspects designed to make it easier for the incumbents to retain power.

Conspicuously ignored was the national consensus—based on the view that Jawara had held on for too long—that holders of the presidency should be allowed a maximum of two terms. Less surprising was the decision to set the minimum age of eligibility for the presidency at 30 rather than 40 (the latter figure would have excluded the youthful Jammeh). Perhaps most controversially, the new Constitution included an indemnity clause freeing every member of the AFPRC of legal accountability for actions taken while in office. This was in spite of (or more accurately, because of) the well-substantiated accusations of massive corruption that had surfaced regarding the AFPRC elite. A related provision declared that no future National Assembly could amend or repeal the indemnity clause.

Although the Constitution included various provisions relating to elections, the precise arrangements for the 1996–97 voting were mostly set by a 161-page decree that the AFPRC released in April 1996 and then kept amending right up to election day. The arrangements that resulted objectively disadvantaged the opposition. Jammeh was allowed to handpick the members of the Provisional Independent Electoral Commission (PIEC), the body entrusted with organizing the elections. (In the event, the PIEC did its best in very difficult circumstances.) In a move to discourage the nomination of opposition candidates, the government multiplied by 25 the deposit required from parliamentary candidates. Any party not having access to state coffers but wishing to contest all 45 constituencies would have needed what, in a poor country like the Gambia, is a truly enormous sum. This meant that no opposition party could afford to put up a full slate of candidates. In addition, the old constituency boundaries were redrawn in ways that blatantly violated the new Constitution's requirement that constituencies "contain as nearly equal numbers of inhabitants as appears . . . reasonably practical." All the political parties that had been represented in previous Gambian parliaments were banned from reforming. Of all the precoup parties, only the PDOIS could participate since it had never managed to win a seat.

Banning applied not only to parties but to individual politicians. Nobody who had ever been a member of any previous government was permitted to run, whether or not they had ever been accused of any wrongdoing while in office. This ban included such experienced individuals as Sheriff Dibba of the National Convention Party (NCP) and Assan Musa Camara of the Gambia People's Party (GPP)—the two main opposition parties of the precoup era—since each man had in the distant past served in a PPP government. Finally, it was announced that campaigning by political parties, which at that stage had still not been permitted to form, would be restricted to a three-week period before the election. In the meantime, Jammeh carried on his own officially nonexistent election campaign.

The Commonwealth, the European Union, the U.S.-based National Democratic Institute, and various Western governments deemed these arrangements so badly flawed that they decided to abandon monitoring efforts, feeling that the dispatch of an observer mission might merely serve to lend the process undeserved credibility. While this reluctance was understandable, the absence of official outside monitors made it easier to commit malfeasance on election day and also deprived the opposition of the protection, however limited, that monitors might have been able to provide during the campaign period.

Campaigns and Elections

With all political parties banned until a few weeks before the presidential election (and all the major precoup parties banned indefinitely), the preparations for contesting the elections were inevitably rushed. To no one's surprise, the July 22nd Movement became the APRC, its new moniker representing a clumsy attempt to evoke the military AFPRC. The PDOIS—the party with the most radical and youthful base of supporters—now ironically found itself the most "senior" party. It was the only one to have contested previous elections, having run losing candidates in 1987 and 1992.

Elements associated with the old parliamentary parties came together to form the United Democratic Party (UDP) under the nominal leadership of Ousainou Darboe, a prominent human rights lawyer who had for a time been jailed by the military regime. Darboe was untainted by any previous government malpractice and had the further advantage of belonging to the Mandinka, the Gambia's largest ethnic group. The only other party to survive until election day was the rather personalist National Reconciliation Party (NRP), led by the flamboyant but politically inexperienced Hamat Bah. It was strongly rumored in some quarters that Jammeh had personally encouraged the formation of the NRP in hopes of splitting the opposition vote.

Presidential nominations were submitted to the PIEC on September 5, and the official presidential campaign ran from September 9 to 24. The list of nominees contained no surprises. The APRC named Jammeh (who had officially retired from the army on September 4), the UDP and NRP put forward their respective party leaders, and the PDOIS tapped as its standard bearer Sidia Jatta, one of its two most prominent leaders.

The brief presidential campaign was far from being free or fair. The government-owned media, especially the recently established Gambia Television, blatantly touted Jammeh's candidacy while ignoring the other contenders. Coverage was so unbalanced that the PIEC officially criticized the state-owned media's bias. Such criticisms were simply ignored and had no effect. The independent press tried to present more balanced coverage, but faced crippling limitations brought on by more than two years of government intimidation. It must also be remembered that while the independent press reaches readers in the urban coastal areas fairly efficiently, distribution is far more difficult in the more remote, upriver areas where most Gambians live. These logistical problems were compounded by a military-dominated local administration supportive of Jammeh and hostile to his opponents.

The APRC held a massive edge in funding and other resources over the opposition, whose campaigns were shoestring affairs dependent upon contributions of money and labor from party members. Blatantly using state funds for partisan activities, the APRC mounted a large and expensive campaign. Although the lack of independent accounting procedures under the military government makes it impossible to calculate exactly how much of the state budget was diverted to Jammeh's campaign, the amount was clearly very large.

The use of government media and the financial dominance enjoyed by the incumbents were not without precedent in Gambian history. The PPP during its heyday had employed similar tactics, albeit somewhat less extensively. What was new was the APRC's massive use of violence and intimidation. Campaign events staged by the opposition, especially the UDP, often became targets of violent attacks by Jammeh supporters. Deaths and serious injuries resulted, though the numbers are a matter of dispute. Soldiers, sometimes in uniform, frequently played a prominent role in these assaults, following which the police would move in to arrest *the victims* for "disturbing the peace."

On occasion, intimidation alone was used. On his tours of the countryside, Jammeh was always accompanied by a large military escort,
often with heavy weapons like antiaircraft guns in tow. It is not difficult
to imagine the effect that such displays of overwhelming power—rather
dubiously justified as necessary for the head of state's personal security—would have on small Gambian villages. Meanwhile, threats against
the life of UDP leader Ousainou Darboe forced him to seek refuge in the
Senegalese embassy on election day.

Given the circumstances, it came as no surprise that Jammeh was declared the winner. Indeed, one of his AFPRC colleagues, Captain Yan-
kuba Touray, had been announcing at campaign rallies that Jammeh
would win whether the electorate voted for him or not! The official
results credited Jammeh with 55.8 percent, with 35.8 percent going to
Darboe, 5.5 percent to Bah, and 2.8 percent to Jatta. According to these
results, Jammeh finished first in 37 out of 45 constituencies, with Darboe topping the remaining eight. Later, an alternative set of results
would leak out suggesting that Darboe had actually defeated Jammeh,
57 to 34 percent. Even observers sympathethic to Darboe greeted these
figures with skepticism, however, since the unbalanced circumstances
of the campaign itself would seem to have made a Jammeh victory inevitable and obviated the need for extensive election-day chicanery.

With the presidential election out of the way, attention focused on
the legislative balloting, which had been rescheduled for 2 January
1997. The deeply flawed nature of the presidential race spurred debate
within opposition ranks about whether it would be advisable to take
part in the legislative elections. Many in the UDP argued that without
strict (and difficult to enforce) guarantees of greater fairness from the
government, participation might serve only to lend a veneer of legitimacy to a thoroughly illegitimate process. As it had in the opposition
debate over the constitutional referendum, the PDOIS took the view
that there was more to be gained from taking part in a flawed process
than from sitting it out. Once the PDOIS leaders had announced their
intention of contesting the legislative elections, the UDP felt that there
was little choice but to follow suit. The disagreement within the opposition camp left behind considerable animosity, making an opposition
electoral pact impossible to arrange.

At the close of nominations on December 4, only the APRC had candidates in all 45 constituencies. Because of organizational and financial
difficulties—and, in some localities, threats—the UDP had 34 candidates, the PDOIS had 17, the NRP had 5, and independents totaled 6. In
5 constituencies, all in Jammeh's home region, the APRC nominee ran
unopposed.

Although the legislative election was far from free and fair, there
was general agreement among the opposition that it marked an improvement over the presidential contest, with lower levels of violence

and intimidation. Nonetheless, significant numbers of UDP activists were arrested, and Gambia Workers' Confederation secretary general Pa Modou Faal, the country's leading trade unionist and a longtime critic of military rule, was detained without charge for most of the campaign period. The UDP parliamentary candidate in the Jarra West constituency, Kemeseng Jammeh, was detained but than released after intervention on his behalf by the PIEC.

As in the presidential election, the APRC campaign made extensive use of state resources. President Jammeh openly told voters that districts returning opposition candidates would get no government development funding. Election day itself was free of major outbreaks of violence. In several up-river constituencies there were cases of known opposition supporters being arrested as they went to vote, *pour décourager les autres*. Such naked intimidation appears to have been largely absent from urban polling stations.

When the results were announced, it again came as no surprise that the APRC had won. Jammeh's group won 52 percent of the popular vote and a 33-seat majority (counting the 5 districts where it ran unopposed). The UDP won 34 percent and 7 seats, with the PDOIS gaining 8 percent and 1 seat; independents, 4 percent and 2 seats; and the NRP, 2 percent and 2 seats. Analysis suggests that voting patterns remained fairly constant from the presidential to the parliamentary elections. Although Jammeh gained a higher percentage of the overall vote than did his party, this was balanced by the lack of opposition in the 5 constituencies in his home region. Most of the opposition victories were in constituencies where one or another of the opposition presidential candidates had outpolled Jammeh the previous September.

Although the opposition parties complained of the illegal inclusion on the voter rolls of foreign migrants (from Senegal, Mali, Sierra Leone, Guinea, and Nigeria) likely to support the APRC, oppositionists broadly accepted that the actual counting of votes had been relatively fair. Given the similarity of voting patterns across the presidential and legislative elections, this might be taken to imply that the counting of votes in the presidential election was also relatively fair. Information remains seriously incomplete, however; thus it is probably most accurate to say that no definitive assessment of the reliability of the voting figures is possible as yet.

A "Moldy Loaf" or No Bread at All?

Even aside from the murky question of the vote counting, it is clear that the 1996–97 elections cannot be seen as representing an authentic and thoroughgoing transition to democracy. The denial of civic freedoms during more than two years of outright military rule was severely inimical to the necessary conditions for a democratic election process.

Continuing official intimidation of opponents made the elections un-
free by any reasonable standard. The new Constitution and the electoral
arrangements had been tailored to favor the incumbent military elite,
which was, in any case, determined to maintain its grip on power regardless of the electoral outcome. During extensive discussions with a
wide range of politically informed and active Gambians in 1995 and
again in 1997, I encountered no one who thought that Jammeh and his
colleagues might actually leave office because of a lost election. The
inner ring of the AFPRC government has remained intact since the
elections; retiring from the army did not mean relinquishing power.

To return to Soyinka's metaphor, these elections clearly represented
a "moldy loaf" for Gambians in terms of a democratic transition. A
crucial question, however, is whether this "moldy loaf" was better than
no bread at all—that is, whether a badly flawed transition was preferable to a continuation of undiluted military rule. My own judgment,
which coincides with that of most Gambian opposition leaders, is that
for all its severe imperfections, the change did mark a limited movement away from military dictatorship and toward a kind of liberalized
authoritarianism. The Gambia is still far from being a functioning
democracy, but it has taken a step in the right direction.

The existence of legal opposition parties and their significant presence in the National Assembly mean that there is a forum available for
critical discussion of public concerns. In other words, new political
space has opened up. It was noticeable during the election campaigns,
for example, that opposition criticisms of the government flourished
with unprecedented vigor and were well reported in the independent
press. Early indications suggest that this process has been carried
through into the debates of the National Assembly, where the opposition has been trying to make the most of its opportunities under the new
constitutional and legal framework.

A look at how the new National Assembly operated during its first
year, however, also shows how hard it is for the oposition to use parliamentary debates to criticize Jammeh and his government. Under Jawara, the neutrality of the speaker of parliament was taken very seriously.
Consultations between government and opposition ensured that the
individual chosen had the support of all sides. This is no longer the
case. The new Constitution mandates that the holder of the speakership
must come from among the ranks of the presidentially appointed MPs.
Speaker Mustapha Baboucarr Wadda (formerly secretary general of the
Office of the President) has used the powers of his office to block
critical motions and pointed questions.

In an effort to get around this obstacle, opposition legislators have
been making the most of the adjournment debates that occur at the end
of each Assembly session, and during which members may raise any issue they choose. While these debates do not permit the introduction of

new motions or the questioning of ministers, they do provide a public forum for the criticism of the government's policies and actions.

The advent of "constitutional" rule has proved to be at best a weak barrier against the regime's authoritarianism. The new arrangements have created an institutionalized form of political space, but the ruling elite has thrown up a variety of obstacles to keep its opponents from using that space. This contest—between a regime determined to shrink the new political space and an opposition eager to expand it—has been the dominant feature of the postelection period. Over the past year, the opposition parties and the independent press have struggled courageously to protect the freedom of political debate amid state repression that has been scarcely lessened since the end of overt military rule. Opposition supporters and independent journalists are still subject to harassment, detention, and even torture.

If one were seeking instructive comparisons in West Africa, the case of Ghana might be worth considering. Ghana's 1992 elections suffered from many of the same defects that were apparent in Gambia four years later. The Ghanaian opposition's objections to the conduct of the November presidential race—won by Jerry Rawlings, Ghana's own civilianized military strongman—led it to boycott the December legislative elections. The wisdom of this tactic is debatable. The Gambian opposition clearly took a different tack by choosing participation rather than abstention, albeit after much discussion (including reflections on the Ghanaian example). The contributions to this volume by E. Gyimah-Boadi and Terrence Lyons clearly show how democratic space opened up in Ghana after the flawed 1992 elections, and how the next balloting four years later marked a significant gain for the cause of democratic governance.[4] While no one should conclude from this that the future trajectory of Gambian politics will necessarily replicate that of Ghana since 1992, the comparison may have some validity.

On a more pessimistic note, the extremely flawed nature of the transition in the Gambia does not bode well for the Nigerian transition, presently set to occur in October 1998. Sani Abacha, Nigeria's military dictator, is widely expected to follow Jammeh's example by engineering his own installation as an "elected" president. Relations between Abacha and Jammeh have been highly cordial over the past few years. In February 1997, Abacha complimented his Gambian counterpart on "the impressive way and manner [in which] your transition program was implemented." In a state visit to the Gambia the following October, Abacha expanded on this theme.

If one also takes into account the manner in which coup leader General Ibrahim Mainassara secured his own subsequent election to the presidency of Niger in July 1996 (an episode with many parallels to the Gambian case), it is plausible to regard Jammeh's "election victory" as replicating a more widespread phenomenon. In the past, single-party elections were the means of choice for African military rulers looking to engineer political legitimacy for themselves. The emerging pattern today involves the use of constrained multiparty elections for the same purpose. To return to Soyinka's metaphor, we are seeing more "moldy loaves" being handed to the voters of West Africa.

The future of the Gambian political system remains uncertain. An optimist might suggest the distinct possibility that the Gambia's opposition parties and civil society can maximize the opportunities created by the recent changes to constrain the Jammeh regime's authoritarian impulses and nudge the political system in a democratic direction. A pessimist might stress the possibility that the Gambia will follow the pattern, visible in Sierra Leone, of coups and countercoups leading to state collapse. Until the military takeover of 1994, the Gambia knew almost 30 years of relatively democratic and stable government. It would be a catastrophe for the Gambian people if their country were now to head in a direction quite opposed to that legacy.

NOTES

1. Wole Soyinka, "The Shape of Things to Come," *Index on Censorship,* September–October 1993, 32–33.

2. For fuller accounts of the coup and the military period, see John A. Wiseman and Elizabeth Vidler, "The July 1994 Coup d'Etat in The Gambia: The End of an Era," *The Round Table,* January 1995, 53–65; and Wiseman, "Military Rule in The Gambia: An Interim Assessment," *Third World Quarterly* 17 (December 1996): 917–40.

3. While one might question the PDOIS leaders' choice of tactics, their integrity is beyond doubt. Having spent nearly a decade opposing the Jawara regime, they declined the cabinet posts that Jammeh offered them after his coup, citing their principled objections to military intervention in politics. Subsequently, they were arrested and detained for deliberately flouting a military decree by continuing to publish their party newspaper *Foroyaa* (meaning "freedom" in the Wolof language).

4. Terrence Lyons, "Ghana's Elections: A Major Step Forward" and E. Gyimah-Boadi, "Ghana's Elections: The Challenges Ahead," *Journal of Democracy* 8 (April 1997): 65–77 and 78–91.

16

NIGERIA: AN END TO THE PERMANENT TRANSITION?

Peter M. Lewis

Peter M. Lewis *is assistant professor in the School of International Service at the American University in Washington, D.C. His recent publications include (as editor)* Africa: Dilemmas of Development and Change *(1998) and (with Barnett R. Rubin and Pearl T. Robinson)* Stabilizing Nigeria: Sanctions, Incentives, and Support for Civil Society *(1998). He is currently completing a book on the comparative political economies of Indonesia and Nigeria.*

As democratic pressures swept Africa in the early 1990s, Nigeria appeared poised for its own passage from authoritarian rule. Rather than joining the "third wave" democracies, however, Nigeria's military rulers annulled a broadly popular presidential election in 1993, giving rise to a harsh new dictatorship. The ensuing crisis accelerated a downward spiral of political disorder, social division, and economic decline.

The death of military dictator Sani Abacha on 8 June 1998 ended a dismal chapter in Nigeria's political life. Although his successor, General Abdulsalami Abubakar, has charted an encouraging new direction, the country confronts formidable challenges of reconciliation and renewal.

In late July, General Abubakar unveiled his government's political agenda. In a televised address, the general pledged to lead the military back to the barracks, and permanently out of political life, in May 1999. He outlined a plan for the country's return to democratic rule through a series of elections and political reforms. This included promises for the release of political prisoners, the promulgation of a constitution, and an open arena for political parties. An independent electoral commission would supervise the program. The ten-month schedule of party registration, conventions, campaigns, and phased elections would conclude with the handover to civilian government.

The general's statement was met with guarded approval from foreign and domestic audiences. For most Nigerians, however, this was a familiar refrain that sparked more suspicion than enthusiasm. Over

Nigeria's 38 years of independence, the armed forces have ruled for all but ten. Generals have held power continuously over the last 15 years. Most of the country's eight military leaders have vowed a return to democracy; so far, only one has delivered. To observers of Nigeria's predicament, the "permanent transition" has become a virtual strategy of military control.[1]

The political situation in Nigeria did not always seem so bleak. The nation's course of decay was not inevitable, although it did reflect deeper historical currents. In the decades since independence, Nigerians have grappled with the management of cultural pluralism, the development of democratic institutions, the terms of civil-military relations, and the oversight of a centralized petroleum economy.

Like most African states, Nigeria was an artificial creation of colonialism. The boundaries established by the British encompassed some 250 ethnic and linguistic groups, among whom the northwestern Hausa-Fulani, the southwestern Yoruba, and the southeastern Igbo became dominant rivals. The arena of communal competition has become more complex as a number of ethnic minorities have asserted themselves politically. During the first decade of independence, the stresses of ethnic and regional contention led to military coups, mass violence, attempted secession, and civil war. Nigeria's existence as a federal state has been preserved, yet sectional tensions have continued to destabilize the nation's politics.

The quest for democratic governance has occupied many leaders since 1966, when the first parliamentary government was overthrown by the military. Since that time, despite an oft-stated commitment to democracy, military rulers have governed for all but four years. The ill-fated civilian Second Republic, modeled on the American presidential system, lasted only from 1979 to 1983. As the armed forces have become habituated to ruling, it has become increasingly difficult to lead ambitious officers back to the barracks. Political entanglements have exacerbated factionalism, corruption, and insecurity within the military.

Economic management constitutes another challenge. The country's emergence as a leading global oil producer in the 1970s gave rise to a centralized, state-dominated economy, in which the allocation of mineral rents is a principal source of growth, class formation, and political control. The vast resources concentrated in Nigeria's rentier state have made the central government a focus of competition and influence. Rivalries among ethnic and regional communities and contention between civilian and military elites have been animated by the struggle for access to state resources.

These dilemmas have converged over the past decade to produce a crisis of governance and civic order. Military dominance has eroded the foundations of democratic rule and weakened civil society. The political hegemony of northern elites has produced growing restiveness among southern groups, raising grave questions about Nigeria's tenuous federal compact. The degeneration of the rentier economy, afflicted by misrule and adverse global markets, has aggravated popular frustration and debilitated the state.

In recent months, Abubakar's transition program has gained acceptance, and many Nigerians have allowed themselves some guarded optimism about political change. The legacy of a decade of predatory dictatorship, however, weighs heavily on the current process. The country urgently needs to reconstruct essential institutions, mend civic morale, and revive the moribund economy. The current regime has lifted expectations, but a derailment of reform could jeopardize Nigeria's viability as a nation.

A Wayward Transition

Nigeria's recent travails are rooted in an earlier failure of political reform.[2] General Ibrahim Babangida assumed power in August 1985 in a nearly bloodless coup that ousted the regime of General Muhammadu Buhari. Initially welcomed as an enterprising reformer, Babangida relaxed many of his predecessor's restrictions on political life and the media, and announced a program of democratic transition and economic liberalization. His personal charm and political dexterity were potent assets in selling his agenda. Many Nigerians hoped for a respite from the ceaseless alternation of military and civilian regimes.

Over time, however, the regime grew increasingly authoritarian and moved away from its commitments to change. Babangida employed political manipulation, inducement, and blunt coercion to secure acquiescence with his programs. Throughout the transition, authorities confined the scope of political debate, participation, and competition. Two officially sanctioned political parties were mandated in 1989, and the transition program was repeatedly amended. The government arbitrarily banned or accredited selected groups of politicians.

In April 1990, the regime foiled a violent, ethnically based coup attempt. A few months later, the Gulf crisis prompted a surge in world oil prices, conferring a new revenue windfall for the government. At this point, the transition stumbled conspicuously, as Babangida's rule became more dictatorial and self-interested. The regime meddled extensively in the political process, and postponed the transition twice more before settling on a deadline of August 1993. Meanwhile, economic management worsened, and there was a marked acceleration of official corruption.

If the military was seeking a pretext for lingering in power, it was aided by the discord and misconduct of the political class. As in previous interludes of civilian competition, politicians treated public office as the route to personal or ethnic gain. The transition was muddied by legal disputes, factional squabbles, and political violence. Babangida added further obstacles by creating nine new states, which increased political and administrative confusion. In a bid to allay suspicion that he harbored a "hidden agenda" to perpetuate his rule, Babangida appointed a civilian Transitional Council in January 1993 to act as a shadow administration until the handover.

The June 12 Crisis

In the early months of 1993, the political parties nominated candidates with an implicit stamp of approval from the military. The center-left Social Democratic Party selected Chief Moshood K.O. Abiola, a popular Yoruba Muslim business magnate. His presidential aspirations were bolstered by his high profile as a media baron and philanthropist, and he formed a strategic ticket with a northerner, Babagana Kingibe. The center-right National Republican Convention selected Alhaji Bashir Tofa, a comparatively obscure business leader from Kano, in the northern Muslim heartland.

Public cynicism toward the transition was eased by two considerations. The contest posed new openings for sectional politics. Southerners were skeptical that northern elites would relinquish political control, but Abiola's candidacy posed an opportunity for a southern presidency. The two-party system, although a military contrivance, encouraged coalitions across regional and ethnic lines. Another encouraging factor was the notable restraint during the campaign by the politicians, who sought to avoid a pretext for additional delays in the transition.

The June 12 election was unexpectedly sound, with little evidence of systematic fraud, vote-rigging, or violence. Returns were quickly compiled by the electoral commission and leaked to the press. The results showed a commanding majority of 59 percent for Chief Abiola, who carried not only the southwestern Yoruba areas, but also several states in the far north, the middle belt, and the minority southeast. The voting pattern also suggested a tentative coalition of ideological progressives from diverse parts of the nation.

The poll was clouded by a flurry of legal challenges, instigated by a shadowy civilian group that campaigned for the perpetuation of military rule. After unsuccessfully seeking an injunction to halt the election, they obtained a ruling against release of the results. Several days later, the regime summarily voided the election. Babangida cited legal and administrative problems as the grounds for annulment. His claim of deference to the rule of law was disingenuous, as the regime ruled by decree, and there was strong evidence that the court actions had been orchestrated by the military.

In the view of most Yorubas, the annulment was a rebuke to their political aspirations by a northern Muslim elite. The 1993 election was

reminiscent of irregular elections in 1965 and 1983, providing further
evidence of the southwest's exclusion from national power. For much
of the Nigerian public, this action represented the designs of an
entrenched military leadership unwilling to cede power or access to the
nation's oil wealth.

In the rioting that soon erupted in Lagos and other southwestern
cities, security forces killed more than 100 people. A loosely knit prodemocracy coalition of human rights groups, trade unions, professional
associations, segments of the media, and fragments of the political
parties pressed for validation of the elections, though it did not have a
distinct strategy. The United States, Great Britain, Canada, and the
European Union protested the annulment and suspended some marginal
aid, but the international response was uneven.

Under pressure from public opposition, foreign censure, and urgings
from elements of the military, Babangida ultimately conceded to the
transition deadline. On 26 August 1993 he resigned from the presidency and the military, transferring authority to a civilian-led Interim
National Government (ING) led by Chief Ernest Shonekan, the head of
the Transitional Council. General Sani Abacha, a Babangida confeder-
ate, was moved into position as Defense Minister in the ING. Abacha's
presence was widely regarded as a military stalking horse within the
civilian council.

Lacking a clear mandate or popular legitimacy, the ING muddled
through for less than three months. Seeking to improve relations with
external creditors, the government attempted to raise domestic fuel
prices. This incited a general strike, and on November 17, Shonekan
was induced to resign by General Abacha. Having already replaced key
Babangida loyalists in the military with his own coterie, Abacha
quickly consolidated his authority.

The Emergence of Predatory Rule

The June 12 crisis aggravated several pernicious trends in Nigerian
politics and society. Having steadily personalized his control,
Babangida ran roughshod over public institutions and civic forces. The
military showed utter disdain for democratic change, revealing stronger
signs of internal factionalism and politicization. In the latter years of
Babangida's regime, a narrow circle of military officers and cronies
also fostered new extremes of economic predation. For their part, the
civilian political class exhibited a disheartening degree of opportunism,
and they did not form a bastion of democratic change. The crisis further
accentuated the alienation of citizens from the state, aggravating deep-
seated regional and ethnic resentments.

These trends worsened markedly under the regime of General
Abacha. Nigerians are accustomed to military rulers and official corrup-

tion, but the degree of political repression, human rights abuses, and wholesale economic plunder seen during Abacha's reign was truly unprecedented. Abacha's concentration of personal power and the efforts to regularize his dictatorship went beyond anything his predecessor had envisioned.[3]

Initially, Abacha's palace coup was not entirely unwelcome, and the General practiced some of Babangida's political craftsmanship. He engaged in backroom discussions with Abiola's camp over the possibility of reinstating the June 12 poll. He also named a mainly civilian cabinet replete with veteran politicians, a prominent human rights advocate, a leading media executive, and a noted economic reformer. Babagana Kingibe, Abiola's erstwhile running mate, appeared as foreign minister. But the direction of the regime became clearer when Abacha discarded Babangida's transition program, scrapping the constitution and dissolving the various tiers of civilian government that had been elected.

The government created a Constitutional Conference to debate the framework for a new political transition. The conference attracted hundreds of politicians and notables through ample government stipends and tacit opportunities for political advancement. This incorporation of civilians, along with other forms of patronage, brought much of the political class into compliance with the regime.

Opposition to Abacha's government was divided and tentative. The dissolution of the political parties depleted an important organizational base for resistance to the military, and selective government repression against labor, students, academics, human rights groups, and the media proved sufficient to quell large-scale dissent. Abiola's contingent had difficulty sustaining broad support outside the Yoruba community. The regional and class makeup of the democratic movement, centered among professionals in Lagos, hindered wider social mobilization and was exploited by the military to isolate dissent.

The regime's economic policies proved ruinous. With considerable input from civilians in the cabinet, the 1994 budget discarded the basic features of economic liberalization and established a populist economic framework, sending the economy into a steep decline. These policies were accompanied by evidence of massive official corruption.

As the first anniversary of the June 12 election approached, the confrontation between government and opposition intensified. In May 1994, the National Democratic Coalition (NADECO), a multiethnic grouping of former politicians and other notables, emerged as a leading force in the prodemocracy movement. From this organizational base, Abiola renewed his efforts to affirm the verdict of June 12. A day before the anniversary, Abiola declared himself the legitimate president of Nigeria, challenging the military to abdicate. He was soon arrested and charged with treason—a capital offense.

Chief Abiola's arrest sparked the most concerted opposition to military rule yet seen in Nigeria. The petroleum workers' unions, NUPENG and PENGASSAN, went on strike in July to protest Abiola's detention and support his mandate. They were soon joined by disgruntled bank employees and prodemocracy academics, as scattered protests and rioting erupted in several southwestern cities. The Nigerian Labour Congress remained on the sidelines. The oil unions' actions were sufficient to paralyze the country during nine weeks of confrontation. Nigeria's oil exports were reduced by a third, and the domestic economy was immobilized by fuel shortages.

Abacha moved aggressively to end the standoff by arresting the leaders of the petroleum unions and sealing their offices. The government also shuttered three independent media companies and issued a decree exempting itself from the jurisdiction of the courts. Democracy activists were arrested under a preventive detention order, and assailants staged attacks on the homes of several dissidents. More than 120 street protesters were killed by security forces in the southwestern cities. By early September, the strikes were broken, and the military government had clearly prevailed.

Repression and Consolidation

In the wake of the strikes, Abacha dismissed civilians from his ruling council, reshuffled his cabinet, and sidelined military personnel whose loyalty was suspect. Activists and journalists were harassed and detained. The Constitutional Conference proceeded, but the government disregarded most of its central recommendations, including appeals for an early return to civilian rule.

In March 1995, the government announced that it had foiled a coup attempt. The regime conducted secret trials for more than 40 alleged conspirators, including retired Generals Olusegun Obasanjo, a former head of state, and Shehu Musa Yar'Adua, Obasanjo's former Chief of Staff and a recent presidential aspirant. Obasanjo and Yar'Adua were both vocal critics of military rule, having supervised the 1979 transition to the civilian Second Republic. The democratic activist Beko Ransome-Kuti was also tried, as were prominent journalists. The tribunal's harsh rulings included the death penalty for Yar'Adua and life imprisonment for Obasanjo, sentences which were later reduced after international protests.[4] In the absence of any public evidence, critics maintained that the incident was simply a ruse for Abacha to purge his opponents.

Continuing to profess his commitment to democratization, in October 1995 Abacha announced a new schedule for transition to civilian rule, set to conclude in three years. The program resembled Babangida's agenda, leading many observers to infer that Abacha held a similar attachment to power. The new transition was purportedly based upon the draft constitution produced by the Constitutional Conference. This document, after subsequent amendments by Abacha, introduced a six-zone regional arrangement and provided for the rotation of presidential candidates among the zones. It also outlined a ponderous executive structure including a president, vice president, prime minister, and deputy prime minister. While the government regularly referred to the 1995 Constitution as a foundation for its political agenda, it did not see fit to publish the document. Throughout Abacha's reign, the constitution was a matter of conjecture rather than law.

On 10 November 1995, in a shocking blow against political dissent, the regime summarily hanged Ken Saro-Wiwa and eight other activists from the Movement for the Survival of the Ogoni People (MOSOP). Saro-Wiwa was a prominent journalist and activist from the minority Ogoni community of southeastern Nigeria. Since 1990 the Ogoni movement, located in a key oil-producing region of Nigeria, had waged an increasingly militant campaign against the government and the Royal Dutch Shell company, protesting the environmental degradation and economic neglect of their area. The government imposed a heavy security presence in Ogoniland, with considerable evidence of human rights abuses.

Saro-Wiwa and 27 compatriots were arrested in 1994 after four local chiefs were killed in riots arising from a quarrel between radical and moderate Ogoni groups. The sudden execution of the "Ogoni 9" after a flawed trial and virtually no judicial review provoked a wave of international condemnation. The United States imposed modest new sanctions, and Nigeria was suspended from the Commonwealth.[5] Although the country was becoming a global pariah, Abacha evidently concluded that the costs of alienating the international community were tolerable, especially since oil sanctions appeared to be politically unfeasible.

The Downward Slide

The execution of the Ogoni defendants signaled that the regime had taken a plainly despotic course. Abacha was an opaque figure, ruling from the fortified Aso Rock presidential complex in Abuja, and rarely appearing in public or traveling abroad. During his entire reign, he did not once visit Lagos, the nation's largest city and its commercial (and former political) capital. He was inaccessible to much of his cabinet and the ruling military council, shielded by his security chief and presidential guard. These elements, along with a few key civilian retainers and business cronies, formed the bulwark of the regime.

Political repression was extended and regularized. An array of restrictive decrees, some inherited and others introduced by Abacha, allowed wide latitude for the security and intelligence agencies. An unaccustomed climate of fear pervaded the country as the government harassed, detained, and assaulted opponents, real or imagined. For the first time in memory, many Nigerians found themselves wary of public discussion and association.

Within the tenuous political space available, a cluster of human rights groups, prodemocracy organizations, and professional and popular associations pressed for democratic change and protested the regime's abuses. Much of the independent media also continued to operate. These activities existed in a gray zone of semilegality, where crossing an invisible line could bring severe consequences.

Unidentified assailants staged a string of attacks on prominent dissidents and former officials. In June 1996, Kudirat Abiola, the activist wife of the imprisoned political leader, was gunned down in her car in an area of Lagos brimming with security checkpoints. In the public's view, these assaults were instigated by the regime, and the use of political assassination formed another new instrument of control and terror.

Social and economic disorder also worsened. Antipathy for the regime was most evident in the southwest, and a series of bombings against military personnel in Lagos and several other cities heightened tensions. Abacha employed a familiar tactic in 1996, creating yet another six new states (bringing the total to 36) with an associated mosaic of local governments. Instead of reducing friction, this instigated new ethnic disputes in the minority areas of the Niger Delta (where oil production is centered) and in other localities, as groups contended over boundaries and resources. The agitation escalated in the face of government repression and indifference. In addition, the Muslim Brothers, a budding Islamist movement led by Sheik Ibrahim Zak-Zaky, came into growing confrontation with authorities in the northern states. A series of protests resulted in dozens of fatalities and more than a hundred arrests, including that of Sheik Zak-Zaky.

These upheavals reflected the impact of economic deterioration. After 1994, the government restored some features of economic liberalization and fostered a slight upturn in overall performance. But these cosmetic improvements could not conceal the underlying rot in the economy. Nigeria's per-capita gross national product declined from a high of $1,000 in 1980 to less than $250 in 1996, a drop of some 75 percent. Productive activities and non-oil exports were stagnant, the financial sector was approaching collapse, and basic services and infrastructure were in an advanced state of decay. Nigerian participation in international drug trafficking and commercial fraud expanded. Political uncertainty and corruption reinforced the country's international isolation. Even the oil industry suffered, as the government failed to pay its foreign partners and to fund the petroleum sector adequately. The leading sign of economic breakdown was the domestic fuel shortage that persisted through much of 1997 and 1998. This fuel drought, in a major oil-exporting economy, was a powerful indication of the government's ineptitude and misconduct.

The official transition schedule plodded along, and the government-controlled electoral commission accredited five political parties in October 1996, conspicuously excluding groups linked to opposition politicians. The new parties were amorphous, both ideologically and in terms of their regional bases. Large segments of the traditional political class were absent. The opposition contemptuously dismissed the official parties as "five fingers of the same leprous hand." Alongside the party structures, a separate campaign emerged to draft Abacha for president, including efforts to create a cult of personality around him.

Successive elections revealed waning popular interest in the transition. The government claimed a large turnout for local elections in March 1996, but results were not fully released or independently verified. State government polls in December 1997 registered a participation rate of merely 15 percent, and in the April 1998 national assembly elections, fewer than 5 percent of the voters showed up. The absence of political alternatives and the growing evidence of Abacha's intention to succeed himself as an elected civilian president inspired public apathy. With typical cunning, Abacha kept silent on the question of his candidacy, while senior officials asserted his prerogative to run, boosters sang his praises, and other aspirants were discouraged from entering the field.

The regime also acted against potential threats. In December 1997, the government announced that General Yar'Adua had died in prison of a "sudden illness." Appalling prison conditions and a lack of medical care provided the most likely explanations for his death, but some opposition figures charged that Yar'Adua, a popular northern political figure, had been poisoned.

Only weeks after Yar'Adua's death, the government uncovered another alleged coup plot. Twelve people were initially arrested in connection with the conspiracy, the most prominent of whom was General Oladipo Diya, Abacha's second-in-command. The others were mainly Yoruba senior officers. Diya's association with the regime made him unpopular in the southwest, but many Yorubas were still rankled by this apparent ethnic purge. In April 1998, Diya and six other defendants received death sentences.

The next step in Abacha's campaign to succeed himself came in April, when the five political parties hastily assembled conventions and each selected Sani Abacha as its presidential candidate. With this "consensus" nomination on the table, the electoral commission suggested that the August presidential election might become a referendum. A group of 18 northern politicians and notables issued an open letter asking Abacha to decline the nomination and allow an open poll. They were soon followed by a larger group of 34 politicians from around the country. Abacha still refused comment, but there was a general expectation that he would accept the nominations in due course.

The denouement came on June 8, when General Abacha died, reportedly of a heart attack. Given the highly personalized and secretive nature of Abacha's rule, many feared that his death would lead to a power vacuum, inciting rivalries and agitation within the armed forces. But the military Provisional Ruling Council (PRC) quickly designated the Chief of Defense Staff, General Abubakar, as successor, observing the chain of command and rebuffing key Abacha loyalists.

The Latest Transition

Years of predatory rule have created a formidable set of difficulties. The abuse of executive power reached a nadir under General Abacha, who created a virtual shadow government around his inner court. The demoralized armed forces have fallen into disrepute. Leading institutions such as the civil service, the judiciary, and the public education system have been seriously undermined. Central elements of civilian rule, including electoral authorities and political parties, have been weakened by repeated manipulation. The political class, tainted by past transgressions and by its willingness to collaborate with military stratagems, is viewed with disdain by many Nigerians.

The country's traditionally vigorous civil society has been subdued by repression and economic malaise. Many of the social and economic foundations that might support a democratic process, including a substantial educated middle class, have eroded. Regional, ethnic, and religious stresses have become more acute, showing the effects of political exclusion and growing popular immiseration. Levels of social trust, always strained in Nigeria, have palpably declined. The economy has collapsed into a listless oil monoculture, suffused by corruption and criminality, and peripheral to most world markets.

These circumstances pose stiff challenges for political transition. The early months of Abubakar's rule, however, witnessed a dramatic shift of direction. The new head of state, an officer with a reputation for professionalism and relative probity, quickly took steps to reverse some of the most unpopular features of the Abacha regime. Shortly after taking power, he freed several prominent political prisoners, including General Obasanjo, Beko Ransome-Kuti, and the oil union chiefs Frank Kokori and Milton Dabibi. In the following weeks, dozens of additional detainees were released, including 20 prominent Ogoni prisoners, and more releases were promised. Inquiries into corruption under the previous regime were pursued with surprising vigor. The regime quietly began discussions with the domestic opposition, including overtures to Chief Abiola, who was still in detention. Abiola's release was widely rumored and eagerly anticipated. The country's diplomatic isolation subsided as senior officials from the UN and the Commonwealth traveled to Abuja.

Despite these hopeful steps, the country was thrown into turmoil when Chief Abiola died on July 7, during a meeting with a high-level diplomatic team visiting from Washington. Official reports attributed the death to a heart attack, but Chief Abiola's family and supporters bitterly reproached the military government for persecution, medical neglect, and possible foul play. Rioting in the wake of Abiola's death claimed at least 60 lives in three southwestern cities, including Lagos. An independent team of doctors performed an autopsy, and certified a heart attack as the cause of death. Suspicion and anger nonetheless persisted throughout much of the Yoruba community.

Notwithstanding this stunning setback, the authorities showed moderation in handling the unrest, which quickly subsided. Within two weeks, General Abubakar announced a new agenda for transition to democratic rule, set to conclude on 29 May 1999. The government scrapped the political parties, elections, and institutions associated with Abacha's program, and promised a more open and fair process of reform. The 1995 draft constitution was to be retained. A new Independent Electoral Commission (INEC), headed by a respected jurist, was inaugurated, and another round of party registration was slated, this time open to all aspirants. The government plan called for local elections in December 1998, state elections in January 1999, and a presidential poll on 27 February 1999, with the handover three months later.

In spite of their deep-seated mistrust of military promises, the Nigerian public and the political class cautiously accepted the new program as credible. By September, 25 aspirant parties emerged in the scramble for registration. Three organizations led the pack. The People's Democratic Party (PDP) included most of the seasoned politicians in the "Group of 34," including Alex Ekwueme, former vice-president in the Second Republic; Adamu Ciroma, a former minister; and Solomon Lar, a former governor. The Alliance for Democracy (AD) attracted many of the (mainly Yoruba) dissident politicians and activists associated with Abiola's cause, including former NADECO chief Abraham Adesanya; Olu Falae, a Minister of Finance under Babangida; former governor Bola Ige; and the dissident Nobel laureate Wole Soyinka. The All People's Party (APP) also boasted many notables, although their acceptance of politicians close to Abacha and the military drove others toward the PDP or the AD. In October 1998, the INEC certified nine parties, including these major groups.

Pressing Questions

Two pressing questions now face Nigeria: whether the government of General Abubakar can see through a workable transition, and whether the current political framework can yield a lasting democratic regime. Abubakar has assiduously tackled political reform and has already undertaken bold steps toward liberalization. Some of these changes are already irrevocable, but others, such as the promise of press freedom and guarantees of unfettered politics, could still be rescinded.

The regime has straggled in significant areas, such as the repeal of restrictive legislation and the removal of noted hard-liners from the upper echelons of the military. This suggests that significant issues remain unresolved and that disagreements persist within the armed forces. There is a concern that hard-liners on the ruling council may seek to obstruct the transition, and a lingering threat that renegade factions could attempt a coup.

If the country can surmount the hurdle of military withdrawal, many problems will arise before May 29, with further questions over the longer term. In the near term, several issues appear salient. The first is the conduct of the elections. The Independent National Electoral Commission appears reputable, but administrative and logistical problems abound. The October voter registration exercise was troubled by reports of disarray and public confusion, and similar problems are likely in the elections themselves.

Regulations to ensure transparency may assist in building credibility. The electoral commission has retained the "modified open ballot," employed successfully in the 1993 elections. This system requires voters to sign in at their polling station prior to voting, followed by balloting at an appointed time. The system preserves the secrecy of the ballot, but hampers fraud at the polling station. The INEC's invitation for formal international election monitoring (a feature absent from the 1993 elections) could provide additional confidence, especially if foreign observers are accompanied by monitors from Nigerian civic organizations. The Transition Monitoring Group, a coalition of domestic prodemocracy and human rights groups, has sought to fulfill this role.

The emergent party system raises another set of questions. The PDP and the APP, with their extensive national alliances, appear likely to form the dominant parties in the new government. Many politicians, however, criticize the electoral rule that parties must garner at least 10 percent of the vote in 24 of 36 states in order to qualify for permanent registration after the December local government elections. Several parties may have a narrower appeal, even though they represent significant portions of the electorate. If important groups are marginalized from the political process, the legitimacy of the transition will be compromised. In a bid to avert this problem, four parties explored an alliance in the weeks before the local government poll. They included the Alliance for Democracy, the People's Redemption Party (led by former governor Balarabe Musa), the United People's

Party (headed by the dissident retired Air Commodore Dan Suleiman), and the National Solidarity Movement. This coalition, encompassing parties with different ethnic and regional bases, echoes previous efforts in Nigeria to forge a broad progressive alliance.

The role of the politicians presents a further concern. Nigeria's civilian political class has inspired little confidence in its ability to represent the public interest and manage national affairs. If elected government is to gain ground, the political elite must obey basic rules of the democratic game. This requires that parties reject electoral manipulation and campaign violence, and avoid recrimination if voting does not go their way. If politicians can reduce their traditional emphases on personalities and ethnicity, and elevate policy concerns, this will go a long way toward building confidence. Although civil society can be invaluable in its watchdog role, politicians must also show self-restraint and public accountability.

The constitutional framework poses important issues. The government has announced that the original 1995 Draft Constitution will be the basis for the new political order, discarding the arcane revisions inserted by Abacha. Nigerian legal experts believe that this could be a workable document, although it includes such controversial provisions as rotation of the presidency among different regions, and the creation of three vice-presidential posts. By late November, the government had not yet formally promulgated the constitution. In consequence, Nigerians still did not know the basic institutions of the new democratic regime.

There is a consensus in Nigeria that the transition cannot await a full constitutional overhaul, but it is essential to institute a mechanism for future reform. South Africa's democratic transition could serve as an example in this regard, as its constitution was finalized during the first term of the new democratic regime. In November, Abubakar's government appointed a 25-member panel to organize debate over the constitution. This could prove useful, although critics observe that the committee falls short of the more inclusive process conceived by advocates of a "Sovereign National Conference" or a new constituent assembly.

Looking to the Longer Term

Looking beyond the May 1999 transition, several issues affect Nigeria's democratic prospects, especially that of ethnic inclusion. The Yorubas bitterly resent the political status quo and are indignant over the June 12 fiasco and Abiola's death. Much of this community will measure the legitimacy of the transition on the basis of their entry into the political mainstream. Recent disturbances among the Ijaw and other minority ethnic groups in the oil-producing Niger Delta have attained the scale of a low-intensity civil war, throttling Nigeria's exports and threatening future stability. Southeastern minorities are seeking political representation and a timely response to their demands for local development and environmental restitution.

The stubborn problems of ethnic power-sharing in Nigeria require changes in both leadership and institutions. There is a prevailing recognition of the need for a "power shift" in the current transition from a northern to a southern presidency. Northern constituencies, however, seek guarantees that a shift of executive power will not permanently handicap their region.

At an institutional level, the unresolved question of federalism is crucial. Many Nigerians, especially in the southern states, stress the need for a devolution of economic and political power, reversing the trend in recent decades toward centralization of resources and authority. In confronting this task, the country can build upon a legacy of constitutional development and refinements in revenue allocation. Existing provisions for federal redistribution could offer a framework for the new regime, although it will be important to provide for additional reform.

The issue of civil-military relations looms as a pivotal concern over the longer term. Although the current transition ensues from a sustained failure of military rule, the armed forces have retained their prerogatives in shaping the pace and content of change. An effective transition requires institutionalizing civilian control and establishing a nonpolitical role for the Nigerian armed forces. At the same time, elements of the military are quietly seeking immunity for past corruption or human rights abuses. The model of political pacting familiar from democratic transitions in Latin America could inspire a dialogue between Nigerian soldiers and civilians.

The battered economy is among the most formidable problems faced by Nigerian leaders. During his reign, Abacha amassed an estimated $6 billion by siphoning public monies, monopolizing patronage, and choking off competing legitimate activities. Reversing the devastation of the economy will require credible policy change and strong oversight, which an insecure or unstable government is less likely to achieve.

For the first time in many years, Nigeria has an opportunity to end its procession of instability and decline. In view of its wealth and its regional importance, the ramifications of success or failure will extend well beyond Nigeria's borders. The current transition may represent the last, if not best, hope for democracy and national stability.

Postscript

The preceding account of Nigeria's political travails concluded in November 1998. In the months that followed, the central features of General Abubakar's transition program were fulfilled, and the outline of political forces in the new democratic republic became clearer. A three-party structure quickly emerged, and a sequence of increasingly problematic elections yielded a presidential victory for a former head of state, retired General Olusegun Obasanjo, running as the candidate of the PDP.

The local government elections, contested by the nine accredited parties on 5 December 1998, attracted modest popular participation, with official returns indicating voter turnout of close to 50 percent. Of the 774 districts in which local governments were chosen, the PDP won 464, nearly 60 percent of the total. The APP won 192 local governments and the AD 109, the latter almost entirely in the six southwestern states.

Only these three leading parties were certified by the electoral commission to contest the state and national elections, and the relative strength that they showed in the local elections was reflected throughout the rest of the transition. In the state government elections of 9 January 1999, the PDP garnered 21 governorships, against nine for the APP and six for the AD. The PDP's margin of victory appeared to be diminishing, however, suggesting possible new opportunities for its rivals. The APP and the AD announced a political alliance, promising a joint effort to secure the presidency. This improbable coalition between the progressive activists of the AD and the traditional cohort of the APP had little evident rationale other than a desire to outflank the dominant PDP.

The APP-AD alliance ultimately settled upon a ticket comprising an AD President and an APP Vice President. This compact was grudgingly tolerated by electoral officials, who refused to permit the alliance candidate to run under a joint ballot symbol, and was challenged by prominent presidential aspirants within the APP, who questioned their party leadership's prerogative to agree to have the APP back an AD presidential candidate.

The nomination processes for legislative and presidential candidates were hasty and chaotic. The selection of candidates was decided by "consensus" among party elders, and the lack of transparency fostered considerable dissension within the parties. The PDP, in particular, was reputedly filled with retired military officers, and there was evidence that several former generals seized their own nominations outright. The party conventions, held only days before the deadline for declaring candidates, were shadowy affairs.

More than a dozen serious aspirants seeking the presidential nominations were quickly winnowed down to four: Olu Falae and Bola Ige for the AD, and Alex Ekwueme and Olusegun Obasanjo for the PDP. The APP-AD alliance chose Falae as its presidential standard bearer, and the PDP selected Obasanjo. With only two weeks to campaign, the presidential race was decided by the relative resources and organization of the parties, rather than by any programmatic or ideological appeals.

While the local and state elections earned generally favorable appraisals from foreign and domestic observers, there was an evident deterioration in electoral conduct during the legislative and presidential rounds of polling. In both elections there was a large discrepancy between the low participation rates observed by election monitors and the official returns, which continually registered turnout close to 50 percent. Reports of electoral irregularities and fraud also increased dramatically. In the absence of a reliable census, a credible voters' register, or independent verification of polling results, there was scant basis for assessing the validity of the official election returns.

The February 27 presidential election proceeded peacefully throughout the country, yielding an official count of 62 percent of the vote for Obasanjo and 38 percent for Falae. Falae immediately challenged the results, lodging an electoral appeal with INEC. International and domestic observers, along with much of the Nigerian media, cautiously endorsed the outcome, if not the conduct of the elections. For many Nigerians, the imperative of completing the transition outweighed qualms about the process.

Nigeria's latest transition essentially constitutes a referendum on military rule. Barring unforeseen events, the current agenda will produce a civilian regime on 29 May 1999. The new government will confront formidable institutional deficiencies, policy problems, and political demands. President Obasanjo's qualities of governance, after a 20-year hiatus in office, are also untested. For a broad segment of Nigerians, the real hope is that civilianization will at least afford time and political space to begin the long process of democratic development.

NOTES

1. These problems are detailed in Larry Diamond, Anthony Kirk-Greene, and Oyeleye Oyediran, eds., *Transition Without End: Nigerian Politics and Civil Society Under Babangida* (Boulder, Colo.: Lynne Rienner, 1997).

2. On this episode, see Diamond, et al., eds., *Transition Without End;* and Peter M. Lewis, "Endgame in Nigeria? The Politics of a Failed Democratic Transition," *African Affairs* 93 (July 1994): 323–40.

3. For an overview of the Abacha era, see Peter M. Lewis, Barnett R. Rubin, and Pearl T. Robinson, *Stabilizing Nigeria: Sanctions, Incentives, and Support for Civil Society* (New York: The Council on Foreign Relations and The Century Foundation, 1998).

4. The sentence for Yar'Adua was changed to life imprisonment, while Obasanjo received 15 years.

5. These events are covered in the report by the Civil Liberties Organisation, *Annual Report on Human Rights in Nigeria, 1995* (Lagos: Civil Liberties Organisation, 1996).

INDEX

Taylor, Charles, xi, 7, 70
Tofa, Alhaji Bashir, 231
Togo, xi, 38, 59–60, 162;
  assassinations in, 51;
  authoritarianism in, 5–6, 49,
  51, 58, 157; coups in, 5;
  elections in 6, 51, 71, 157;
  national conferences in, 5, 69;
  civil society in, 38
Touray,Yankuba, 223
Touré, Sékou, 64
Traoré, Moussa, 51
Tsikata, Kojo, 180
Tunisia, 64, 71–72, 76
Tutu, Desmond, 38

Uganda, xi, xiii, xxi, 46, 72, 74–
  76, 206, 211; authoritarianism
  in, 59, 65, 203; constitutions
  in, 75, 204, 207, 210, 212–13;
  corruption in, 44–45, 205,
  214; coups in, 22, 204; donor
  funding in, 202, 213; ethnic
  conflict in, 204; elections in,
  9, 22, 57, 201–2, 208–9, 212;
  election monitoring in, 201,
  209; and Great Britain, 201–
  3; national conferences in,
  213
United States, 14–15, 59, 69, 72,
  219, 232; and Ethiopia, 7–8;
  and France, 12; and Kenya,
  190; and Nigeria, 235
University of Cape Town, 112
University of Ghana, 174
Upfront (newspaper) (the
  Gambia), 217

Verwoerd, Hendrik, 117–18

Wadda, Mustapha Baboucarr, 225
Walle, Nicolas van de, 10, 12, 21
Wamalwa, Kijana, 193–94, 197
World Bank, xix, 42, 67, 69, 77,
  160, 189
World War II, 64, 119, 217

Yar'Adua, Shehu Musa, 5, 234, 237
Young, Crawford, ix, 105

Zakaria, Fareed, 14–15
Zaire, 9, 64, 74; assassinations in,
  54; authoritarianism in, 49, 57;
  coups in, 23; elections in, 9,
  22–23; media in, 56; national
  conferences in, 69. See also
  Congo-Kinshasa
Zafy, Albert, 26, 28
Zak-Zaky, Ibrahim, 236
Zambia, xi–xii, xxiii, 12–13, 39,
  54, 58; authoritarianism in, 6,
  13; civil society, 38–40;
  constitutions in, 6, 29, 37;
  coups in, 43; election
  monitoring in, 38; elections in,
  6, 25–27, 29, 32, 38, 51–52,
  69, 71, 144, 181; media in, 35;
  nongovernmental
  organizations in, 40
Zambian Post, 35
Zenawi, Meles, xi, 8, 59
Zeroual, Liamine, 73
Zimbabwe, x, 44, 58, 72, 149;
  authoritarianism in, 54; civil
  society in, 38; economic
  growth in, 121; elections in,
  32, 71; nongovernmental
  organizations in, 38
Zwelithini, Goodwill, 101